LEARNING TO TEACH MUSIC IN THE SECONDARY SCHOOL

This third edition of *Learning to Teach Music in the Secondary School* has been thoroughly revised to take account of the latest initiatives, research and scholarship in the field of music education, and the most recent changes to the curriculum. By focusing on overarching principles, it aims to develop reflective practitioners who will creatively and critically examine their own and others' ideas about music education, and the ways in which children learn music.

Providing an overview of contemporary issues in music teaching and learning from a range of perspectives, the book focuses on teaching music musically, and enables the reader to:

- place music education in its historical and social context
- consider the nature of musical knowledge and how teachers can facilitate their students to learn musically
- critically analyse the frameworks within which music teachers work
- develop an understanding of composing, performing and responding to music, as well as key issues such as creativity, individual needs and assessment
- examine aspects of music beyond the classroom and how effective links can be made between curriculum music and music outside of school.

Including a range of case studies, tasks and reflections to help student teachers integrate the theory and practice of music education effectively, this new edition will provide invaluable support, guidance and challenges for teachers at all stages of their careers, as well as being a useful resource for teacher educators in a wide range of settings.

Carolyn Cooke was previously Lecturer in Music Education at The Open University, UK, and is currently completing a PhD in Music Education at the University of Aberdeen, UK.

Keith Evans is Senior Lecturer in Music Education at the University of Greenwich, UK.

Chris Philpott is Reader in Music Education at the University of Greenwich, UK.

Gary Spruce is Senior Lecturer in Education at The Open University, UK, with responsibility for Music Initial Teacher Education (ITE). He is also director of the University's PGCE programme.

LEARNING TO TEACH SUBJECTS IN THE SECONDARY SCHOOL SERIES

Series Editors: Susan Capel and Marilyn Leask

Designed for all students learning to teach in secondary schools, and particularly those on school-based initial teacher training courses, the books in this series complement *Learning to Teach in the Secondary School* and its companion, *Starting to Teach in the Secondary School*. Each book in the series applies underpinning theory and addresses practical issues to support student teachers in school and in the training institution in learning how to teach a particular subject.

LEARNING TO TEACH MUSIC IN THE SECONDARY SCHOOL

A companion to school experience

Third edition

Edited by Carolyn Cooke, Keith Evans, Chris Philpott and Gary Spruce

Routledge
Taylor & Francis Group

LONDON AND NEW YORK

Third edition published 2016
by Routledge
2 Park Square, Milton Park, Abingdon, Oxon OX14 4RN

and by Routledge
711 Third Avenue, New York, NY 10017

Routledge is an imprint of the Taylor & Francis Group, an informa business

First edition published by Routledge 2000
Second edition published by Routledge 2006

British Library Cataloguing in Publication Data
A catalogue record for this book is available from the British Library

Library of Congress Cataloging in Publication Data
Names: Cooke, Carolyn, 1980– | Evans, Keith, 1958– | Philpott, Chris, 1956–
| Spruce, Gary.
Title: Learning to teach music in the secondary school: a companion to
school experience/edited by Carolyn Cooke, Keith Evans, Chris Philpott
and Gary Spruce.
Description: 3rd edition. | London; New York: Routledge, 2016. |
Series: Learning to teach in the secondary school | Includes bibliographical
references and index.
Identifiers: LCCN 2015044452 (print) | LCCN 2015048620 (ebook) |
ISBN 9780415713085 (hardback) | ISBN 9780415713092 (pbk.) |
ISBN 9781315621203 (ebook)
Subjects: LCSH: School music – Instruction and study – Great Britain.
Classification: LCC MT3.G7 L43 2016 (print) | LCC MT3.G7 (ebook) |
DDC 780.71/2 – dc23
LC record available at http://lccn.loc.gov/2015044452

ISBN: 978-0-415-71308-5 (hbk)
ISBN: 978-0-415-71309-2 (pbk)
ISBN: 978-1-315-62120-3 (ebk)

Typeset in Interstate
by Florence Production Ltd, Stoodleigh, Devon, UK

CONTENTS

ILLUSTRATIONS

Figures

Tables

Boxes

Tasks

CONTRIBUTORS

Carolyn Cooke - University of Aberdeen
Alison Daubney - University of Sussex
Julie Evans - Canterbury Christ Church University
Keith Evans - University of Greenwich
John Finney - Cambridge University
Duncan Mackrill - University of Sussex
Chris Philpott - University of Greenwich
Gary Spruce - The Open University
Ruth Wright - The University of Western Ontario, Canada
Sally Zimmermann - Royal National Institute for the Blind

SERIES EDITORS' PREFACE

The third edition of *Learning to Teach Music in the Secondary School* is one of a series of books entitled 'Learning to Teach (subject name) in the Secondary School: A Companion to School Experience', covering most subjects in the secondary school curriculum. The subject books support and complement the generic book *Learning to Teach in the Secondary School: A Companion to School Experience*, seventh edition (Capel, Leask and Younie, 2016), which deals with aspects of teaching and learning applicable to all subjects. This series is designed for student teachers on different types of initial teacher education programmes, but is proving equally useful to tutors and mentors in their work with student teachers.

The information in the subject books does not repeat that in *Learning to Teach*, but extends it to address the needs of student teachers learning to teach a specific subject. In each of the subject books, therefore, reference is made to the generic *Learning to Teach* text, where appropriate. It is recommended that you have both books so that you can cross-reference when needed.

The positive feedback on *Learning to Teach*, particularly the way it has supported the learning of student teachers in their development into effective, reflective teachers, encouraged us to retain the main features of that book in the subject series. Thus, the subject books are designed so that elements of appropriate theory introduce each topic or issue, and recent research into teaching and learning is integral to the presentation. In both the generic and subject books, tasks are provided to help you to identify key features of the topic or issue and apply them to your own practice. In addition, the requirement for material to be available to support student teachers' work at Master's level in PGCE courses in England has been met in the latest editions by the inclusion of advice about working at this level. The generic book referred to above also has a companion reader (*Readings for Learning to Teach in the Secondary School*) containing articles and research papers in education suitable for 'M'-level study.

We as editors have been pleased with the reception given to the earlier editions of this book as well as to the *Learning to Teach* series as a whole. Many subject books have moved into their third or fourth editions and others are in preparation. We hope that whatever initial teacher education programme you are following and wherever you may be situated, you find the third edition of *Learning to Teach Music in the Secondary School* supports your development towards becoming an effective, reflective teacher of music. You should also find the companion practical book, *A Practical Guide to Teaching Music in the Secondary*

School, of value. Many of the authors contributing to the *Learning to Teach* series are also contributing to the research summaries on www.MESHGuides.org. The MESHGuides build on the subject series and are intended to support you to develop evidence-informed practice throughout your career. Above all, we hope you enjoy teaching music.

Susan Capel and Marilyn Leask
October 2015

Introduction

Learning how to teach music

Carolyn Cooke, Keith Evans, Chris Philpott and Gary Spruce

This book is intended as a companion and resource to those who are learning how to teach music in secondary schools. It is intended to provide support, guidance, ideas and challenges for beginner teachers and teacher educators wherever they may find themselves. The multitude of routes into teaching, and the variety of contexts in which learning to teach music can occur, mean that beginner teachers and teacher educators all have very different needs. It is hoped that the book will prove useful to learning how to teach music across the various routes and contexts. We also hope that qualified music teachers are able to use the content and tasks to extend and refresh their ongoing professional development.

Many aspects of learning how to teach are covered in the generic book *(Learning to Teach in the Secondary School: A Companion to School Experience* – Capel, Leask and Turner 2013, sixth edition) and do not necessarily need a musical perspective here. For example, *some* aspects of behaviour management have cross-subject implications and are covered more than adequately in the generic book. We concentrate here on those aspects of learning how to teach that have significant implications for the music teacher.

This book does not take you stage by stage through the process of learning how to teach music (even if this were possible); instead, it is intended to be used after you have 'audited' your own particular needs in your own specific circumstances. For example, the chapters can be read in preparation for, or as a response to, learning inside or outside the classroom and the tasks can be used as part of a 'development plan' by tutor, mentor or beginner teachers. The text covers skills, knowledge and understandings that allow you to develop music pedagogy targets and, although not specifically designed to do so, will facilitate your progress towards the standards for qualified teacher status (QTS).

Many of the tasks ask you to share your thoughts and findings with other beginner teachers, qualified music teachers and mentors. However, while engaging with a community of practitioners will be important to your learning, it is *often very difficult* for music teachers to meet face to face (there could be only one teacher in a department), and the current diversity of routes into teaching exacerbates this issue for beginner teachers where the existence of a group learning together is increasingly rare. It is here that the power of digital media comes to the fore, and we encourage you to develop your own community of practitioners (even if you find yourself in a group) through, for example, social media and contributing blogs to various music education websites, where you can share your ideas and obtain feedback on them.

Primarily this book aims to identify musical and pedagogical principles that underpin effective music teaching and learning. In doing so, we have intentionally avoided details of particular curricula, policies or syllabi (for these often change), although there are times when we use such details as examples or case studies when making broader pedagogical points. This allows the book to be used in a wide range of learning contexts and national frameworks, and across age groups. However, it is therefore necessary for the reader to reflect on how these principles could apply to their own contexts and statutory responsibilities, although we believe that the quest for a 'musical' music education transcends published standards, curricula and syllabi.

Some of the chapters are unashamedly theoretical in outlook. We believe that theory and practice are inextricably linked, for theory always underpins practice. We do not use the concept of theory here to mean anything distinct from practice, but as the *rational* basis for practice. All teachers have theories about the nature of children, the importance of the subject and the nature of learning in their subject, upon which they base their everyday work. These theories often remain intuitive, and Swanwick emphasises the same point when he suggests that

> no human mind is free from the impulse towards theorising, any more than human physiology can get by for long without breathing – (teachers) are implicitly working to theories about music and educational processes, whether or not they declare them publicly.
>
> (Swanwick 1988: 6–7)

Learning how to teach any subject involves a willingness to reflect on and evaluate theory and practice. The cycle of *plan-act-reflect-evaluate* is important in the development of teachers in all contexts. Indeed, all teachers have a professional obligation to their youngsters to become better practitioners, and it is the aim of this book to be part of the developmental cycle. In this sense, learning to teach music is a 'lifelong' process. The tasks are designed to support this developmental cycle through encouraging you to respond to your ongoing experience as a music teacher by integrating theory and practice. Furthermore, the questions and activities allow you to respond to the themes and issues presented at a variety of different levels. As a graduate, it could be that you are keen to gain level 7 credits (M level) as part of becoming a music teacher, and with the right support the tasks will facilitate you to develop the skills of synthesis, innovation and creativity that define postgraduate work.

The chapters in this book adopt a variety of positions on the nature of music, musical knowledge, musical learning and musical development, i.e. they expound particular theories of music education. These 'positions' constantly confront you with the problems, difficulties and issues that surround the complex job that is music teaching, and require that you reflect on your developing practice. You may not agree with every position adopted in this book, but it is important that you reflect on and review what you do believe. This process helps to underpin your beliefs with a strong philosophy of music education. This is important, for experience suggests that the best music teachers are those who have developed for themselves well-reasoned positions on learning and teaching in music. The strength of such teachers is enhanced if, at the same time, they are receptive to the theories that underpin the good practice of other music teachers.

There are at least three very good reasons for developing a personal philosophy of music education. First, your theories underpin the successful planning and execution of your lessons. Second, by having a personal philosophy of music education you are empowered to critique and take reasoned decisions about policy, curriculum design and musical experiences for your pupils. Such empowerment is critical in ensuring that policies and other people's agendas positively impact on musical learning, rather than inadvertently diminish it. Third, having a reasoned philosophy enhances your power to convince others of the value of music at school and its importance in the wider society.

An important starting point for any personal philosophy of music education is your own experience as a pupil, student or teacher. It is likely that your biography will be an important influence on the way you think about music and the teaching of music.

Task 0.1 helps you to reflect on your own music education.

Task 0.1 An initial statement

From your experiences as a teacher and student of music, answer the following questions:

- What makes a good teacher?
- What makes a 'musical' music lesson?

On the basis of these reflections, write an initial statement that identifies the sort of music teacher you would like to become. It will be interesting to revisit this task during your development as a teacher.

Further reading

Elliott, D.J. (1995) *Music Matters: A New Philosophy of Music Education*, Oxford: Oxford University Press.
Swanwick, K. (1988) *Music, Mind, and Education*, London: Routledge.

In the early chapters of both of these books the authors make a strong claim for the importance of theory in music education and also the need for a coherent philosophy to underpin and inform our practice.

1 The place of music in the secondary school

Ideology - history - justification

John Finney

Introduction

This chapter sets out to stimulate thought about the place of music in the secondary school, to consider what role it might play within a general education and to do this within a historical perspective. Particular attention will be paid to some of the beliefs and ideologies, including dominant ideologies, that continue to shape current thought and practice. This in turn will lead to a consideration of the kinds of justification made for music as a subject of the curriculum.

Objectives

By the end of the chapter you will be able to:

- discuss with other beginner teachers, with music teachers and school administrators the value placed on music education in the secondary school;
- examine critically the validity of arguments supporting the place of music in the secondary school;
- distinguish between justifications made for music education and music educational advocacy;
- read with insight official documents defining the place of music in school and its contribution to the whole curriculum;
- create in outline the case you would want to present in support of musical study, whether in a job application letter, at interview or at a meeting of parents and governors.

A moral and political question

Writing in the fourth century BC, Plato saw music as educating the soul, as affecting human character and the whole personality. Music could be of good and bad character. Music's modes and rhythms were to be selected with care. Some were vulgar, some sentimental, not all were equally civilising. After all, the modes had been named after tribes of people, some to be admired, some not. A mode was constructed out of musical proportions, some able to bring about the harmony of mind, body and soul, some not; some able to bring about perfection, some not. In this way of thinking, music education was in need of regulation (Plato 1982).

Plato's ideal state required men of courage, disciplined in war, reflective in peace, physically agile and politically adroit. Thus, the character of boys should be developed through modes that were modest, simple and masculine rather than violent, effeminate or fickle. Music, like the other arts, touched emotion, affected mood and character, and in Plato's theory of knowledge had low status. Music was less cognitive than other subjects and potentially dangerous. A music education, then as now, was wholly implicated in the moral and political life of society and of greater or lesser interest to those who wished to educate, manipulate and govern. From earliest times music had been recognised as a medium through which to induct and socialise each new generation into the norms, values and aspirations of a society. However, that this process should take place in schools attended by all young people is a relatively new practice. As nineteenth-century Europe embraced the idea of mass education, so in 1870 universal education was established in England. Music in the form of singing was officially sanctioned in schools.

Music, high status, exclusive

The idea of music as a subject of study, as having a distinctive contribution to make to the whole, had emerged from antiquity. One form of this conception, frequently referred to, was what became known as the Seven Liberal Arts. Here the curriculum was divided into lower and higher divisions: the trivium (grammar, logic and rhetoric) and the quadrivium (arithmetic, astronomy, geometry and music). The trivium was concerned with the arts of language, leading to the mastery of self-expression and understanding of the human mind. The quadrivium, on the other hand, took the learner out into the world of ideas and abstractions and here music was given high status, a subject to be engaged with by a few initiates thought qualified enough to probe the mysteries of the universe and to search for ultimate truths.

There was thought to be interconnectedness between disciplines, and this involved a search for common patterns and analogies. This concern for overall coherence was matched by the counterbalancing features of the two divisions. There was the trivium's sacredness and the quadrivium's secularity, the trivium's reaching inward and the quadrivium's reaching outward, keeping the knower in relationship with what was known. The linguistic nature of the trivium was complemented by the quadrivium's concern with the numerical, the spatial and the temporal. It is tempting to seek parallels with modern ideas of curriculum balance and coherence, but these are made with caution.

Of enduring interest is the character given to music in the scheme. Music is given high status through being recognised as a natural science and for its abstract qualities, rather than as an art and as a source of self-expression. In all this, the idea that music is a temporal art bringing time and space to order remains fundamental to much thought about music: to be and become musical requires organising time, and a musician's craft requires playing with time as well as playing in time.

Task 1.1 What kind of subject is music?

How do you view music as a subject of study?

Make contact with another beginner music teacher. Decide on one of the following talking points and, through discussion, find arguments for and against the statement selected:

- Music is a subject that enables self-expression.
- Music is a subject with a strong mathematical orientation.
- Music is by its nature an exclusive subject.
- Music is a subject that orders time and space like no other.
- Music is not a subject but an activity to participate in.

Revisit this task at the end of the chapter.

The Seven Liberal Arts proved to be a prototype of what came to be thought of as liberal humanism and the idea of a liberal education able to bring about understanding of ourselves and the world in which we live. In this view, education, and with it music education, had intrinsic worth, with the potential to open the mind to creative possibilities and meetings with the unexpected. This was an education that, through its rigour, discipline and training, was thought to be liberating, while serving the common good.

The aim of Plato's regulation of music was to preserve the state, to ensure social order and to establish and sustain a common culture. In more recent times, and now with music as a school subject, this expectation continued to be placed upon music, and this focused on which music was taught and the repertoire of music used. In suggestions made to music teachers by the Board of Education in 1927, the following recommendation is made:

> As a rule the music first learned by children should be drawn from our Folk and Traditional songs. These are the true classics of the people, and form the foundation on which a national love of music can be built up . . . a pupil whose memory is stored with these songs from his earliest school days has the best protection that education can give against the attractions of vulgar and sentimental music when school days are over; and it is not always realised how strong and vital a tie between the members of a school, a college, or even a nation may be formed by their knowledge of a common body of traditional song.
>
> (1927: 253)

Here is a conviction that, through singing, shared identities would be formed and a national community of common values created. Music education was in this way conceived of as an education in citizenship and in many respects as an education to be regulated in the way that Plato had proposed. Vulgarity and sentiment in music militated against 'good taste', and 'good taste' was related to what was civil and civilising. An ideology with a long history was being sustained. But there was to be a change of mood. Task 1.2 asks you to consider music as a civilising influence, drawing on your own experiences of music education.

Task 1.2 Music as a civilising influence

Based on your in-school observations, consider:

- To what extent do you consider the issue relevant in the light of what you have observed in school?
- To what extent do you think the task of music education is to educate taste?

Exchange your views either face to face with another beginner teacher or via social networking.

Concessions and change

By the 1950s a curriculum had evolved to which His Majesty's Inspectorate referred as 'singing plus'. Singing, the appreciation of music and the acquisition of a clearly defined set of skills, techniques and repertoire of music were the common fare of music classrooms following the Second World War. However, experience often resembled a narrow course of musical training. Overemphasis on technical matters frequently got in the way of musical experience and enjoyment. While the Board of Education of 1927 had called for careful management of repertoire, the Scottish Education Department in 1955 called for concession. Writing of the choice of music for instruction in listening, music teachers were given the following advice:

> At first it should not be too unlike that which the pupils are accustomed to hear in the cinema or at home. The lively polkas and graceful waltzes of Strauss, for example, are a means of capturing the interest of the pupils who may not respond so quickly to the music of Bach and Beethoven. The simple classics should remain the foundations of good musical training, but the interest of the pupils in contemporary popular music should not be ignored. When they leave school – indeed, while they are still at school – the pupil's interest is drawn towards this very attractive, although perhaps ephemeral, music, which forms so large a part of their musical experience. The schools' obligation is not to dissociate itself entirely from this kind of music but to teach some discrimination in sorting out the good from the bad.
>
> (1955: 218)

The statement is carefully crafted and offers helpful principles that we all might easily commend:

- Recognise the interests of young people.
- Acknowledge their prior knowledge and experience beyond school.

- Move from the known to the unknown.
- Nurture critical judgement and discrimination.

Task 1.3 Enduring principles?

Observe in school and note ways in which these principles work in practice.

Discard one of the above principles that you consider least relevant to a music education today. Replace it with one of your own.

However, in place of former censorships, a patronising attitude to the value of popular music had emerged. As the 1960s and 1970s unfolded, young people were not slow to recognise this. A survey of the attitudes of *Young School Leavers* (Schools Council 1968) showed music given lowly status as a school subject. A pupil of the time reflects:

> It was 1965 and our music teacher tried some experimental lessons when we got to Year 9. We were invited to bring our favourite records to the lesson. I brought Bob Dylan's 'She belongs to me'. I remember thinking this was a really worthy piece of work because both the words and music had been created by Dylan. This encapsulated my ideal of individual expression and what I considered to be authenticity. The piece connected with my interest in surrealism too. The teacher noted the harmonica playing with some disdain: 'It's just suck-blow, suck-blow.' We seemed to be in parallel universes. The teacher always kept a tight lid on discussion to avoid tribal warfare.
>
> (Interview 2004)

Task 1.4 How was it for you?

Make contact with somebody who was at school in the 1960s or 1970s. Find out what they remember most about their music lessons in school. What long-term influence has school music had on their lives?

Use the following prompts to help the process of determining positive as well as negative responses:

- Did lessons leave you feeling musical?
- Did you make up music?
- What is recalled from the listening repertoire experienced?
- Are there songs from school days still in your head?
- Was there a most memorable lesson?

The curriculum offered was experienced as increasingly irrelevant by the young people for whom it was designed. A gap had grown between policy makers, teachers and youth. Children were changing faster than schools, and new technologies provided young people with the means of organising their own music education. The terms 'good music' and 'good taste' became problematic. Music in secondary school was experienced by the majority, and in particular by older students, as anything but liberating, rather a training in skills and techniques largely considered as irrelevant, or at best relevant to a minority. Like music in the medieval quadrivium, the subject was in danger of becoming exclusive. Responses to this crisis of confidence illustrate well the forging of fresh ideologies and the emergence of competing visions of how music should be thought about, what a music education might consist of and what might be the right place for music in the secondary school.

The creative turn

The most influential of these new ideas came from the composer-educator John Paynter, who, leading a major curriculum development programme at York University, drew on innovative classroom practice. Teachers following the principles of Carl Orff, for example, had developed small-group music making, and, while taking care to teach instrumental techniques, they nurtured improvisation and composition and were willing to build on the ideas of young people. The York Project, as it came to be known, developed the slogans 'Music for the Majority' and 'All Kinds of Music'. Paynter's chief enemy was music education reduced to a narrow course of musical training where tutored skills and proficiencies dominated, to the exclusion of imagination and creativity. This was 'Music for the Minority'. Paynter set about emphasising music as a central element in a general education, and this had the potential immediately to raise the status of music within the secondary school. This brought musical improvisation and composition to the fore, as well as the art of interpretation in the performance of music. Why, for example, should these arts depend upon the acquisition of conventional skills in notation reading and writing? Tutored skill in music reading might or might not assist in this. Paynter was proposing the dissolution of the theoretical–practical divide and the integration of technical and expressive matters: 'Children need the creative stimulus of "using" the skills they have acquired *as* they acquire them. We must try, therefore, to provide opportunities for interpretive decision-making even at the most elementary levels' (1982: 123).

Emphasis was placed on the development of the learner's ability to grow in discernment and in the capacity to make informed judgements of his/her own. In particular, giving the learner freedom to make decisions about 'how music should go' in the context of composing music provided the learner with the opportunity to know music from the inside. In this view, releasing creativity and imagination was essential to the notion of being musically educated. Task 1.5 asks you to reflect on your own views of creativity and imagination in music.

Task 1.5 Creativity and imagination in music

- In what situations do you consider yourself to be most musically creative?
- When is it that you feel most musically alive?
- To what extent have you gained knowledge of music from the inside through your performing, improvisation, listening and composing?

Compare your responses to these questions to those of another music teacher.

The arts: a common purpose

The creative banner was taken up by others and notably by Malcolm Ross, an arts educator who declared a common purpose for the arts: the education of feeling (Ross 1980). For Ross, as for Paynter, music lagged hopelessly behind the way other arts subjects were conceived and taught, a point repeated by Ross in 1995. A favourite metaphor was to view the music classroom as a museum and the music teacher as the curator. This was not how it was in art, drama, dance or English lessons. If music shared a common purpose with the other arts, and if this involved engaging at a feelingful level, exploring subjectivity and learning to master the art of self-expression, then thinking of the music teacher as Kapelmeister was inappropriate. We were moving a long way from a programme of training and from music's earlier place within the natural sciences. In fact science, in its apparent claim to objective truth and mastery of the natural world, was seen as opposed to the claims of feeling made by the arts. The arts, so it was argued, existed to provide an antidote to those subjects defined by rules and right answers, and where knowledge was 'impressed' on the learner.

Task 1.6 Rules and right answers

In school, observe lessons across a range of subjects. Can a case be made for strongly distinguishing the arts from the rest of the curriculum? Are the arts concerned with a distinctive kind of knowledge and way of understanding?

Form a small group of young people and ask them how they view music, the other arts and other subjects as sources of knowledge and understanding as well as ways of learning. How is their learning different in different subjects across the curriculum?

For Herbert Read (1943), an education that emphasised feeling and expression constituted an aesthetic education, and this was fundamental to general education in fostering growth of what is individual in each human being. Read believed that only by placing the arts at the heart of the curriculum could a more democratic society be attained. Here was the conviction that before people could co-operate effectively with other people, they must understand themselves. Involvement in the arts demanded exploration of personal ideas and feelings. The most important consideration was the learner and her potential to be an 'artist'. This approach was to be referred to as 'child-centred' and 'progressive', and placed existing norms and values, as well as heritage and tradition, in a supportive, even subordinate, rather than a leading role.

These kinds of development in thinking had the potential to bring the arts closer together. Indeed, the growing belief that the arts formed a coherent area of the curriculum was marked by the proliferation of terms such as 'combined arts', 'integrated arts', 'expressive arts', 'creative arts' and 'performing arts'. Yet, just precisely how teachers of the arts were to forge closer relationships within the classroom was to prove problematic, for while the arts in broad terms might share a common purpose and support each other in providing for a creative-aesthetic education, the arts are not interchangeable. Music won't be learnt by studying art or drama. Each arts subject has its own distinctive set of skills and procedures. At the same time, each art form, and music is a good example, thrives in the context of other arts, as evidenced in opera, rap, dance music, song, mood music, film and video, and the perpetual visual spectacle from which the performance of music derives meaning.

Task 1.7   Music and the other arts

In school, examine the stated aims of arts subjects in order to find out to what extent they share a common set of beliefs. Use the questions below to create a table setting out your findings:

- Is there planning for cross-arts learning?
- In what ways do arts subjects connect a) explicitly, b) implicitly?
- At what stages of secondary school are relationships made?
- What opportunities are there for students to work through the other arts in music lessons?
- What opportunities are missed for collaboration across the arts?

Music as social symbol

For others, the idea of 'creative music', whether in conjunction with the arts or not, failed to recognise music as socially located, arising from social structures affecting the conditions of its practice. And this was one way in which to explain the persistent patronising attitude to popular music, for it was high culture that continued to call the tune, claiming seriousness over the triviality of popular music and setting out the criteria by which all music could be judged. It was serious music that was believed to have transcendent qualities, enabling works of art to be moved to a special realm of aesthetic contemplation and beyond the social milieu of everyday life. In all this, it was the individual's inner life that could be enriched, safe from the contradictions and injustices of the social world. This dominating ideology, with its roots in the liberal humanist tradition, came under scrutiny from critical theory, whose task was to expose taken-for-granted ideas that serve to make legitimate unequal forms of social relations (see Gibson 1986).

At the same time, a new approach to the sociology of knowledge raised questions about what counted as school knowledge and, in particular, why some knowledge was given high status. In the case of music, this knowledge came most obviously through an adherence to a notated tradition, a canon of works and a set of associated performance practices. As such, it was unable to value diverse musical traditions and in particular contemporary practices, and this led to a culture clash with young people's way of perceiving music and valuing musical experience (Vulliamy 1978). How was the music teacher to give value to those children who imitated the vocal inflections of popular singers, if what was valued related to criteria derived from the western classical tradition?

In this view, music education needed to free itself from the long-established formalities of the western classical tradition. Notation, for example, so it was argued, stood between the learner and real musical experience and knowledge that were socially constructed. Pop, rock and blues, as well as music from 'unsung' sub-cultures and diverse ethnic groups, were the means by which to liberate, loosen the structures of schooling and change society. John Shepherd was among those who maintained that music is ultimately and inherently social. Society is in music, music is in society. This proposal challenged the dominant belief that western European high art held the key to some higher or ultimate reality inaccessible through other music (Shepherd *et al.* 1980). Here was a good example of the way in which dominant ideologies were believed to work. It was an illusion to suggest that music had innate meaning or that musical values existed in a vacuum, separate from the conditions that brought them into existence or the circumstances in which they continued to be practised. The ways in which prevailing ideologies were able to legitimise some music and not others had been exposed (Vulliamy and Shepherd 1984). Task 1.8 asks you to consider your own musical education in relation to these ideologies.

Task 1.8 Dominant ideologies

To what extent did your music education emphasise one particular set of musical practices and criteria for success? How has this affected your musical development and the way you think about/relate to music today?

Where possible, share your answers with another beginner teacher.

A moderating voice

Keith Swanwick (1979) had provided music teachers with a carefully argued model of music education in which the processes of performing, composing and listening gave direct access to aesthetic experience, knowledge and meaning. These processes, of course, would require support from enabling skills and knowledge about music. However, Swanwick was opposed to thinking of music as a social symbol and unconvinced by loosely defined ideas about creativity and self-expression. Nevertheless, the individual came before the social, and it was each person's capacity to animate the physical properties of sound, hearing tones as if they were tunes and tunes as expressive shapes, that in turn found fresh relationships as if they had a 'life of their own'. It is these processes of symbol and metaphor making that have the capacity continually to transform experience and to engage with our personal and cultural histories (Swanwick 1999).

Swanwick's caution about creativity and self-expression represented a concern that the arts become devalued by an insistence on their subjective natures. Music was a part of the objective world – a form of discourse. The idea is expressed elegantly here:

> Music maintains its foothold in formal education not because it gives some kind of direct sensory pleasure, or enhances the public image of a school, or because some few students may eventually earn a living in music-related occupations. It persists in our

educational systems because it is a form of human discourse as old as the human race, a medium in which ideas about ourselves and others are embodied in sonorous forms, ideas that may be simple or complex, obvious or enigmatic. And insight into these ideas – as into any significant idea – can be intrinsically rewarding.

(Swanwick 1997: 4)

In presenting music as 'a great symbolic form' and 'a discourse as old as the human race', Swanwick sought to strengthen the place of music in the secondary school, giving it the kind of significance that can be attached to other 'great' symbolic forms such as mathematics, the humanities and science, for example. By implication, there are greater and lesser symbolic forms. Swanwick is reminding us that every known human culture has valued music, that as a cultural form music is something that is inherited and passed on, a form of human expression universally experienced. Music is of greater cultural significance than basket weaving, for example.

Hard and soft justifications

Justifying music in this way sought to go beyond what Philpott thinks of as those 'soft' justifications that have grown exponentially at the beginning of the twenty-first century. These focus on the power of music to affect lives and shower benefits on those who engage with it. Focusing argument upon the benefits of music draws forth two obvious objections. In the first place, such benefits are unlikely to be solely the province of musical engagement, and second, such benefits are likely to be contingent upon particular circumstances and conditions. Music on its own is powerless to make things happen (DeNora 2006). Nevertheless, considerable energy is currently directed towards identifying what is thought to be 'the power of music'.

In the book *Music Education in the 21st century in the United Kingdom*, Susan Hallam sets out evidence showing the impact of music upon the intellectual, personal and social development of children. Claims are made upon perceptual and language skills, literacy, numeracy, intellectual development, general development, creativity and social and personal development (Hallam 2010). While such claims undoubtedly form strong advocacy for engagement in musical activity, this approach works with an unrealistic and naïve conception of what music is in the world (Philpott 2012). The point is sharply made by Philpott in pointing out that while music may be good for you, music may equally be bad for you, and further recognising that music can be tribal, exclusive and enshrine prejudice; manipulative of behaviour; gendered; reflective of social structures; propagandist; and can enshrine ideology.

In this way of thinking, music is already in the world, living within complex webs of meanings and continually being understood and re-understood, interpreted and re-interpreted. In extending Swanwick's idea of music as a great symbolic form, Philpott now proposes conceiving of music as a language. Unlike other claims on music as a language, this is not to see in music the properties of speech, such as speaking tempo, vocal pitch and intonational contours, which can be used to communicate attitudes or other shades of meaning; nor is it to see in music grammar, syntax or dialect characteristic of a musical style; but more fundamentally to see music as a language in itself, as characterised by an openness to acquired and multiple interpretations where meaning and value are determined by usage in particular contexts. Music, rather than being something that is good for you and a source of enduring comfort, becomes yet more powerful when thought of as a subject that engages critically with political and ideological issues. Music is no longer part of a therapeutic education but a critically alive worldly education that thrives on suspicion and critique. In this way music becomes a hard-edged subject. To think of music as simply a source of benefits, while superficially attractive, may serve to undermine harder and more substantial justifications.

Task 1.9   Justifying music

In light of the above discussion, examine the statement below introducing the 2007 edition of the National Curriculum for Music.

> Music is a unique form of communication that can change the way young people feel, think and act. Music forms part of an individual's identity and positive interaction with music can develop young people's competence as learners and increase their self-esteem. Music brings together intellect and feeling and enables personal expression, reflection and emotional development. As an integral part of culture, past and present, music helps young people understand themselves, relate to others and develop their cultural understanding, forging important links between home, school and the wider world. (See http://webarchive.national archives.gov.uk/20130401151715/http://education.gov.uk/publications/eOrdering Download/QCA-04-1374.pdf)

- To what extent do you think this an adequate justification for music?
- Is the distinction between hard and soft justifications helpful?

Music education now

The 2007 edition of the National Curriculum for Music referenced above had been preceded by three other editions, the first in 1992 following the Education Reform Act of 1988. While the Act gave music a place for all young people between the ages of 5 and 14, it drew in new assessment structures, regimes of testing and school inspection linked to the idea of school improvement. As the 1990s progressed, old concerns re-surfaced. Despite the subject's re-orientation in the 1970s and 80s, culminating in the establishment of GCSE music and its composing, performing, listening template, and reinforced in the National Curriculum Programme of Study, there was scant evidence that this had enhanced the status of the subject in the eyes of young people.

Questions were being asked as to whether music as a once-a-week classroom event was capable of having the life and vigour experienced by young people in their bands, orchestras, choirs, rock groups and private listening. For students of secondary age, music was a source of cultural energy, self-expression and identity formation. Was it time to listen to the ways in which young people justified their own music education programme, with its complex range of informalities, formalities and unintentional learning experiences?

While the official response was represented by the launch of a National Strategy for Music at Key Stage 3 (see http://3.hants.gov.uk/music), an alternative and radical response came from The Paul Hamlyn Foundation in the form of Musical Futures (see www.musical futures.org.uk), offering ways of working informally within the formal structures of the school. The question 'Whose music?', asked thirty years earlier, was now addressed by recognising the musical interests, tastes and identities of the student.

At the same time, music education's cause had been taken up by government, culminating in a Music Manifesto (DfES 2004, 2006a), and in 2007 the not inconsiderable sum of £332 million was allocated to the subject's development. This gave rise to a number of initiatives, notably the Sing Up and Wider Opportunities programmes. All this brought music education into the public sphere, where the voices of an ever-widening range of interest groups advocating the benefits of music became prominent. Advocacy, thought of as a necessary strategic tool in the art of political persuasion central to securing funding and recognition, became a relentless feature of ongoing discussion surrounding the value of a music education. As the art of political persuasion, advocacy requires the skilful use of rhetoric involving the use of claims not always able to stand up to careful scrutiny. The process of making a reasoned justification, mindful of ideological positions, which we are here engaged in, is of a different order.

The incoming Conservative-led coalition government, mindful of sustaining support for music education, commissioned the making of a National Plan for Music (see https://gov.uk /government/publications/the-importance-of-music-a-national-plan-for-music-education). Key themes were inclusion and participation, expressed as the opportunity for all to learn a musical instrument. By 2013 a new National Curriculum for Music had been written. In view of the focus of this chapter, the curriculum's purpose of study deserves careful attention, as you will explore in Task 1.10.

Task 1.10 Purpose of study

Music is a universal language that embodies one of the highest forms of creativity. A high-quality music education should engage and inspire young people to develop a love of music and their talent as musicians, and so increase their self-confidence, creativity and sense of achievement. As young people progress, they should develop a critical engagement with music, allowing them to compose, and to listen with discrimination to the best in the musical canon.

(www.gov.uk/government/publications/national-curriculum-
in-england-music-programmes-of-study)

Examine this statement in the light of what you have read and thought above, bringing to the fore (1) what might be a defensible justification for music and (2) dominant music educational ideologies of the past.

Now make clear what you consider to be a cogent statement of purpose fit for a letter of application for a teaching post and which would serve as the basis for a public presentation to parents and school governors.

Summary

This chapter has addressed the ways in which music education has been thought about over time and the ways in which it has been justified. We have seen that the justification for music in education:

- has a long and winding history tied to social systems and political arrangements;
- has been influenced by the power of ideas often serving particular interests, both individual and group, that have shaped ways of thinking about music and music education;
- has been conceived of as a civilising influence, a shaper of character, a marker of the educated citizen, a great symbolic form, a language or indeed as just something that is good for you.

Whatever the justification, there remains a call to each new secondary school music teacher to ask: 'Why music?' Our responses can quickly resort to enthusiastic rhetoric and vague advocacy or draw upon too many diffuse claims and arguments. We should take time to rehearse our case and be able to defend it in theory and practice.

Further reading

Cox, G. and Stevens, R. (2010) *The Origins and Foundations of Music Education: Cross-Cultural Historical Studies of Music in Compulsory Schooling*, Bloomsbury: London.

Philpott, C. (2012) The justification for music in the curriculum: music may be bad for you, in C. Philpott and G. Spruce (eds) *Debates in Music Teaching*, London Routledge: London, pp. 48-63..

These readings allow you to gain a fuller perspective on the history of music education in England, ideologies and justifications.

2 Culture, society and musical learning

Gary Spruce

Introduction

The relationship between music, society and culture has attracted considerable attention over recent decades. Among others, Blacking (1987), Leppert and McClary (1987), Shepherd (1991), Martin (1995), Small (1977 and 1998), Scott (2000), DeNora (2000), Laughey (2006) and Street (2012) have all published substantial work in this area. Small (1977), Green (1995 and 1997) and Woodford (2005) have adopted a specifically educational focus, with Green publishing significant research on the relationship between music, gender and education (e.g. Green 1997) and Woodford on the links between music education and democracy (2005). The work of all these writers is based upon a belief that music can be understood fully and, by implication, taught effectively if only one takes into account the social, political, cultural and economic factors that impact upon its production, dissemination and reception.

Objectives

By the end of this chapter you should be able to:

- describe how culturally constructed assumptions about the nature of music have influenced the development of the music curriculum and the way in which it has been taught;
- explain how music has been used to create and perpetuate social divisions;
- define how a cultural and social perspective can inform the music curriculum and its teaching, leading to a wider range of musics, musical skills and understanding being valued and celebrated.

Context and background

Parallel with the development of a sociological perspective on music and music education was the emergence in the 1990s of what came to be called the 'new musicology'. This sought to challenge the assumed and seemingly self-evident greatness of western art music through showing that such 'greatness' is socially constructed and sometimes retrospectively applied. For example, Tia DeNora has persuasively demonstrated how, in the case of Beethoven (arguably the paradigm of the 'great' composer), 'the very notion of greatness was tailored to "fit" the forms that Beethoven produced' (DeNora 1996: 169). Drawing on ethnomusicology and the emerging discipline of music sociology, the 'new musicology' argued that western art music must be studied and understood not as the products of individual genius but in relation to the values, mores and, for example, gender relationships and musical practices of the society within which it was created and from which it emerged.

This approach generated considerable controversy among musicologists in that it challenged what Regelski (2005: 221) calls the 'aesthetic ideology' of musical study, which is based upon the belief that musical meaning and value are contained within, and articulated exclusively through the sounds (sonic materials) of, music. Music then undergoes a process of reification (of objectification) where meaning is understood as fixed within its objectified form - typically 'the score'. Reification leads to the notion of autonomy (is unaffected by and *transcends* time and place) such that, for example, a performance of a Beethoven symphony in early nineteenth-century Vienna has the same musical meaning as a performance at a 'Proms' concert in 2015, because musical meaning is contained exclusively in the score and the sounds of the music. The impact of this aesthetic ideology on music education has resulted in a focus on the study of the sonic materials of music (the ubiquitous 'element of music') and the musical score as an autonomous entity - as a kind of musical text or vehicle for carrying musical meaning. (We shall explore this idea more fully later in the chapter.)

One of the most significant outcomes for music education of the socio-cultural and 'new musicology' perspectives, and as a reaction to the approach to music education underpinned by the 'aesthetic ideology', was the emergence of a 'praxial' approach to music education. Originating in the work of David Elliott, and particularly his seminal book *Music Matters* (1995), 'praxialism' challenges the 'aesthetic' perspective on music and music education by arguing that music makes its meaning not simply through the organisation of its sonic materials but also (and arguably primarily) through the ways in which people use it and the meaning they ascribe to it through these uses; in other words, through musical *practices*. Music, it is argued, does not have an autonomous existence or possess autonomous value, but rather its existence and value derive from the contexts in which it takes place and the purposes to which it is put.

A praxial approach to music education is embedded in the belief that musical under-standing is developed not solely through the examination, exploration and 'appreciation' of the objects of music (often in the form of a score), but through an understanding of the 'practices' of music - of the ways in which people engage with it. This approach rejects the idea that there are musical universals that can be applied to all musics but argues that, for example, conceptions of 'musical excellence' are situated within and are specific to particular musical contexts, practices and traditions, e.g. conceptions of excellence in blues music are underpinned by different musical values from conceptions of excellence in classical or gamelan music.

The praxial philosophy of music has had significant influence on music education. For example, its impact can be observed in the English secondary national strategy for music programme foundation subjects (2006b) and also some informal music approaches. However, some of its proponents have been criticised for caricatured descriptions of other approaches to music education (Swanwick 1999). There is also a danger that praxial approaches can result in the 'freezing' of musical practices at a particular and arbitrary point in time in order to make them teachable, thus negating the essential dynamism of many musical practices within social groupings. Furthermore, in Elliott's conception of praxial music making, performance is given primacy over other activities such as composing, which has become an important part of the tradition of English music education in recent years.

Nevertheless, with these reservations noted, this chapter will argue that long-standing beliefs and assumptions about music, which are often rooted in the 'aesthetic ideology', have influenced, often negatively, the way in which music is taught, resulting in the exclusion of many young people from formal music education. It will consider the ways in which the assumptions underpinning the aesthetic ideology have come to be seen as self-evident and suggest strategies for addressing some of the negative impact this has on music teaching and learning.

It is important to note that in critiquing the impact of the aesthetic ideology on music education and positing the idea of a more praxial approach, this chapter too promotes a particular ideology, which equally is open to critique. In the final activity of this chapter, you will be invited to make such a critique. We want you to begin, however, by reflecting on your own musical studies from a social and cultural perspective.

Task 2.1 Your own musical studies

Think about your own musical studies, perhaps through focusing on a musical work that you have studied in detail. Briefly note down those aspects of the music that were considered to be important and the kinds of questions that were asked about it in any examination you took. Was the focus of the study on just analysing the music, or was any attention paid to the social and cultural context in which it was created and performed or the practices underpinning it? What do you feel is to be gained (if anything) from exploring music's social and cultural context?

Why is a socio-cultural perspective important in music education?

Perhaps the question that needs to be asked at the outset is how an understanding of the links between society, culture and music might help music teachers meet of the challenges of teaching music in the twenty-first century.

First – and most obviously – music permeates almost every aspect of everyday life. It is present as we shop, eat in restaurants or cafés, drink in bars, watch television or films, work out in the gym and travel on the Underground. All kinds of music are now instantly downloadable onto a multitude of mobile technologies, meaning that, if we wish it to be, music can be an almost permanent presence in our lives.

Discos, nightclubs and bars also employ particular types of music to create an 'appropriate atmosphere', and music is used to enhance state, religious and sporting occasions. DeNora (2000) has pointed out that there is a natural tendency on the part of humans to 'comply' with expectations created by the use of particular music in specific social contexts; think, perhaps, of music at a funeral or wedding. Such compliance is rooted in our formal and informal musical enculturation, where we learn to associate certain musical gestures with particular ideas, emotions or occasions. Music can also affect patterns of consumption, either through the association of a piece or style of music with a product or, more significantly, where a musical genre/style is used to create a group identity, which is then further articulated through, for example, choice of clothing. Consequently, as DeNora goes on to say, 'control over music in social settings is a source of social power; it is an opportunity to structure the parameters of action' (DeNora 2000: 20). Given that most of our (and young people's) encounters with music take place in such settings, it is important that we (and they) gain some understanding of how music operates in these social situations and how responses and actions can be influenced by it.

Second, 'society' is not an homogeneous entity, but rather a collection of disparate social groupings based most commonly on class and/or ethnicity, but also involving religion, gender, family and peer groups, with a person typically being a member of more than one group; the way in which these groups use and practise music is one means by which they create and express their identity. As Green and O'Neill put it, 'Social Groups can be identified partly in terms of their different musical production, distribution and reception practices' (Green and O'Neill 2001: 26). It is these that underpin the praxial philosophy of music education. An important part of a music education is supporting young people in understanding how these production, distribution and reception practices impact on how music is understood and makes its meaning. Through gaining an understanding of the musical practices, tastes and values of these different social groupings, teachers can also begin to address one of the key reasons given for the low esteem in which curriculum music is held by some students: that it makes so few connections with the music they encounter outside school.

Task 2.2 Young people and 'their' music

Construct a list of questions that could form the basis of a discussion with teenagers about their musical tastes and preferences. These questions might include:

- the kinds of music they listen to;
- what they find attractive and interesting about that music;
- how (if it does) the music emables them to identify as members of a particular social group;
- whether consumption choices are made which are linked to this music, e.g. types of clothing, drink, magazines, nightclubs.

Third, schools are social arenas within which particular values and norms are transmitted. Those social groups, which can influence most effectively the organisation of schools and what is taught within them, are best positioned to ensure that the values that serve their interests are those that are promulgated within schools and come to be seen as self-evidently good. Formal education is a means by which children are *enculturated* into the values and norms of the dominant culture, and music has traditionally been an important means of reflecting and articulating these norms and values. Green, for example, has demonstrated how school reinforces gender stereotypes and assumptions about musical practices that are rooted in the traditional practices of western classical music:

> [school] takes part in the perpetuation of subtle definitions of femininity and masculinity as connotations of musical practices, linked to musical styles in which pupils invest their desires to conform, not . . . to the school only, but to the wider field of gender and sexual politics.
>
> (Green 1997: 192)

Once more, an important part of music education is to develop students' (and perhaps our own) understanding of how music can perpetuate arguably undesirable stereotyping and sustain oppressive hegemonies. Freire refers to this as the process of conscientisation, whereby learners come to understand and develop their awareness '. . . of the power relationships that impact their lives and those of others' (Spruce 2015).

Finally, and arguably most importantly from an educational perspective, the way in which we actually think about music – the way in which we construe and construct its meaning – is culturally and socially rooted. At a very basic level, our recognition of music as sad, happy, martial, romantic etc., although often seemingly natural and self-evident, is *learnt* as part of our (often informal) enculturation into society. More significantly, the music that is typically and unquestioningly assumed by many to have the highest status – music of the western classical tradition – has attained this hegemonic status through its association with a dominant cultural order and has come to be one means by which such a hegemonic order is maintained. Whereas the overt dominance of classical music in the music curriculum is, for the most part, a thing of the past, we are still to a great extent held in its thrall. It still exerts its influence through the assumptions we hold about music: assumptions about the way in which musical quality is best evaluated; about the way in which it communicates its message and how music is best experienced. Such assumptions inevitably influence the way in which music is taught in schools, and it is important that we recognise, understand and are aware of these so that we control them, rather than they us.

Task 2.3 Musical value and musical meaning

Note down on a piece of paper your thoughts about:

* the criteria by which you evaluate the quality of a piece of music;
* how you feel music communicates its message;
* the way in which music is best experienced.

As you read through the rest of the chapter, keep referring back to your responses, noting whether or not your initial thoughts change.

The ideology of autonomous music

The language we use to describe music tells us much about the way we think about it. With this in mind, do Task 2.4 below (which in any other context is not recommended as a model of good teaching!).

Task 2.4 Talking about music?

Insert the missing word to complete the following sentences:

- Please _____ all your music to next week's rehearsal.
- Compose a _____ of music for the opening of the new school music block.
- Buy a _____ of Beethoven's 'Moonlight' Sonata from your local music shop.
- Listen to as many musical _____ by Elgar as possible.

It is likely that the words you inserted into the sentences were, respectively, 'bring'; 'piece'; 'copy'; 'works'. This is the way we tend to talk about music; or at least about western art music. We speak of *bringing* music to a rehearsal, of playing or composing a *piece* of music, of buying a musical *score* or *copy* and of hearing a musical *work*. The use of these terms (piece, score, copy, work) suggests that we think of music (at least subconsciously) as a kind of imaginary 'object' – something we can 'hold', like a jug. Now clearly music is not the same as a jug, as the essence of it – sound – cannot be 'held' in the same way as one can hold an object. However, the fact that we tend to think of music as an object tells us much about our underlying assumptions concerning the nature of music, the way in which music articulates its meaning and – perhaps most importantly – the criteria we use instinctively to apportion musical value. This then influences the way in which we interact with music and, of course, the way we *teach* it.

So, how did we end up thinking and talking about music in this arguably rather odd way? And, perhaps more importantly, why does it seem so natural to do so? Certainly we have not always thought of music like this. Until the late eighteenth century, music was thought of as a *performance* art rather than a *productive* art. Composers created a *performance* to fulfil the needs of a particular social occasion, often within the context of the court or church. They did not think they were engaged in producing an *object*.

However, during the late eighteenth century there developed the notion of 'fine art'. Fine art drew a distinction between art and craft: the latter was valued in terms of how well it fulfilled a primarily utilitarian function, while the former was evaluated in terms of its aesthetic merit. It was, essentially, the beginning of the ideology of 'art for art's sake'. Here the art object is understood and valued not in terms of its 'usefulness', or for its accuracy as a representation of something external to it, but as an autonomous creation to be valued in terms of the success with which it organises its basic materials into a formally satisfying and therefore (by definition) beautiful whole. The craft/fine art distinction was replicated in music through drawing a distinction between music that was of sufficient quality to enjoy an *autonomous* existence and music whose function was essentially social: the music of the streets, fields and coffee houses.

Art music reflected the object arts, in that meaning was understood to be articulated exclusively through the relationship and interaction of the musical materials. Consequently, the 'objectification' process – the codification of music into a score – took on much greater significance. Whereas, prior to the end of the eighteenth century, the score had acted only as a general guide to performance, it now came to be seen as definitive, encapsulating the musical meaning – the 'score' and the 'music' were perceived as virtually synonymous. Musical activity was now thought of as something that must naturally and inevitably result in a product; an object in the form of a score.

Musical autonomy and social stratification

The development of the ideology of autonomous music coincided with the emergence of a middle class seeking a cultural and social identity that would mark them out from the labouring classes – a cultural identity that through its inherent 'sensitivity' and 'sensibility' could be characterised as essentially superior to that of the working classes and be used as a justification for the unequal distribution of wealth and power. Autonomous art music – and particularly 'the score' – provided one particularly effective means of articulating this identity and distinctiveness.

A score, like any other object, can be marketed and access to it controlled through the application of market forces. Once music has been objectified, it can act, as memorably described by Everitt (1997: 26), like a pre-cooked frozen meal, capable of being reconstituted at any time and in any place. Having control of the time and place in which the performance takes place made it possible to exclude the 'hoi-polloi', so that identification with this music could be reserved exclusively for the middle classes. Performances of art music took place at pre-arranged times, in venues often specifically constructed for the purpose, where access could be controlled – often by levying a fee for entry. Brewer notes how:

> concerts . . . were organised as a series for which one had to pay a full season's subscriptions . . . Grand musical occasions, such as St Cecelia's Day concerts held in Salisbury Cathedral . . . charged entrance prices in excess of the seasonal fee to a subscription series.
>
> (Brewer 1997: 535)

Simply put, the working classes were charged with not being sufficiently sensitive to appreciate autonomous art music but economically barred from proving otherwise. Classical music, its forms, procedures, modes of production and dissemination, became intrinsically linked to middle-class social and cultural identities and thus became a potent tool of social stratification and one means by which a cultural hegemony could be constructed.

Maintaining the social hegemony: music education in the early twentieth century

Allsup argues that, '. . . for a ruling class to survive or reproduce it needs to pass down its culture through some form of education' (Allsup 2003: 8). From this, it follows naturally that western art music has traditionally been seen as the most appropriate music for the school curriculum – and in some schools this remains so. Where other music was admitted into schools (such as folk music), it was seen primarily as a stepping stone on the way to engagement with high art music. The basic premise was that all music could, and should, be evaluated according to the principles, practices and procedures of autonomous art music, irrespective of the music's genesis and original intended function.

The music that working-class children experienced outside school, which was part of their cultural identity (the music of the streets and music halls), did not meet the criteria of value as predicated by autonomous music and was therefore seen as unworthy and even degenerate. W.G. Whittaker in *Class-Singing* (1925) writes that:

> It would seem incredible that the head mistress of a kindergarten should use the sentimental rubbish of a well-known popular contralto for a school repertoire, that one should find a music hall song which runs, 'strolling round the town, knocking people down, We all got drunk etc' used as marching tunes, yet these are actual examples of what is perpetrated in the sacred name of education.
>
> (Whittaker 1925: 105)

At the time, Whittaker's outrage would have seemed quite justified. During the latter part of the nineteenth and early part of the twentieth centuries, the Platonic notion of the power of 'good' music to have a positive impact on the moral character of the nation's youth came to be seen as one of the main purposes of music in schools. The editorial of the first edition of the *School Music Review* in 1892 stated that: '. . . the beneficial influence an early taste of music might exert upon the choice and character of the amusements of the people cannot seriously be disputed' (Russell 1987/97: 52). A.T. Cringen in *The Teacher's Handbook of the Tonic Sol-fa System* (1889) wrote that 'Progressive teachers . . . are now fully alive to the beneficial effects of the study of Music as a refining, moral influence in the schoolroom and the home' (Crowe 1996). Singing was seen as particularly beneficial in that it not only provided 'the most valuable means we know of introducing children to music of sterling value and of forming taste' (Whittaker 1925: 106), but was also invaluable 'for the education and character building value of the stirring words that are sung' (Crowe 1996).

Refined taste and moral rectitude were defined as that which reflected middle-class values and norms and consequently reinforced the predominating social order. The potential, particularly of songs, to affirm the social and cultural status quo was not lost on those who developed music materials for schools. Crowe (1996), for example, quotes from a songbook used in Canadian schools in the early part of the last century, words and music by one Mr Henry Sefton:

> My hands how nicely they are made, To hold, to touch and do:
> I'll try to learn some honest trade; That will be useful too;
> My eyes, how fit they are to read, To mind my work and look;
> I ought to think of that, indeed, And use them in my book.
>
> (Sefton: 'Three Part Songs': 15)

A socio-cultural perspective on contemporary music education

One of the most significant changes in school music over the past thirty years or so is the broad range of musical traditions and style that most children now encounter as part of the school music curriculum. Popular musics and music from around the world, as well as traditional music and western art music, are an important part of the music curriculum in most schools, and students' entitlement to a broad and balanced music curriculum is enshrined within the English National Curriculum for Music (2013b).

That western art music no longer exerts the explicit dominance over the music curriculum as once it did is therefore beyond question (at least in most schools). Indeed, there is a fear, expressed perhaps most recently in an Ofsted inspection report into music in schools (2013), that the pendulum has swung too far away from 'classical' music and that 'classical' music has been pushed to the peripheries of the music curriculum in schools. This concern is evident in the most recent version of the National Curriculum for Music in England, which now includes the stipulation that pupils 'listen with increasing discrimination to a wide range of music from great composers and musicians' (2013b).

However, as Green argues, the legacy and dominance of western art music is not over-come simply by a change in repertoire. As she says, 'the question is not one of content but of pedagogy' (Green 1997: 145). In this final section we consider aspects of pedagogy which, although continuing to be influenced by the traditions of western art music, can, through adopting a socio-cultural perspective, become more relevant, inclusive and, above all, musical.

Musical literacy

A philosophy of music education predicated upon the western music tradition inevitably places great importance on the 'score'. To understand the score is to understand the meaning of the music, so the argument goes. Iain Kendall espouses such a view when he writes:

> The child who cannot read music is in a very similar position to the child who cannot read words. He simply does not know what a wonderful world exists beyond the barrier of the symbol – the secret code which he cannot crack. Between him and incredible spiritual wealth stand five lines and some dots with tails.
>
> (Kendall 1977: 31)

More recently, a similar sentiment was expressed in an inspection report into music education in English schools. Here, once again the lack of 'theoretical' understanding is perceived as *inevitably* presenting a barrier to musical understanding:

> The Year 3 cohort, as their final lesson in a singing unit, sang in three part harmony to the whole school. The teaching was expert and encouraging and the quality of the pupils' performance truly excellent and uplifting. But, as the teacher and the hub leader recognised, the pupils had not seen the notation of the song, learning to sing it by copying the teacher. The pupils were in the dark about the chord sequence, time signature and melody that they had sung so beautifully.
>
> (Ofsted 2013: 26)

The belief that 'musical meaning' resides within the notated form of music (its objectification) and that the key to that meaning lies through the decoding of this notation has exerted an almost hypnotic power over music education, causing us often to ignore the fact that musical knowing is, primarily, embodied knowing: we demonstrate musical understanding through doing and making music. Views such as those expressed above have sometimes led to notation being taught as an abstract concept separate from any musical context. To be able to read staff notation is perceived as having intrinsic value, with no need for it to be linked to a particular musical activity or practice.

A further consequence of this focus on notation is that we have come to think of musical literacy in very narrow terms: the ability to read staff notation. The emphasis on staff notation as a process of decoding pre-existent musical scores has led us to ignore, and consequently fail to teach, the many other ways in which notation is used in the musical world. Fautley(2013) expresses this well when looking back over the role that different forms of notation have played in his musical life:

> I also learned alternate notations – guitar chords, and like hundreds of other children of the third quarter of the twentieth century, I learned to play the electronic organ using guitar chord symbols. Simultaneously doing 'academic' music the translation of chord symbols into roman numerals was straightforward, and, later, figured basses seemed to me to be built on the same sets of premises. At the time I played in orchestras using notation, dance bands using a hybrid of staff notation and chord symbols, and in the pit for shows from charts entirely consisting of chord symbols. But I've also played in acoustic folk bands, rock bands, and, for a brief while in the wacky 80s, kraut-rock inspired synth multitracking, with none of the above. Many of these non-formal musickings were undertaken with musicians far better than me who could 'just do it', some of whom were kids in my classes.
>
> (Fautley 2013)

Task 2.5 The diversity of musical notations

Think of the ways in which you have worked with different forms of notation or with staff notation in ways other than simply realising a 'score'. What kinds of musical learning and skills did these engender?

Take one of the examples that you have identified and work this up into an activity or lesson for some of the students you teach. Share your ideas with other beginner teachers either in seminars/meetings or through a blog post.

Most damagingly, however, the emphasis on musical literacy implies that those who don't read music are musically illiterate; and one sometimes hears highly skilled musicians from other musical genres and cultures describe themselves as such. However, such a view is predicated upon a restricted and culturally self-serving view of what counts as 'literacy'. As Kwami points out:

For the majority of the world's people, musical literacy does not involve the ability to read and write music ... For many, musical literacy operates as the ability to communicate with others through music in a practical way. ... internalisation, is a process that characterises this type of musical literacy. ... A second factor is improvisation ... Other facets of this musical literacy involve dance, movement and language which feature to a greater extent elsewhere than in the Western classical tradition, the main currency of the school curriculum.

(Kwami 2001: 144)

Kwami's point is that we need as teachers to adopt a much broader view of what constitutes 'musical literacy'. Musical literacy is not the ability to read staff notation but to be able to communicate and respond to music. Task 2.6 asks you to consider what a broader view of musical literacy might mean in practice.

Task 2.6 Teaching without recourse to notation

Imagine that you are teaching the first lesson in a sequence of lessons on the 'blues'. The first lesson has within it aspects of listening, performing and composing. You have decided to teach the lesson without recourse to notation. Outline the activities you might ask the class to do and the teaching strategies you would employ. Draw on Kwami's description of different kinds of 'musical literacy' to help you do this.

Then think how you might introduce appropriate notation into a lesson on the 'blues'. Adopting a more 'praxial' approach, find out about the ways in which blues and jazz musicians use notation (when they do) and draw on this in your teaching. What do you think students will gain from engaging with notation in this way?

Set works

The tradition of 'set works' is rooted in this idea of musical meaning being exclusively contained within the score. Let us think for a moment about the way in which set works are typically taught, e.g. a movement from a symphony. The teacher typically focuses on the music's thematic content, the way in which instruments are used and combined, the harmony and rhythm and how these relate to each other; thought is given to key relationships, harmonic function and structure. Even where the production of the symphony is closely related to contemporary events (say, the depiction of Stalinist terror in Shostakovich's *Tenth Symphony*), consideration of these aspects is peripheral to analysing the relationships of the musical elements to each other. Such an approach is predicated on an understanding that musical meaning resides, essentially, within the score as an objectification of the music. Little attention is paid to the social context of its composition, performance and reception or the extent to which the music articulates any extrinsic message.

Let us consider now a different way in which a set work might be approached; one that takes into account the social context of its creation. Here the set work is Bach's *Fifth Brandenburg Concerto*. At the end of the first movement there is a long cadenza for the harpsichord. This cadenza is notable for two reasons: first, its length in proportion to the rest of the movement, and second, the way in which an instrument that normally plays a supporting role is suddenly brought to the fore. Clearly this work is analysable in terms of the autonomous working out of its materials. However, conventional analysis only tells us the 'what' of the music, not the 'why'. *Why* Bach chose, at this time, in this place and in this piece, to compose a cadenza that is disproportionate to the rest of the movement, modulates to keys that are well beyond the expectations of the period and focuses on an instrument that (in orchestral music, at least) had hitherto been kept well in the background. Such questions are not answerable simply through analysing the music as an autonomous object or wholly explained as Bach 'intuiting the way to new modes of expression, opening up musical vocabulary, simply as a result of his genius' (Gaines 2004: 133). A different perspective is required; one that is provided by looking beyond the musical object to the social context of the music's composition.

Susan McClary, in 'The blasphemy of talking politics during Bach Year' (1987) (a seminal work in the emergence of the 'new musicology'), suggests that what Bach is doing in this movement is challenging the social norms, conventions and hierarchy of the Brandenburg Court. In her analysis, the flute and violin (the main solo instruments) represent the conforming members of society who are allowed limited freedoms within the tightly drawn parameters of courtly society. However, the harpsichord 'hijacks' the music and, in doing so, directly challenges both musical and courtly conventions and the social hierarchy that underpins them:

> the flute and violin drop out, inconclusively, one after another, exactly in the way an orchestra would if one of its members started making up a new piece in the middle of a performance. . . . They fall silent in the face of this affront from the ensemble's lackey . . . Certainly, social order and individual freedom are possible but only as long as the individuals in question . . . abide by the rules. What happens when a genuine deviant (and one from the ensemble's service staff yet!) declares itself a genius . . . and takes over?
>
> (McClary 1987: 40)

This cultural perspective tells us more about the revolutionary nature of this cadenza than any amount of abstract analysis of its 'autonomous' form. It provides an explanation of why Bach breaks conventions so dramatically *in this work, at this time and in this place*. In other words, it links a work to its social context. This is not to suggest that analyses like this should be used exclusively, any more than one should rely wholly on analysis of the autonomous object. The one perspective does not exclude the other. Both go hand in hand, enriching our and our students' understanding of the music.

Task 2.7 Applying a social and cultural perspective

Choose a piece of classical music that you know well. Briefly analyse it in terms of its structure, key relationships, harmony and rhythm. Now research the background to its composition, performance and reception, focusing not on biographical details of the composer, but on the social milieu in which it was created. Finally, decide how you might use the results of your research to develop students' understanding of the music.

Non-western musics

Asked why music from other cultures should be included in the music curriculum, music teachers might reply that it enables children to gain an understanding of other cultures and an awareness of and respect for ethnic and cultural diversity. However, as Green points out, there is little research to demonstrate how or whether this occurs (Green 2001: 57). Indeed, it is highly questionable whether simply coming into contact with music of other cultures (simply brushing against it) really has any significant impact on children's understanding and awareness of cultural diversity.

It might also be argued that taking music from a different cultural context and then engaging and evaluating it purely in terms of dominant cultural norms (e.g. those of western art music) is little more than cultural imperialism and will inevitably result in the music being perceived as inferior or primitive. Developing children's cultural awareness and under-standing through music therefore involves integrating into the curriculum and its teaching not just the musical artefacts of other cultures, but also their practices, procedures and processes, i.e. adopting a praxial approach.

The procedures and processes of music from other cultures are often radically different from those of western music. Many musical cultures have different conceptions of musical time and space, beat and pulse. The temporal organisation of most western art music is 'linear': we think of music as progressing through time, e.g. sonata form. However, other musics (such as Indian classical music and minimalism) operate on cyclical principles. Western music's typical emphasis on the first and third beats and its predilection towards 'regular' pulse is not reflected in, for example, 'reggae' where the emphasis is on the second and fourth beats or 'in African traditions [where] what we have may be closer to a medieval scenario of tempus perfectum and imperfectum – of "twos and threes"' (Kwami 2000).

Providing opportunities for young people to engage with music on its own terms means that they are able to demonstrate their musical knowledge, skills and understanding through means other than the skills *exemplified* through western musical practices. Those who demonstrate their music skills best through aural learning and improvisation (skills exemplified in most popular and non-western musical styles) are then given the opportunity to excel, while those who are skilled in western music are given the chance to develop other ways of understanding music and being musical. Restricting the curriculum to one that is underpinned exclusively by the 'aesthetic ideology' can result in a curriculum that is narrow and over-specialised and within which many students 'fail'. This leads inevitably to disillusionment with curriculum music.

Adopting a praxial approach to music teaching, which takes into account music's original mode of production, dissemination and reception, can help children develop a deeper understanding of other cultures. Young people who are given the opportunity to work with music in ways similar to how its originators worked with it may develop an understanding of the many different ways in which music is created, disseminated and received. This then leads to a greater empathy with both the music and the culture from which it has emerged. Such teaching is, we would argue, more inclusive as it recognises and celebrates both musical and cultural diversity.

Focusing on the modes of production, distribution and reception and on musical practices and the values that underpin these practices (i.e. adopting a praxial approach) allows for conscious links to be made between different musical practices on an equal footing; what Kwami describes as an 'intercultural' rather than a 'multicultural approach' (2001). This approach also allows for different kinds of musical learners to succeed, as musical achievement can be demonstrated across a much wider musical canvas. At the same time, non-western musics are granted equal status in the classroom, not simply through *asserting* it to be so, but by integrating into the curriculum the ways in which those cultures communicate musically.

The opportunities offered by a music curriculum that has cognisance of the cultural and social genesis of music is one that is less about inducting children into a specific set of musical and cultural norms and values and more about facilitating entry into a range of musical practices. It is, as Kwami puts it, about '. . . trying to understand the music in a manner similar to that of the people from whom it originates or belongs' (Kwami 2001: 145). For as Small says, in order to really understand what music's meaning is, we should not ask 'What does this musical work mean?' but rather 'What does it mean when this performance takes place at this location at this time, with these people taking part, both as performers and listeners?' (Small 1999: 19). This, in a sense, is the essence of the praxial approach to music education.

Task 2.8 Adopting a praxial perspective to plan for music learning

Imagine that you are going to use popular music or non-western music as the basis for a sequence of lessons. Research the social and cultural background of the music. Plan an outline for these lessons that shows how you will develop students' musical skills, knowledge and understanding through activities that reflect the ways in which the music is created, disseminated and received.

Robert Walker sums up the challenges of the praxial approach to music teaching when he writes:

> For music educators, the message is that we in music do far more than merely teach skills and techniques. Music cannot speak its profound message about the society it lives in merely from the sound. The sounds of music can only become valuable in education when they are explained in terms of the belief and knowledge systems of the society which alone enables us to endow them with meanings.
>
> (Walker 1996: 15)

However, to achieve this means revisiting what we consider as norms. It means revisiting musical ideas that have been taken for granted. This is the challenge.

Task 2.9 Critiquing the critique

To what extent do you agree with the arguments put forward in this chapter for a 'praxial' approach to music education? Do you think this approach has anything to offer to your own teaching and the music education of the students you teach? What do you think are the deficiencies in the arguments presented here and do you feel that the critique presented of the 'aesthetic ideology' is a fair one?

Spend some time thinking about your responses to these questions and then share and discuss them with other (beginner) music teachers either face to face or via a blog post.

Summary

In this chapter we have suggested that:

- a too narrow conception of what music is can lead to an impoverished model of music teaching and learning;
- music teaching that is informed by a socio-cultural and praxial perspective has the potential to be more inclusive – to celebrate and value a wider range of musics, musical skills and musical understanding.

Further reading

Cheetham, J. (2013) An after school rock school investigated: why are they here?, in J. Finney and F. Laurence (eds) *MasterClass in Music Education: Transforming Teaching and Learning*, London: Bloomsbury, pp. 151–156.

DeNora, T. (2003) 'Music sociology: getting the music into the action', *British Journal of Music Education*, 20, 2: 165–177.

Finney, J. (2009) Cultural understanding, in J. Evans and C. Philpott (eds) *A Practical Guide to Teaching Music in the Secondary School*, Abingdon: RoutledgeFalmer, pp. 28–35.

These chapters and articles offer a sound background to the issues and ideas surrounding a socio-cultural perspective on music and music education.

3 The what, how and where of musical learning and development

Chris Philpott

Introduction

Musical learning is complex. However, it is important for the music teacher to formulate an understanding of the nature of learning in music if they are to plan lessons and units of work that enable young people to become progressively more accomplished composers, performers and responders to music.

In this chapter we address four related issues in order to help you build an understanding of the nature of musical learning:

- What is there to learn? What is the nature of musical knowledge?
- How do young people learn? How do they learn what there is to know?
- Where do they learn?
- How does their musical knowledge develop?

For the purposes of this chapter, learning is defined as having taken place when a change has occurred in the behaviour, attitudes or values of young people through the development of different types of musical knowledge. As we shall see, sometimes learning is intentional, where the learner sets out to learn and/or a teacher sets out to bring about learning. However, it is often the case that learning takes place that was not intended by the learner or teacher, for any musical experience can be a source of knowledge. Furthermore, there are many complexities surrounding musical learning, as identified by Hallam (2001). These include:

- the learners' characteristics, i.e. their level of development, prior knowledge, age, gender, motivation and self-esteem;
- the learning environment, i.e. society, culture, school, home and peers;
- the teaching environment and teacher characteristics.

Teaching constitutes the intentional strategies employed to create and sustain an environment to bring about learning; creating the optimum conditions for learning. Given the complexity of musical learning, music teachers have a professional responsibility to make meaningful connections between their own teaching and the learning of their students.

Objectives

By the end of this chapter you should:

- know how music can be differentiated into different types of knowledge;
- understand how these knowledge types can inform your objectives for planning music lessons;
- know how musical knowledge is learnt;
- know that musical knowledge can develop in both formal and informal settings;
- know how the learning of musical knowledge develops;
- know how learning in music is potentially transferable to other areas of learning.

What is there to learn? The nature of musical knowledge

What is there for the musician to learn? What is the nature of musical knowledge? Answers to these questions are particularly important when you are setting objectives for learning in your classroom.

Task 3.1 Musical knowledge 1

What different types of musical knowledge have you needed to learn in order to become a successful musician? Think back to your own musical development and try to place these into categories or types of knowledge. Discuss this with another beginner teacher and compare ideas.

Music teachers are always engaging with the questions found in Task 3.1 (consciously or not) when deciding what to teach, how to frame learning objectives, how to bring about learning and how to 'measure' musical learning. To some extent the learning you expect in your music lessons will be dictated by the intuitive assumptions behind your answers to these questions.

As a model to structure our considerations here, three different types of musical knowledge can be identified, which have been adapted from the work of Reid (1986) and Swanwick (1988).

Knowledge 'about' music

This might be referred to as factual knowledge, that is, factual knowledge about composers, about style, about theory, about musical concepts. While developments in music education over the past fifty years have explicitly moved us away from an over-reliance on factual musical knowledge to practical engagement, 'facts' have an important role to play in informing our understanding of music. Knowing *that* a song is in verse-chorus form or *that*

Mozart was a prodigy or *that* a diminished seventh is a pile of minor thirds can enhance our understanding and enjoyment of music. However, facts about music are only 'musical' in as much as they are derived from and related to the sound of music itself. Facts about music are only given meaning by real music, without which they are not distinguishable from historical or theoretical (albeit interesting) trivia.

Knowledge 'how'

This could be termed 'know-how' and is clearly an important dimension of musical knowledge. Musicians might have 'know-how' in the following areas:

- technical know-how (knowing how to do this or that on an instrument or digital system);
- technical skill (the physical or intellectual capacity to carry this out);
- aural discrimination (knowing how to distinguish between sounds);
- perceptual know-how (for example, knowing how to recognise a 'drone');
- presentational know-how (how to present a piece to an audience);
- notational know-how (reading and writing music);
- craft skills (knowing how to make music sound in a particular way).

Clearly some of these skills are closely linked; for example, an aural dictation exercise can test discrimination, perception and notational 'know-how'. It is also clear that learning facts 'about' music without the 'know-how' to recognise their embodiment in music can be a sterile process. Furthermore, 'know-how' can remain intuitive. For example, many young people immerse themselves in particular musics and while they may 'know how' to recognise the main features, they may not necessarily have the desire or skills to 'name' what they hear.

Knowledge 'of' music

This form of musical knowledge is a knowledge 'of' music by direct acquaintance (see Reid 1986). It implies the building of an understanding relationship with the music, in the same way that we get to know a person or a face. We might not be able to say what we know or even demonstrate it, yet the relationship with 'this' piece of music cannot be denied. Indeed, this is the only way that we can account for youngsters developing musically without any formal music education. Young people arrive at secondary school with a good deal of intuitive understanding (knowledge 'of' music); in particular, they understand 'their' music and use it to make sense of the world. Clearly our knowledge 'of' music (our understanding relationship with it) is differentiated by 'how' and 'about'. Knowing *that* we are listening to an Irish rebel folk song and knowing *how* to identify the structural elements, of course, enhances our understanding of the work. However, formal know-how and factual knowledge are not *essential* to this understanding. Young people (and indeed us all) build significant relationships with pieces of music without any formal understanding about the music or how it is put together. This is not to say that their relationship, their knowledge 'of' the music, is not underpinned by much *intuitive* 'know-how'.

Task 3.2   Musical knowledge 2

Complete the following with examples from your own musical knowledge:

1   I know that (Eminem is a rapper) . . . .
2   I know that . . . .
3   I know that . . . .
4   I know how to (recognise a tri-tone). . . . .
5   I know how to . . . .
6   I know how to . . . .
7   I know (Wagner's 'Ring' cycle in the same way I know a person)
8   I know . . . .
9   I know . . . .

Once you have completed this task, discuss the following questions with another beginner teacher. Is it possible to rank these types of musical knowledge in any order of importance? How are they related? Do we need to learn 'know-how' before we can build meaningful relationships with music?

The knowledge types in action

Our observations on the different types of musical knowledge and their relationship are clearly important when planning objectives for music lessons and when understanding the potential strategies for achieving these. For example, the traditional song in Figure 3.1 can be used with students to develop knowledge 'about' music, knowledge 'of' music and the 'know-how' of music (see Table 3.1).

Figure 3.1 Traditional song (to be sung as a round)

Table 3.1 The knowledge types in action

Knowledge 'about'	Know 'how'	Knowledge 'of'
What a round is	How to sing and recognise a round	The expressive shape and character of the music
What counterpoint is	How to breathe in the right places	The expressive potential of the music (what would happen if we sang it as a strident march or as a lament?)
What 4 time is		
Others?	How to sing in ensemble	
	How to conduct in 4 time	Others?
	Others?	

As can be seen from Table 3.1, you can develop your students' technical musical knowledge (factual and know-how) as well as their knowledge 'of' the music as they build an understanding relationship with the expressive and structural character of the music. Task 3.3 asks you to consider these knowledge types in relation to your own teaching.

Task 3.3 The knowledge types in action

Using the example in Figure 3.1 and Table 3.1 as a model, take a musical activity of your own, such as the learning of a song, and try to analyse which aspects of the knowledge types can be developed when young people engage with this work. Try to turn this analysis into a lesson plan that addresses learning objectives in relation to all of the knowledge types.

Musical knowledge and objectives for the music lesson

Swanwick (1979) makes a strong case for placing knowledge 'of' music at the centre of music education. He argues that our relationship with music is at the core of why we engage with music at all, i.e. it means something to us! He does not deny the interplay of the knowledge types, yet believes that knowing about music and the know-how of music services our foundational knowledge 'of' music. For this reason he believes that developing relationships with music through immersion in listening, responding, composing and performing should be at the heart of the objectives of every music lesson. For Swanwick it is impossible to imagine a 'musical' lesson that deals only with knowledge 'about' or technical know-how divorced from the context of making or listening to music. However, learning 'about' and 'how' can take place in parallel with building meaningful relationships with music.

When designing lesson objectives in relation to the knowledge types, Swanwick suggests that the following priorities should be observed:

- Category 1 objectives: for students to recognise, identify, understand and use expressive gestures and structures in a range of styles (primarily knowledge 'of' music).
- Category 2 objectives: for students to engage in skill acquisition and literature studies; to assemble and categorise information (mainly concerned with knowing 'how' and knowing 'about').
- Category 3 objectives: for students to develop skills in human interaction (cooperation and sharing) (Swanwick 1979: 67).

Swanwick is quite clearly saying that developing knowledge 'of' music underpins music education. While he recognises the interrelationships between the knowledge types, he believes that categories 2 and 3 *service* category 1 objectives, that is, those objectives that aim to develop a student's meaningful relationships with music. However, it has been notoriously difficult to plan for category 1 objectives in the classroom. While many music educators have placed knowledge 'of' as an ultimate aim of music education, there has been less agreement on how to achieve it. Metcalfe (1987) has shown that while the history of music education is littered with good intentions, many music curricula have become reductionist about musical knowledge, assuming that the only way we can teach music is by breaking down the holistic experience into chunks of knowledge 'about' and knowledge 'how'. Writers such as Reimer (1989) have suggested that in order to plan for knowledge 'of' music, we must return to the nature of music itself. He asks us to consider how we understand music; what do we mean when we say we know a piece of music? Clearly, such knowledge does not merely amount to knowledge 'about' or 'how', for this would exclude the intuitive musical understandings that young people bring with them to the classroom.

Task 3.4 Swanwick's hierarchy

What are your thoughts about Swanwick's hierarchy? To what extent can category 1 develop without 2 or 3? Do we need to learn 2 and 3 before we can achieve 1? Is it possible to have category 1 learning as your overriding priority? What are the priorities of the department in which you are working? Discuss these questions with other beginner teachers and/or your school-based mentor.

There are many other accounts of musical knowledge that you should explore to inform your understanding of music education. For example, while Swanwick has been used here as a case study example, the work of David Elliott (1995, and his subsequent writing) has also been influential in this regard. Elliott focuses his attention on what he calls a *praxial* philosophy of music education, where the central concept of musicianship is underpinned by procedural knowledge that is further differentiated into interrelated knowledge types such as formal, informal, impressionistic and supervisory knowledge.

In both of these accounts, musical knowledge is seen as being at the core of music education, and the nature of musical knowledge is derived from the essential nature and practice of music itself. They aim to answer the question: What is it that we need to know in order to behave as a musician when listening, responding, composing and performing?

We now turn our attention to how musical knowledge is learnt.

How do we learn musical knowledge?

There has always been controversy surrounding how young people learn their musical knowledge, and the following questions have exercised music educators for many years:

- What is the relationship between informal, intuitive, encultured learning and formal training and instruction?
- What account should teachers take of informal, intuitive and encultured learning?

Whatever our answers to these questions, it is clear that the 'how' of musical learning is as complex as musical knowledge itself.

Enculturation and instruction

One of the main concerns for how we learn in music is the relationship between 'encultured' learning and 'instructional' learning. 'Enculturation' happens without conscious effort. This is learning that is 'caught' by being part of the culture, i.e. the music that is always around us. For example, we might 'catch' how rap works and even be able to perform and compose it. The 'instructional' aspects of musical learning take place as a result of the intentional efforts of teachers and/or learners. For example, we might be taught how to analyse the technical aspects of rap and how to develop our skills of performance in rap. There is an ongoing debate that surrounds the relationship between 'enculturation' and 'instruction', with some suggesting that enculturation and instruction are quite separate, and that the latter is essential to making sense of the former. Others believe in the necessary and parallel interplay between each, while some espouse the need to trust the encultured learning of youngsters as fundamental to how they learn. The tensions in the debate about encultured and instructional musical learning can be found in Table 3.2, while Task 3.5 asks you to consider these issues in relation to your own experiences of music education.

Table 3.2 Some tensions in debating the *how* of musical learning

Encultured learning	*Instructional learning*
Osmosis (caught)	Instruction (taught)
Youngster led	Teacher led
Encounter	Instruction
Knowledge of music	Knowing the about and how of music
Intuition	Technique and analysis
Informal	Formal

Task 3.5 Encultured and instructional learning

Using a four-point scale where 1 is closest to *encultured learning* and 4 is closest to *instructional learning*, rate:

- music education at your school as a child;
- music education at your placement school;
- the music education you would like to promote.

Where do you find the majority of your answers? What are the differences between your answers for each? What does this activity tell you about your views of music education in relation to your past and current experiences?

What is clear is that these complexities need to be understood by teachers and taken into account when facilitating musical learning. Not to do so may cause the disjuncture between the various aspects and moments of musical learning and the consequent alienation and poor motivation of youngsters, and this is a situation that has often dogged 'classroom' music in the past. However, current effective practice suggests that formal instruction and enculturation *can* co-exist in the classroom and where knowledge types develop alongside and in parallel with each other. The theoretical resolution of the tensions of how we learn can be found in the broad concept of constructivism.

Constructivism

Constructivism is a theory of learning that embraces both enculturation and instruction. This theory of learning assumes that learning takes place when existing knowledge interacts with new learning experiences. Learning is not seen as a passive process but one in which the learner actively engages in the construction of knowledge. Young people need to feel responsible for their learning, and their teachers need to facilitate learning experiences that encourage ownership and the productive interplay of enculturation and instruction.

Sloboda (1985) refers to intuitive musical learning as 'enculturation', which he maintains happens in 'waves' without conscious effort or instruction in the early years of life. The 'formal' aspects of music education are, he maintains, concerned with training and skill acquisition where skills are formed out of habits which become automatic after repetition. Sloboda deals with these two aspects of musical learning quite separately. He embraces our knowledge 'of' music through our intuitive 'enculturation', and skills ('know-how') through training and instruction. Sloboda suggests that we cannot progress significantly from the encultured state unless we engage with high-level skill development, and that the role of formal education is to provide this training at various levels. For Sloboda a new type of learning takes place after initial immersion in the culture, and on this analysis formal instructional learning is in a linear and sequential relationship to informal and encultured learning.

Swanwick (1988) has also developed a constructivist theory of musical learning in which the knowledge types are integrated into a spiral of musical development. For Swanwick, learning from instruction and enculturation can take place in parallel. He suggests that music lessons should contain a productive tension between musical encounters (enculturation) and instruction and yet where knowledge 'of' music is at the centre of all musical learning. That is, we can only make sense of instructional 'know-how' and knowledge 'about' music by building meaningful encultured relationships with it.

Social learning

Implicit in the constructivist work of both Sloboda and Swanwick is the important dimension of *social learning*, and this has important implications for music teachers. Clearly, all learning takes place within specific social and cultural contexts, and we are subjected to models of musical practice as part of both enculturation and instruction.

At the heart of social learning is what Elliott calls 'procedural knowledge'. That is, how to behave musically within a particular culture, and for him, this learning can only develop in conditions where 'real' music is being made in 'real' circumstances, and where 'the heart of the music curriculum (is) a musical teacher inducting students in to musical practices through active music making' (Elliott 1995: 285). Plummeridge also takes up this point when he maintains that:

> the central aim of music education is to engage youngsters in practical activities through which they will come to learn and internalise the procedures of the discipline. In this way they develop musical thinking . . . Procedures have to be taught . . . but there is a sense in which they are 'caught' . . . people come to understand the methods, or procedures, of music by working with others who are on the inside of that discipline.
>
> (Plummeridge 1991: 29)

Indeed, in much 'community'-based music education, such as brass bands and church choirs, learning is based upon a healthy mixture of formal induction into musical practices and the 'catching' of musical learning by 'osmosis', by just being there! The implications of social learning for music teachers are as follows:

- The music teacher is a model for students' learning.
- The models we provide need to be as musical and as authentic possible.
- Students bring much social learning with them.
- Students can also be musical models for the learning of others (their peers and the teacher).
- The school and classroom can been seen as a community of musical learning.

Task 3.6 Social learning

What are the implications of social learning for music education and how might the theory influence the way you teach? Prepare some notes as the basis for a seminar/discussion with other beginner teachers.

Another dimension to the constructivist take on how we learn in music is the issue and debate surrounding informal and formal learning.

Informal and formal learning

As we have seen, some musical learning takes place by being immersed in the 'culture', and this is known as enculturation. For example, by being exposed to music in our everyday lives we all develop an intuitive sense of the syntax and grammar of various musical styles, traditions and genres. There is a sense in which we cannot help this happening to us and, as such, this learning is 'informal', i.e. it is not based upon formal instruction.

There is, however, another notion of 'informal' learning abroad, which is more intentional on the part of young people. For example, this can be found when young people play, sing and compose music by themselves in their own time. The nature of learning in these circumstances has come to be known as informal learning. While enculturation, and what we have come to call informal learning, are closely related concepts, the latter is, as has been said, more obviously intentional.

In many ways the tension between the formal and informal has been at the core of the history of music education in England for the past fifty years or so. Music has often been reported as the most unpopular subject in the school curriculum and yet paradoxically the most important to young people outside of school (see Schools Council 1971; Harland *et al.* 2000). Indeed, the history of music education in the late twentieth and early twenty-first centuries can be seen as a series of attempts to 'heal' this alienation (see Philpott 2010).

Most recently the pedagogy of self-directed learning (a pedagogy of informal learning) has been developed as a possible solution to ongoing issues of pupil alienation from school music. This is exemplified in the work of Lucy Green and *Musical Futures* (see Hertfordshire Pathfinder Project; www.musicalfutures.org; Green 2008). As part of this project, Lucy Green used her work on how pop musicians learn (Green 2001) to research a classroom pedagogy that exploits informal learning processes, i.e. the processes that some popular musicians appear to employ when learning in music:

> Playing music of one's own choice, with which one identifies personally, operating both as a performer and a composer with like minded friends, and having fun doing it must be high priorities in the quest for increasing numbers of young people to benefit from a music education which makes music not merely available, but meaningful, worthwhile and participatory.
>
> (Green 2001: 16)

Green has developed five principles for self-directed (sometimes called informal) learning and pedagogy (see Green 2008: 9–10):

- Young people work with music chosen by themselves that they enjoy and identify with.
- Young people work in the main aurally through listening and copying.
- Young people work with peers in groups chosen by themselves.

- Skills and knowledge are gained in a haphazard fashion with whole 'real' pieces at the core.
- Listening, performing and composing are integrated throughout the learning process.

Crucial to developing this informal pedagogy is the role of the teacher. Self-directed learning draws upon and promotes informal learning and thus aims to begin with the musical ideas and knowledge of the youngsters themselves. The role of the 'teacher' in the learning process is relatively non-interventionist, where teachers are seen as facilitators and a resource for the young people to draw on. The 'new' relationships outlined in the project (student–student, student–teacher) are key to ownership of the music and of the musical learning. The expectation of the teacher is to:

- establish ground rules for behaviour;
- remind students of the ongoing task at the start of each session;
- stand back and observe what the young people are doing;
- empathise with the perspectives and goals students set themselves;
- diagnose students' needs in relation to these perceived goals;
- offer suggestions and models for them to achieve their self-set goals;
- be available for help but not for instructing in the 'normal' way.

It is clear that this approach is in stark contrast to the 'formal' notion that the teacher decides what needs to be learnt and then plans a set of instructional strategies to make this happen. While the results of the research have been encouraging in terms of achievement, increased participation, ownership of the learning and breaking the cycle of alienation from school classroom music, critics remain concerned about what would appear to be a reduced role for the instructional interventions from a professional music teacher (see Cain 2013).

Task 3.7 Informal self-directed learning

How much of your own learning has been self-directed and 'informal' in this way? Can you identify which aspects of your musical learning have developed as a result of this?

How can constructivism provide a resolution to the apparent tension between formal learning (initiated by teachers) and informal learning (initiated by young people)? Folkestad (2005, 2006) has recognised that the relationship between the formal and the informal is immensely complex. He maintains that an understanding of the relationship between the formal and the informal is crucial to understanding all musical learning, and he proposes the following distinction: formal learning can be characterised as the intentional predetermined sequencing of learning activities by 'a person who takes on the task of organising and leading the learning activity' (2006: 141). Teaching is always part of the formal moment, whoever does it.

Informal learning can be characterised as being 'not sequenced beforehand' and occurs during '*self chosen and voluntary activity*' (2006: 141).

Task 3.8 Formal and informal learning

Using Folkestad's analysis discussed above, list examples under the following headings:

- Formal learning in school
- Informal learning in school
- Formal learning out of school
- Informal learning out of school

For Folkestad, the crucial issue is the intentionality of the learner. Formal learning is found when the minds of young people and teachers are directed towards learning *how to play music*. Informal learning is found when minds are directed towards *playing and making* music. Furthermore, 'what characterises most learning situations is the instant switch between these learning styles and the dialectic interaction between them' (2006: 142).

We can characterise this switch as 'flipping', for example, when a band improvises over a riff but then stops while one member teaches the others how to play a chord. Most musicians of all types will have experienced 'flipping', although the 'formal' moment is often so prioritised in music education that the informal experience can be 'buried' (see Finney and Philpott 2010). And so for Folkestad, the relationship of formal to informal is not a dichotomy but a continuum, 'and that in most learning situations, both of these aspects of learning are in various degrees present and interacting . . .' (2006: 143).

In relation to the 'how' of learning in music, 'flipping' is another manifestation of constructivism. However, it is important to make the point that formal instructional learning (how to play) is most likely to be accepted when it is perceived to be needed by the youngsters themselves, arising out of their encultured, informal interests (focused on playing and making music) and thus *owned* by them.

The how of musical learning is of course differentiated by where musical learning takes place, and it is to this that we now turn.

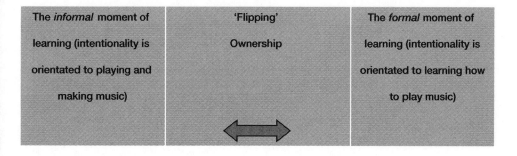

The *informal* moment of learning (intentionality is orientated to playing and making music)	'Flipping' Ownership	The *formal* moment of learning (intentionality is orientated to learning how to play music)

Figure 3.2 A model for musical learning

Where do we learn musical knowledge?

There would appear to be three interrelated contexts and settings for musical learning: formal, informal and non-formal, and yet these should not be confused with formal and informal learning.

Formal contexts

Formal contexts for musical learning include all of those settings where music education is planned for as part of statutory provision. This includes schools and colleges delivering the National Curriculum for Music and local authority music services offering tuition on a variety of instruments.

Informal contexts

Some musical learning takes place through being immersed in the 'culture' (enculturation). For example, by being exposed to music in our everyday lives we all develop an intuitive understanding of various musical styles, traditions and genres. There is a sense in which we cannot help this happening to us and the setting is 'informal'. Another example of the 'informal' context can be found when children organise to play, sing and compose music as individuals or in a group, e.g. using IT sequencing software or when forming a band that rehearses in a bedroom.

Non-formal contexts

The non-formal contexts for learning are an area for ever-increasing attention in music education. These include traditional settings such as choirs and brass bands but also:

- youth groups;
- community bands and choirs;
- community productions;
- visiting artists to schools.

A significant development here is the growth of the relationship between non-formal contexts and formal contexts where, for example, visiting artists and professional orchestras run workshops and longer-term projects in schools. Furthermore, it is clear that in terms of both learning and teaching, more and more activity is taking place in the various intersections and not in discrete sectors. The challenge for the secondary school music teacher is to take account of these contexts and settings in their own planning for musical learning. Figure 3.3 aims to show this relationship.

It is important that music teachers are aware both of the relationship between the various contexts and also how to exploit the synergies between them, as you are asked to explore in Task 3.9.

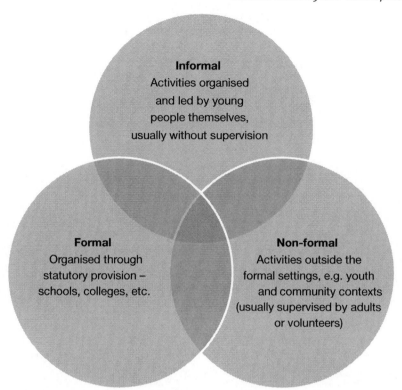

Figure 3.3 Formal, informal and non-formal contexts for music learning

---

Task 3.9 Contexts for musical learning

Using these three contexts for musical learning:

(a) Audit your own learning in each setting; what musical knowledge have you developed in each?
(b) Identify ways in which the learning from one setting has informed or underpinned learning in another.
(c) List three implications of this analysis for planning for musical learning in your classroom.
(d) Have you observed any music teaching that has managed to take account of each context?

While the setting has often dictated the bias towards *how* we learn (e.g. formal learning in formal settings), there is no necessary and causal link between the where and how (and indeed the what) of musical learning. As Folkestad has noted, the *how* is related to an intentional orientation to learning and not *where* we are learning. Children might be engaged in all three contexts and could bring learning from each to the others. For example, both formal and informal learning can take place in any physical space and are not limited to the school-home/community dichotomy:

> [I]t is far too simplified, and actually false, to say that formal learning only occurs in institutional settings and that informal learning only occurs outside of school . . . what are described as formal and informal learning styles are aspects of the phenomenon of learning regardless of where it takes place.
>
> (Folkestad 2005: 283)

Figure 3.4 illustrates how all types of learning can take place in all contexts.

Context for learning *Type of* *Learning*	Formal context e.g. school music classroom	Informal context e.g. four friends form a pop group	Non-formal context e.g. local brass band
Formal learning (An orientation to learning *how to play* music)	A teacher leads a lesson on the nature and structure of Rondo form	One of the group asks a friend to teach her how to play two chords on a guitar to go with one of the songs	An experienced cornet player begins to teach a child the rhythm of a part from a piece the band are studying
Informal learning (An orientation to *playing and making* music)	Composing a Rondo with a small group of peers	The group learn a new tune together in a garage after school	The child sits in on a rehearsal even though s/he cannot yet play the part

Figure 3.4 The types of musical learning and contexts

Task 3.10 The types of musical learning and contexts

(a) Using a blank version of Figure 3.4, try to fill in each section with an example of your own.
(b) Using either the example above or your own from (a), outline how you would plan to integrate each into your teaching. For example, if you were teaching a unit of work on 'Rondo', how might you integrate the learning and experience of the pop group or the cornet player?

We have explored the types of musical knowledge and how and where these might be learnt. We now turn to how young people develop musically.

How does musical knowledge develop?

Why is a theory of musical development important to music teachers? You can use a theory of musical development to:

- recognise what it means to be musical;
- recognise that some young people are more or less musically developed than others;
- inform your short-, medium- and long-term planning, including that which occurs around transitions between key stages;
- evaluate the impact of your teaching;
- help you assess both formatively and summatively.

We have identified that musical learning can be both intuitive and formal, encultured and instructional. Theories of musical development can provide us with a framework for understanding the role of both the informal and the formal in musical development. For example, the sequence of learning is vital to successful teaching, and thus a theory of development helps you to decide if you are 'putting the cart before the horse'. The wrong sequence of learning can demotivate and alienate youngsters.

Task 3.11 encourages you to engage with the notion of musical development, first through your own intuitive perceptions and then through some influential models of development. You will be asked to apply these to practice in your schools and to reflect on their usefulness.

Task 3.11 Musical development

(i)   For the ages c5, c8, c11 and c15, draw up a table that shows your intuitive sense of how musical knowledge, learning and engagement will manifest itself in young people in terms of (a) the sorts of music they listen to; (b) the sorts of comments they might make about music; (c) what you might notice about their singing or other performances; and (d) what their compositions will be like.

(ii) Once you have done this, compare your answers to Table 3.3.

(iii) In Table 3.3 there is a summary of some models of musical and artistic development (these have been simplified for the purposes of the task). After carrying out the following tasks, prepare answers to share with other beginner teachers:

 - Identify any broad similarities between the theories.
 - Identify any contradictions.
 - Do any of the theories confirm or contradict your own experience thus far?

Table 3.3 Some models of musical and artistic development

Ages	0-4	5-9	10-15	15+
Swanwick (1988)	Materials: impressed by the use of extremes of sound, for example dynamics, timbre. Rambling exploration of instruments for the voice	Expression: gross musical gestures, for example loudness to express the words of songs. Later on, musical conventions appear, for example metrical four-bar units	Form: experiment with structure, for example surprise and contrast. Later a desire for and empathy with authentic structures from immediate culture, e.g. the pop song	Value: music becomes special, with personal significance and may even become discursive on own and others' work
Parsons *et al.* (1978)		Children see artistic objects in terms of their own experience	Understanding the 'rules' of public use of artistic symbols	Understanding that a wide variety of traditions and styles exist
Shuter-Dyson and Gabriel (1981)	Very young children (0-1) react to sounds. Older children (2-3) reproduce bits of songs	Beginning to understand basic sound elements; discriminating pitch and rhythmic perception	Perception and skill improvement, i.e. tonal and rhythmic. Harmonic sense is established	Increase in the cognitive and emotional response to music
Sloboda (1985)	Enculturation: spontaneous acquisition of musical skill. Lack of self-conscious effort and explicit instruction	Enculturation: children do not aspire to improve their ability to pick up songs, yet they do improve	Training is self-consciously engaged with. Experiences are specific to a subculture but based on the foundation of enculturation	Training: contributing to a depth of knowledge and accomplishment in a narrow skill area. Developed through instruction
Ross (1982)	Sensory engagement; early relationships to the mood of the music	Doodling and mastery of sound patterns	Emergence of musical procedures, conventional competence and association with idiom	Personal expression, embodying meaning, a vision and significance

Despite the differences in emphasis between the theories, it does seem that there is a broad sequence to musical development; it is not random. It is, however, important to emphasise that any ages attached to musical development need to be read with considerable caution. You are likely to find students of vastly different developmental stages in the same class.

Musical development, assessment and transitions between key stages

Young people develop musically, and even if you do not have a fully worked out 'theory', it can be seen from some of the tasks carried out that we all make intuitive assumptions about musical development that inform our everyday work as a music teacher. This is especially the case in relation to assessment in the music classroom.

In our summative assessment *of* musical learning, different levels or stages of development will, for example, underpin the criteria we use to make judgements about compositions and performances. Models of musical development are inherent in the criteria that we use, whether they are derived from a national curriculum or examination assessment regime or invented by teachers and students in response to 'local' units and lessons. Every summative judgement in assessment of learning is a statement about the musical development of the students involved.

Levels and/or stages of musical development also underpin formative assessment *for* learning in the music classroom. When we ask questions, give feedback, provide models and set targets for students, we intuitively engage with our sense of musical development as part of the formative discourse that is assessment for learning (see Philpott 2009).

Furthermore, assessment of learning and assessment for learning are vital tools in planning for transitions between units of work, from one school year to the next and at the transitions between key stages. These tools provide us with ways of coming to know the developmental stages of our students such that we can manage their musical learning, and facilitate the development of their musical knowledge. While more detail can be found on these themes in Chapter 13 on assessment, you will need to be aware of both the implicit and explicit relationship between the development of musical knowledge and assessment.

Finally, we turn to an aspect of musical learning that has taken on an increasing importance in advocacy for music in the curriculum, that is, the transfer of learning in music to other areas of knowledge, skill and understanding.

The transfer of musical learning

One of the justifications for music in the curriculum is that learning *in* the discipline leads to a good deal of learning *through* it; in other words, there is transfer to other areas of the curriculum and to general student development. While you should exercise caution in being over-reliant on justifying music in terms of its influence on learning in other subjects, there is some evidence for such effects. It has been claimed that music education might have positive transferable effects in the following areas:

- aural perception;
- performance in mathematics;

- spatial reasoning;
- creativity;
- aural and visual memory;
- literacy skills;
- intellectual development;
- language skills. (Hallam 2015)

Task 3.12 The transfer of learning

Can you to add to the list of transferable learning?

Have you experienced/observed any of these transferable effects of learning through your experience of music? How and why do you think this effect has occurred? Try to give specific examples from your own learning or that of students at your school. Record what you have noticed and discuss this with another beginner teacher or with your mentor.

Research into the transfer of learning in music education is a strong theme for much current research, where the outcomes are used to make a positive case for the extrinsic importance of music in the secondary school curriculum. However, the evidence needs to be read critically, especially where such justifications overshadow those for the intrinsic value of music itself.

Summary

In this chapter we have seen that:

- musical knowledge can be differentiated into different types;
- knowledge 'of' music is particularly important in a constructivist approach to musical learning, where young people build meaningful relationships with their own music and the music of others;
- musical knowledge is developed through the interplay between encultured/informal/intuitive learning and formal/instructional learning;
- the informal and formal musical learning of young people can be developed in many different contexts;
- an understanding of musical development is vital if you are to plan and assess the development of musical knowledge in your classes;
- and finally, learning in music can have important transferable effects to learning in other areas of student development, that is, learning through music may contribute to learning across the curriculum.

Further reading

Hallam, S. (2015) *The Power of Music*, London: International Music Education Research Centre (iMerc).

This is a comprehensive review of research on the impact of music on the intellectual, social and personal development of young people.

Hargreaves, D.J. (1986) *The Developmental Psychology of Music*, Cambridge: Cambridge University Press.

Hargreaves offers a comprehensive overview of psychological issues that impinge on musical learning.

Swanwick, K. (1979) *A Basis for Music Education*, Windsor: NFER-Nelson.
Swanwick, K. (1988) *Music, Mind and Education*, London: Routledge.

These seminal publications develop an influential theory of musical knowledge, learning and development.

4 Language and learning in music

Chris Philpott with Keith Evans

Introduction

All teachers are charged with the development of their students' language, and it is inevitable that they will write and talk about music when composing, performing and responding. However, our primary concern in this chapter is how spoken and written language can be used to promote the development of musical learning. Language is one way (although by no means the only way) that we can develop our knowledge and understanding in music.

There are three assumptions made in this chapter in relation to the use of language about music:

1   Intuitive, 'literary' language *and* the language of conceptual, technical analysis are both important ways in which we can talk and write about music.
2   When learning to use language about music, there is a developmental shift from the intuitive to the technical.
3   These two assumptions are important factors for the way in which we plan and prepare for teaching and learning in music.

Intuitive language and technical language are not mutually exclusive. Indeed, much of this chapter explores the relationship between these two and the way in which each can be used to talk and write about music, and thus extend our understanding *of* music.

Objectives

By the end of this chapter you should be able to:

- understand the relationship between language and learning in music;
- facilitate students to use both literary and technical language to make their musical understanding and learning explicit;
- understand the sequence of learning implicit in the use of language about music;
- understand the role of musical criticism in music teaching, learning and assessment.

Using language about music

Your students can talk and write about music! It is quite natural for them to do so, even though they may not have a technical vocabulary to describe what they hear. Furthermore, just because students cannot use a technical vocabulary does not mean that they have not *heard* or *understood* the content of the music. Youngsters intuitively understand and can describe the contrasting sections of 'Chop Suey' by the Armenian-American band System of a Down. They can hear and sense the 'build-up' in the opening of Richard Strauss's 'Also Sprach Zarathustra'. They know that much heavy metal has drive and raw energy. As a teacher you ignore these intuitive understandings at your peril, for they are responses to music itself and represent genuine musical understanding. Indeed, by the time students reach secondary school they have much intuitive understanding and varying amounts of 'technical' vocabulary to describe their musical experiences.

Students need to be given opportunities to 'describe' their intuitive musical experience. How can this be done? How can you help them to make their understandings explicit through language? At this stage we are not *necessarily* concerned with technical vocabulary, for analysis does not necessarily involve its use. It is also important to realise that intuitive responses to music are not somehow 'lost' once we become technical or conceptual, but are always the primordial source of our understanding when we respond to music.

Task 4.1 Describing music

Choose a piece of music and try to describe what it is like without the use of technical vocabulary. What is the music like? What happens in the music? How does the music sound?

When a class or group are listening and responding to music in school or during micro teaching, try asking these same questions of them or of fellow beginner teachers. Ask them to write down their responses. What sorts of language do they use?

In relation to this primordial understanding, Swanwick (1979) helpfully distinguishes between music meaning something 'for' us (our personal subjective response, likes, dislikes, conjured images, connotations and so on) and meaning 'to' us (the objective existence of particular expressive gestures and structures in the music which have brought about this personal response). For example, a particular piece of music might mean little 'for' us (in terms of personal response) but could mean plenty 'to' us (in terms of identifying the musical gestures and structures used). When asking students to respond to music, you can move them from the response 'for' us, which is likely to be individual and subjective, 'to' the recognition of what actually happens in the music, which might be common to many in the class. The ability to put technical, analytical 'names' to this experience will vary from student to student, but is not a necessary condition of describing the music. While 'naming' can undoubtedly enrich musical experience, the 'names' do not form the life blood of the experience itself. Your students can use 'literary' language to describe their intuitive experience of meaning 'for' and 'to' them.

Supporting the use of 'literary' language

One way in which the use of 'literary' language about music can be encouraged is through the use of adjectives, either freely generated by the students themselves or prompted through adjective groups provided by the teacher. These adjective groups can promote confidence in the use of language to describe music. For example, in Table 4.1 later in this chapter (based on 'Bohemian Rhapsody'), the voice-quality boxes might contain words such as *harsh, smooth, powerful, aggressive, crying* and the class can be asked to circle the quality they hear in each section and/or add their own words.

Task 4.2 Using adjective groups in worksheets

Choose a piece of music with distinct sections and provide a range of adjectives for the class or group to choose from when describing the music. Try this out with a class or other beginner teachers.

Another way to unlock your students' intuitive responses is to ask them to compare pieces of music, and this approach can be a very fruitful way of getting them to talk about music. For example, a class could be tasked with comparing:

1   two pieces of music in a similar style, e.g. Courtney Pine's version of 'C Jam Blues' and Dave Brubeck's 'Take Five';
2   'cover' versions of a pop song;
3   different variations on a well-known theme;
4   recordings of Balinese and Javanese gamelan;
5   similar types of piece within the same work, e.g. choruses in Handel's *Messiah*.

Task 4.3 Comparing music

Develop a worksheet that asks for a comparison between two pieces of music. You can scaffold responses through, for example, the use of adjective groups and/or allow students to undertake a free description of what they have heard.

While we are not yet explicitly concerned with the technical concepts of musical analysis, your students quite naturally talk about these when describing their intuitive experience. They will write and talk about pitch, structure, consonance and dissonance (even if they do not use these words), for they are natural sonic and expressive categories when describing the qualities of music. However, they will often use 'literary' descriptions such as 'dark', 'smooth then spikey' or 'clashing' when engaging with these qualities. These intuitive understandings can be a gateway to more technical analysis and the introduction of musical vocabulary, *when the students are ready.*

Language and the sequence of musical learning

Given some of the links we have made between music and language, it is important to reflect on the sequence of learning.

When we learn our spoken and written language, there is a clear sequence in which we move from the sounds of the words to their meaning in the written form. The same might be said for music, i.e. that we need to internalise the sounds and meanings of music if the technical 'names' or notations are to mean anything to us. The point here, in terms of the sequence of learning, is that sounds and intuitive musical meanings come before written notations and technical analysis. Indeed, the maxim of the 'sound before symbol' is now common to the philosophy of many music educators. In the same way, as part of the musical development of our students, we can move *from* intuitive and literary responses *to* more technical understandings.

Language and the development of a musical 'vocabulary'

As musicians, it is easy to slip into the use of technical language and expect our students to understand these 'shortcuts'. One way round this is to provide, wherever possible, musical models of the things we are talking about, and also carefully audit and purge our own language of technical jargon. Most musical phenomena can be described using 'literary' non-technical language, in much the same way that we can all use literary language to describe our musical experience. In a sense we must, as teachers, try to remember how we first learnt to understand music if we are to help students to progress.

Of course, as teachers we do have a duty to introduce musical vocabulary, although only after careful preparation, taking due account of the sequence of musical learning and making sure there has been significant exposure to a musical correlate for what we are introducing (such as a musical model for a 'drone'). Technical and conceptual understandings can grow out of our intuitive relationships with music, both of which can contribute to analysis (see Figure 4.1). For example, a student who is being taught to play in 3 time needs to be immersed in the sense and feel of pulse and music in 3 time before the 'naming' makes any sense.

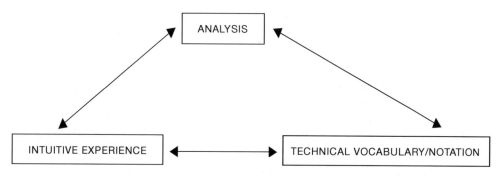

Figure 4.1 Intuition, analysis and technical vocabulary

The implications of what we have said thus far for you as a music teacher are that you need:

1   An ability to actively talk and write about music yourself. You must be good at what you are asking the children to do, that is, the analysis of musical works using literary and technical language.
2   The skills to be able to identify and describe important features in musical works for new learning and reinforcing past learning.
3   The ability to break down your own responses into a form that can be readily understood, and be able to talk about music in such a way that the 'language' used is appropriate for the age and ability of the students. For example, a technical reference to 'rising and falling scalic patterns followed by a perfect cadence' might mean little to students, but they *are* able to hear and talk about such an event. They can hear music that rises and falls and comes to a solid ending, which amounts to the same thing but without the technical language. However, once the up and down patterns have been assimilated, we *might* then talk of 'scales' as a development of technical vocabulary, which can be reinforced later and over time.
4   The awareness not to dismiss a particular response just because it did not use the 'right' word. You need the sensitivity to ask and understand why students have responded in a particular way.
5   The ability to ask questions that help students to develop musical vocabulary from intuitive understandings. For example, before asking 'What form is this piece in?', the question 'What happens in this music?' could be more appropriate.

Based on our observations thus far, we can recognise that the sequence of musical learning moves: from intuitive musical experience to technical vocabulary and back to an enriched experience (see Figure 4.1).

Confusions and misconceptions when using language about music

In developing a technical, musical vocabulary you need to be aware that there are some confusions and misconceptions over the use of certain words and concepts that are common to students and teachers alike. Box 4.1 and Task 4.4 help you to consider these, for an appreciation of such misconceptions is important to how you respond to the learning needs of individuals.

Task 4.4 Confusions and misconceptions when using language about music

Read Box 4.1. Have you any experiences of such 'confusions' thus far in your experience? Have any others caught your attention? Discuss your examples with your mentors and other beginner teachers.

**Box 4.1 Possible confusions when talking about the musical 'elements'
(aka the 'interrelated dimensions of music' in the current
English National Curriculum)**

Pitch

'High and low': This needs care and clarification, as some students think of these words as meaning high and low volume (and with good cause). Also, questions regarding pitch need to be targeted; for example, 'Can you name a high-pitched instrument in this piece?' Asking 'What is the pitch of this music?' will almost always elicit the answer 'High and low'!

Dynamics

'Volume' or 'loud and soft': This needs careful separation from language used to describe pitch (see earlier). Is the opposite of 'loud' actually 'quiet'? Also, in general usage, 'soft' can relate more to texture.

Texture

There are several responses here, ranging from basic 'thick' or 'thin' (referring to the density of the sound) to more specific descriptions addressing the organisation of musical strands (e.g. monophonic, homophonic, polyphonic, heterophonic).

Timbre

While timbre refers to the quality of the individual sound or collection of sounds, it can get muddled with certain definitions of texture.

Be sensitive to what children say or write about music. They may not necessarily be 'wrong' but merely using their words in a particular way. You should also clarify what you mean by your use of certain words. Do not assume that they, or indeed experienced musicians, know what you mean!

Worksheets and using language about music

A worksheet is a useful tool for eliciting responses to music. It is possible to construct worksheets that offer students the opportunity to use both literary and technical vocabulary. Indeed, this approach allows differentiated language to be used about the music, and this could be directed through a grid analysis. Table 4.1 exemplifies this structured approach when responding to Queen's 'Bohemian Rhapsody', although the grid can be easily adapted to cover other pieces or several pieces for comparison, as you will be asked to do in Task 4.5.

Table 4.1 Worksheet idea: a grid analysis of music

'Bohemian Rhapsody' by Queen						
This piece falls naturally into five sections A–E. However, the headings on the grid should be appropriate to the music being used and how you want to direct the responses.						
Section	*Instruments*	*Voice quality*	*Speed*	*What happens to the volume?*	*Mood/ atmosphere*	*Other comments, for example special effects*
A B C D E						

Task 4.5 Grid analysis of a piece of music

Design a worksheet in grid form for a class in Year 7 to respond to a piece of music. Do not assume an understanding of technical vocabulary.

Plan a similar exercise with a Year 11 group about to take their GCSE listening paper. What different approaches did you take for each year group? If you had a chance to use them, what were the differences in responses?

Student talk

Clearly, much of the language that takes place in the music classroom is between peers while making music, and we should not underestimate the value of this talk in the process of musical (and linguistic) learning. Auker (1991) makes the point that the most effective music teaching is that which allows students to make music. However, he also recognises the importance of language to musical learning, especially the 'exploratory talk' that takes place between them. Barrett emphasises that the quality of student talk has important consequences for the process of learning, and suggests that:

> Talk arises spontaneously from the creative music experience. Talk occurs when the child selects and organises information in order to ensure its transmission with clarity and accuracy. The child must assume responsibility by initiating talk while working co-operatively on a music task, by sustaining talk and where necessary, by concluding talk.
>
> (Barrett 1990: 71)

Barrett feels that in such situations pupil talk is quite natural, especially when they are engaged in 'the musical challenge'. She is concerned that the quality of both musical and linguistic experience is served by such talk. When responding to music, she maintains that the following categories of language are quite naturally used:

- investigative language;
- hypothetical language;
- imaginative language;
- descriptive language;
- analytical language;
- interpretative language;
- comparative language;
- reflective and evaluative language.

We suggest that you investigate pupil talk in the classroom, using the Barrett classification to analyse your findings. Task 4.6 will help you to do this.

Task 4.6 Listening to student talk

Listen to some students talking while they are composing or putting together a performance. Be sensitive to the effect that your presence will have on their talk. You might pick up only snatches of conversation from different groups. Use Barrett's categories of talk to analyse the language that you hear. Compare your observations with other beginner teachers, either face to face or via social media.

Your role as a teacher is one of facilitator in creating the conditions for talk between peers to take place. Auker believes that the quality of talking here is fundamental to the quality of the musical product, and maintains that:

> a better product will in fact emerge if we take seriously the role of language in the music lesson, because, lacking the musical vocabulary – it is through spoken language that children can begin to explore and share what they have to offer in terms of musical creativity.
>
> (Auker 1991: 166)

How is it possible for you to further facilitate student talk in your classes? One approach is to take the view that music education is musical criticism, both for you as teacher and for the students in your classes.

Music education as musical criticism

The implication of much of what has been said so far is for music education as musical criticism, with both the teacher and the youngster as music critic. Musical criticism does not necessarily involve us in making judgements about the value of a piece. The concepts of good and bad are not always useful constructs for the language of musical learning.

Swanwick finds that there are five dimensions or categories of musical criticism into which talk and writing (pupil and teacher) usually fall. These categories are:

- control of sonorities (the tone and quality of sound itself);
- expressive characterisation (the character of the music);
- structural relationships (how the piece hangs together, evolves, uses and so on);
- personal evaluation;
- historical and technical context. (Swanwick 1991)

Indeed, Swanwick maintains that there is no critical comment about music that does not fit into one or other of these categories, and that they fundamentally underpin our intuitive understanding of music even if we do not have the technical vocabulary to describe them. Engaging in music education as musical criticism for yourself is one of the first steps to encouraging the students in your classes to become music critics.

Task 4.7   Musical education as musical criticism

Use the Swanwick model of musical criticism to observe how different teachers discuss music with their classes.

Try to place the comments made by you and them into the categories provided by the model.

Do comments fall into certain categories more often than others? What are the implications of this and does it matter?

Repeat the exercise to analyse a range of worksheets that ask for a response to music.

Language and assessment

It is worth mentioning here the inevitable links between responses to music, language and assessment. Through students' responses to musical works, in both formal and informal situations, you can come to understand their learning and development. Their responses to music and the way they talk about it can become one of the foundations for your assessment practice. In both formal and informal situations, their appraisals of music, their appraisal of themselves and your appraisal of their work can form the basis of assessment. In this sense there is a very close connection between assessment, appraisal and musical criticism. However, you should not rely only on your students' use of language in order to 'know' them and their work. Performances and compositions stand freely as the most important manifestations of musical understanding, without the need for words of description, analysis or explanation.

Other forms of responding to music

Much of this chapter has been about young people responding to music through language, such that they can make their understandings explicit. The work of Flynn and Pratt (1995) suggests that 'getting at' music through language is a limited vision of response and appraisal. The implications of this work is that there are other ways or 'languages' through which we can access and develop understandings of music, such as through visual language, the language of movement, drama and forms of notation. These are all important, for there is nothing especially useful about verbal language that means it is superior to other forms, other than its convenience and dominance in our culture as a mode of communication. The forms of response allow intuitive understandings to be made explicit in ways that are not limited to a 'musical vocabulary' or even literary description. We suggest that you try out this approach through Task 4.8.

Task 4.8 Responding to music in different ways

Choose a piece of music that you know well and construct a sequence in which you challenge your class to respond to it through language, and at least two other forms of response.

An example might be the opening of 'Confutatis' from the *Requiem* by Mozart. The initial ABAB is differentiated by, among other things, contrasting use of male and female voices, dynamics and melodic shape. Your class could be asked to draw a picture inspired by this music (what is it that the pictures and music share?). They could be asked to compose a piece inspired by the music or the picture they have drawn. They could be asked to move in response to the various sections.

Learning how to notate music

Finally, it is worth a brief consideration of the learning and teaching of notation, based on our observations about the nature of and sequence of language and musical learning. While the case for teaching notation is well documented (and a National Curriculum requirement), there are many attendant problems for you as a music teacher. For example, what is the relationship of notation to a musical idea? When should notation be taught? How should notation be taught? What forms might notation take?

It must be emphasised that notation itself is *not* musical language but *a* written form of it and is thus subject to our observations on the sequence of learning noted earlier, i.e. when moving from the intuitive to the technical. To ignore this connection is to court the possibility of your students failing to learn anything at all, and thus becoming demotivated and alienated from music lessons. In light of these observations, we must ask ourselves what are the 'basics' in music education. In language, we seem to develop our sense of words before we learn how to write them down, as we have noted earlier. The process of learning appears to be from sounds and meanings to written signs, a principle that can also underpin musical learning. In relation to notation, the best way to learn how to understand and use written signs is by being immersed in relevant musical correlates, and always moving from the intuitive to the technical.

Task 4.9 Notation

List all forms of musical notation you are aware of. Which of these have you seen used and encouraged in school?

How is staff notation taught and reinforced in your school?

Devise a way of teaching a simple aspect of rhythmic notation, e.g. crotchets and quavers, in a way that is faithful to the notion of 'sound before symbol'.

Summary

In this chapter we have seen that:

- we have an intuitive understanding of music that underpins any technical understanding;
- when using language about music, we need to recognise these two types of understanding;
- the process of musical learning is from intuitive experience to a more conceptual and technical understanding and back to an enriched musical experience;
- the development of our use of language in response to music follows this sequence;
- you need to develop the professional skills to bring about musical learning in the classroom through your own use of language in teaching, planning and developing resources;
- music can help with the development of youngsters' spoken and written language and vice versa;
- there are important implications for music education and assessment as a form of musical criticism;
- musical understanding is not exclusively shown through talk or writing, as there are other 'languages' through which a response can be made to music;
- finally, the learning and teaching of notation is subject to the same sequential principles noted in this chapter about the relationship between intuitive and technical understandings in music.

Further reading

Auker, P. (1991) 'Pupil talk, musical learning and creativity', *British Journal of Music Education*, 8, 2: 161–166.

Barrett, M. (1990) 'Music and language in education', *British Journal of Music Education*, 7, 1: 67–73.

These two articles examine the role of talk and language about music in the mutual development of music and literacy skills.

5   What is a music curriculum?

Carolyn Cooke with Gary Spruce

> The school curriculum, construed as what is intended to be learned and what is actually learned, constitutes an important means by which educational transformations occurs. This is the point where theory meets practices, where ideas and beliefs are actualized in the phenomenal world. (Jorgensen 2003: 72)

Introduction

As a beginner teacher going into school for the first time, perhaps as part of a course of initial teacher education, it is likely that you will be presented with some form of 'curriculum document' for music. This might be a fully worked out 'scheme of work' or simply a list of topic or unit headings, e.g. 'The Elements of Music'; 'The Blues'; 'Minimalism', with bullet point lists of learning outcomes. If it is for a class preparing for an external examination, you might be given just the examination syllabus or specification. You will be asked then to use this document as the basis for planning music lessons and/or units of work. Your success as a beginner teacher, and how well you 'fit into' the music department, may be dependent on how effectively your lessons and your teaching are seen as reflecting the perceived intentions of that document.

This conception of 'curriculum' as a document that specifies what teachers will teach (and sometimes how they should teach) and what students will learn and know (e.g. a national, school or subject curriculum) is the way in which 'curriculum' is typically understood within government policy and media and political discussions and debates. Consequently, this conception of curriculum has come to dominate educational discourses, such that it is difficult, perhaps, to contemplate other ways of thinking about what a curriculum might be, might do or for whom it might be for.

However, is such a document the sum total of what a curriculum is? If asked, 'What is your school's music curriculum?', would it be sufficient to offer in response a copy of the national curriculum or even the school's curriculum document or scheme of work? We suggest not. In this chapter we propose a much broader and richer conception of what is meant by a 'music curriculum'. In doing so, we prompt some fundamental questions about the purposes, ideologies and values that underpin conceptions of the music curriculum and, in particular, who the music curriculum is for. We will suggest that the music curriculum is more than simply a fixed and static document that teachers use as a template to guide their teaching, but rather has the potential to be a dynamic phenomenon that emerges from the interactions and interrelationships between teachers, learners and what there is to be learnt. We will argue that a curriculum conceived in such a way has the potential to empower teachers and to address some of the issues that cause many young people to become disenchanted with, and alienated from, the formal music curriculum in schools.

Objectives

By the end of this chapter you should:

- be able to examine critically your own views about the purposes and aims of a music curriculum;
- understand different conceptions of the curriculum and the potential implications of these for music education;
- understand how young people *experience* the curriculum and how they see their role within it;
- understand what an emergent music curriculum might look and sound like within the classroom and how it might be enacted.

Your beliefs about the music curriculum

Conceptions of what the music curriculum is – or should be – are inevitably underpinned by particular beliefs and values – and particularly *musical* beliefs and values. As Regelski says:

> The most basic curricular thinking involves the question: Of all that can be taught, what is most worth learning? There is always more to teach than time and resources permit, and decisions concerning what to teach and for what ends involve important questions about the value of music and, hence, of music education.
>
> (2005: 220)

Before beginning to explore and critique different conceptions of curriculum, we want you to examine your own beliefs about what a music curriculum should be, what it should do and who it is for. A starting point for such thinking is to acknowledge that these beliefs almost inevitably, and legitimately, are rooted in your own previous experiences (both positive and negative) of music education and being a musician. These experiences will colour your evaluation of, and attitudes towards, different kinds of, and approaches to, music curricula. One can never uncouple oneself completely from one's previous experiences (and neither should one try to), but acknowledging their existence is an important first step towards reflecting critically upon them and being open to alternative visions of – in this case – what a music curriculum might be. These alternative visions will emerge, inevitably, from changes to official policy but also from schools, other teachers, your reading of research and scholarship but, perhaps most importantly, from the young people themselves – if we are prepared to listen to what they have to say. It is by understanding our existing views, where they stem from and actively researching and trying alternatives that we can develop music curricula to best support the students we teach, as Task 5.1 will help you begin to consider.

Task 5.1 Your own experiences of a music curriculum

(a) Construct a table like the one below. Then, thinking about your own experience as a young person of the music curriculum in school:
   - In the *first* column, list the different contexts in which you learnt music. These might include a whole-class curriculum, an instrumental or vocal lesson curriculum or exam curriculums.
   - In the *second* column, note down the kind of learning that took place in these different contexts. What kinds of musical learning were developed in each one?
   - In the *third* column, describe your experiences of these contexts. Were they positive or negative experience for you, and why?

Musical context	Learning	Experiences

(b) Now write a statement – perhaps in the style of a blog post – that outlines your current thinking about what is important to a successful curriculum, using the sentence stems:
   - 'An effective music curriculum for teachers should . . .'
   - 'An effective music curriculum for young people should . . .'

Be clear about why you think you hold the views that you do and how your own experiences as a young person, musician and, if appropriate, as a teacher have influenced these views.

   Find an opportunity to discuss your views with other (beginner) teachers, either online in seminars or in schools. Where there are differences in points of view, try to identify what these result from.

The music curriculum as object – implications of curriculum reification

At the beginning of this chapter we suggested that 'curriculum' is commonly understood as being synonymous with a 'curriculum document'. This document then acts as a template for what is to be taught and learnt (e.g. the National Curriculum). In academic literature, this conception of the curriculum is typically referred to either as 'curriculum as content', where the document limits itself to specifying the knowledge and skills to be learnt (e.g. examination specifications), or 'curriculum as product'.

'Curriculum as product' builds on 'curriculum as content' in identifying not only what is to be learnt but also how content and learning experiences are sequenced (pedagogical aspects) and how learning is recognised and evaluated (assessment). As its name suggests, 'curriculum as product' is concerned primarily with the achievement of '. . . some kind of desirable end product' such as '. . . knowledge of certain facts, mastery of specific skills and competencies, and acquisition of appropriate attitudes and values' (Abie 2014: 153).

The characteristics of 'curriculum as content' and 'curriculum as product' and some of their manifestations in music curricula are described in Table 5.1 and explored in Task 5.2.

Table 5.1 The music curriculum as content and product

Curriculum as . . .	Characteristics	Examples from music education
Content	Limits itself to specifying the knowledge to be studied and learnt	• GCSE and A Level music examinations • Graded music theory exams • Graded instrumental and vocal examinations • The most recent English National Curriculum as a document
Product	Learning objectives are identified and set, a plan is devised for achieving these objectives, the plan is implemented and the outcomes measured. This 'managerial' approach to education underpins the 'performativity' agendas described above	• The English National Curriculum as 'delivered' through school curricula. • Commercial curriculum packages • Performance-based curricula (e.g. the American Band method)

Task 5.2 Exploring curriculum as content and product

Go to the document or website for an A level or GCSE specification that you are, or might be, teaching. Analyse this in detail in terms of the characteristics of content and product-driven curricula identified in Box 5.1 below. What particular musical values and beliefs about what important knowledge and skills do you think are being promoted through the specification? To what extent do you feel that these values and beliefs are able to accommodate and support the development of all musical learners?

Both 'curriculum as content and 'curriculum as product' are what might be described as *reified* forms of curriculum. One of the ways in which 'reification' can be understood is as a process whereby essentially abstract phenomena are treated or thought of as concrete objects. In music, reification has occurred where we come to think of 'music' and the 'score' as being synonymous. A consequence of reification is that meaning is seen as being inherent in the reified form of the abstraction (the score or curriculum document) and consequently remains fixed in all times and places.

This unquestioning acceptance of this reified conception of the curriculum comes across in the way in which music teachers often talk about the curriculum. (See Box 5.1.)

Box 5.1 Teacher statements about curriculum

(a) 'The curriculum tells me what musical genres to teach and when.'
(b) 'The curriculum is a document that helps me to plan lessons in the correct sequence so that the young people develop the skills and knowledge they need to work towards the end of term assessment.'
(c) 'The curriculum outlines all the musical learning that takes place over the key stage.'
(d) 'The curriculum tells me how to teach using the department's resources.'
(e) 'The curriculum makes sure all young people achieve the stated outcomes by the end of the term.'
(f) 'The curriculum has stayed pretty much the same for the past five years after a big rewrite we did to incorporate more group work.'

What is evident in the above statements is that irrespective of whether the music curriculum is 'imposed' (e.g. national curricula or exam specifications/syllabi) or created by the teachers, it is thought of in a reified way and becomes something that teachers carry out as a well-tested master plan (another reified concept), which will guarantee that students learn and predefined outcomes are met. Teachers then become what Savage, perhaps a touch tendentiously, describes as '. . . a white-van curriculum delivery service, dropping off pre-ordained packages of curriculum content within a set timetable of deliveries' (Savage 2013: 85) with young people as 'curriculum consumers' (Philpott 2012: 154).

The attraction for teachers of thinking about the curriculum in this reified way is that it allows for 'the curriculum' to be prepared prior to its enactment within the classroom. Learning outcomes and teaching strategies can be identified and content selected and structured away from the immediacy of the classroom moment. Reified conceptions of the curriculum are also attractive to commercial organisations, which can produce off-the-shelf 'curriculum packages' to be purchased by schools for implementation in the classroom. Reified conceptions of the curriculum are also politically powerful tools (which is why this conception of the curriculum has dominated contemporary curriculum policy), as it allows for governments and other powerful groupings to exert direct influence over a curriculum's content, pedagogy and assessment and the learner dispositions it promotes.

In this reified form of curriculum, where they are treated simply as 'curriculum consumers', young people come to see the curriculum as something in which they have little investment; as something that is 'void of self' (Giddens in Schmidt 2005: 5). This lack of investment is further aggravated by the way in which reified conceptions of the curriculum promote the idea that the music curriculum is only that which happens within the school (i.e. that bit which can be controlled); and this comes through clearly in the teacher statements in Box 5.1.

However, we know that young people are active as listeners, performers and composers beyond the classroom during their teenage years (Hargreaves and Marshall 2003; Lamont *et al.* 2003; North *et al.* 2000) and that this has a significant impact on how they relate to music in the formal classroom setting. If young people come to believe that they have little investment in, or ownership of, the curriculum, and that the curriculum ignores their musical life outside school (which contributes significantly to their musical identities), this can easily result in alienation from the curriculum and from formal music education in school.

Curriculum as a lived experience

So what is the alternative? Pollard and Triggs suggest that the curriculum can be conceptualised in four ways:

1   The *official curriculum*: this almost always exists as a document and sets out the knowledge to be acquired, the sequence of learning, assessment etc. This is what we have chosen to call the 'reified curriculum'.
2   The *hidden curriculum*: everything that is learnt that isn't an explicit part of the curriculum but may have a profound impact on the young person's attitude towards education and learning.
3   The *observed curriculum*: what is observed happening in the classroom.
4   *Curriculum-as-experienced*: what the young people connect to, how they 'live' the curriculum both official and hidden. (Pollard and Triggs 1997)

What Pollard and Triggs are suggesting here is that a reified curriculum can only ever tell us part of the story of what goes on in the music classroom. To understand a curriculum we need to triangulate how the curriculum is described in documents and conversations based on reified conceptions of the curriculum with what can be seen to happen in the classroom *and* what young people actually experience (see Figure 5.1).

Pollard and Triggs bring into the curriculum equation the hitherto missing element of the young people themselves. To understand their lived experiences of a music curriculum will involve careful attention to their musical responses to the curriculum but also to how they tell of their experiences verbally. As a beginner teacher and throughout your career, conversations with young people are an excellent starting point to begin to understand how they have 'lived' the curriculum, as you are asked to do in Task 5.3.

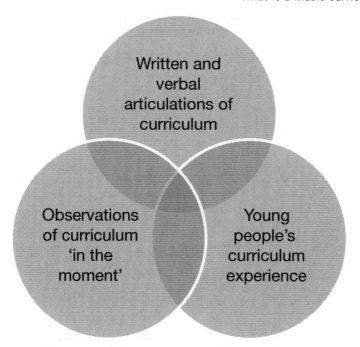

Figure 5.1 Understanding the curriculum

Task 5.3 Talking with young people about the curriculum

Spend time with two students in different year groups, talking to them about their experiences of the curriculum in your setting. You might ask questions such as whether they have been given information about the music curriculum and, if so, what? What information are they given at the start of a new unit about what they will be doing? How do they see their role in the curriculum? What types of experiences do they value? What do these positive experiences have in common (if anything)? What musical experiences do they have beyond class? Do they feel connections between the musical experiences they have in and beyond the classroom?

Talking with young people about their lived experiences of the curriculum provides a valuable insight into their views about the curriculum, but only into the issues that they can express verbally. Asking any young person to recall and describe accurately their musical experiences, using terminology that avoids ambiguity for either party, is a tall order. Moreover, such conversations still tell us little about the way in which the curriculum is *enacted* within individual classrooms with individual teachers and individual students. The curriculum comes alive only in the moment, and it is in that moment that we come to know what the curriculum actually involves and what those involved actually believe the curriculum to be. We are not referring here to the moment decisions are made about the curriculum map in a planning session, the buying of resources or the writing of curriculum documents for parents or young people, or even the planning of individual lessons, but the momentary, spontaneous, improvisatory interactions that happen with students in the classroom each minute of a lesson.

As we begin to explore what a curriculum created 'in the moment' might mean in practice, it becomes more obvious that reified conceptions of the curriculum are inadequate for describing what actually happens when the curriculum is enacted in the classroom, as they fail to take account of the complex, unique ways in which a music curriculum as a lived experience brings together different influences. What it fails to recognise is the resulting myriad of different personal experiences and outcomes that impact on the music curriculum in the classroom. In particular, it fails to recognise the role young people have as co-creators of the curriculum through their contribution and effect on these moments.

The act of young people creating the curriculum

Central to a non-reified conception of a music curriculum is the belief that young people play an active role in *creating* the curriculum. This is a radically different approach from the curriculum-as-content and curriculum-as-product approaches which so dominate educational policy and discourse. We are not suggesting here that young people are not already given the opportunity to do this in most, if not all, music classrooms. No matter how content or product-driven the curriculum is, students' interactions with each other, the musical resources and the teacher at any particular moment will inevitably lead to them exert influence on what happens in the music classroom and therefore be active creators of their curriculum experience. What we are arguing for here is a greater recognition of this influence and an approach to the music curriculum that deliberately sets out to promote this kind of engagement and create an environment in which young people explicitly recognise the role they can play.

If young people are to play such a role in the construction and realisation of the curriculum, it requires us to rethink conventional conceptualisations of the role of the teacher and the learner, the nature of musical knowledge and the interrelationships between these. Above all, it requires us to understand how complex social and contextual factors shape the curriculum.

Cornbleth, in addressing this complexity, defines curriculum as 'an ongoing social process comprised of the interactions of students, teachers, knowledge and milieu' (Cornbleth 1990: 5). Here she is putting young people, teachers, knowledge and the broader context (milieu) in which the curriculum is happening in equal relationship. This context might include, among other things, the learning environment, the resources and the particular nature of the time and day (see Figure 5.2). However, she is arguing that none of these individual factors, such as those identified in Figure 5.2, or even them all together, forms a curriculum. Cornbleth is suggesting instead that it is the *interactions between* these factors that create a curriculum through an ongoing, ever-developing *social process*.

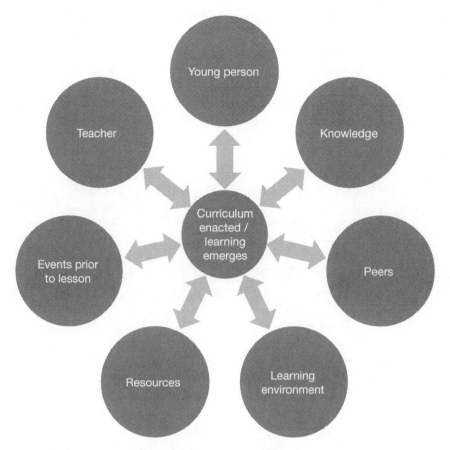

Figure 5.2 Interactions leading to an emerging curriculum

Task 5.4 Interactions within a lesson

Think of a music lesson that you have observed or taught yourself. Make a more detailed version of the diagram in Figure 5.2 showing the interactions that occurred during that lesson.

  You could include the following to help you start:

- the experiences and views of the music teacher about the unit (what understanding, knowledge, skills are important?);
- the prior experiences and views of the students about the unit;
- the experiences of the students during the unit;
- the musical experiences of the students in and out of school;
- the resources available to the students and teacher;
- the influence of other students in the class;
- what teachers from other classes have shared about how they approach this unit;
- the time and place of the lesson.

Wegerif describes such interactions as 'dialogic spaces' where there is a 'dynamic continuous emergence of meaning' from the 'interplay of two or more perspectives' (Wegerif in Spruce 2015: 297). Wegerif is suggesting here that the interplay between young people and resources, young people and teacher, young people and their peers, young people and the learning environment all involve the coming together of different perspectives. As Spruce argues, each perspective brings with it particular historical, cultural, political, philosophical and experiential dimensions in a complex interplay, which is influenced by and itself influences the moment of interaction. Consequently, each interaction is unique to the individuals involved and to the moment in which it occurs (Spruce 2015: 298). In other words, every individual, and every individual moment in which the music curriculum is enacted, will produce a different musical outcome or new musical learning unique to that moment, as it brings together a particular set of variables that are unlikely to be re-created in a different moment.

Doll uses the term 'dancing curriculum' (Doll in Fenwick *et al.* 2011: 37). This term provides a useful metaphor to help us explain these ideas, where knowledge is constantly moving and interacting with resources, materials, the environment, each other and the teacher. The curriculum, as it is constantly being influenced by these interactions, is never fixed or static, but always evolving, creating new moments that can lead to new interactions and new learning. This isn't to say that there is no place for teacher planning and preparation; indeed, the teacher role becomes vital in helping choreograph the dance, enabling new interactions to occur and providing the environment, resources and activities to stimulate these interactions into creating the curriculum experience. As Beghetto argues, '. . . moments of creative potential . . . emerge in everyday routines, practices and planned experiences' (Beghetto 2012: 134). What becomes the teacher's responsibility is to ensure that such routines, practices and planned activities provide rich and diverse interactions that enable young people's knowledge to keep evolving, or *emerging from* their lived experiences.

Recognising the central role young people have as co-creators of their own lived experiences through their interactions with teachers, each other, resources and the environment and to understand their learning as *emerging from* these interactions is to challenge us to imagine a different way of planning, teaching and interacting. The final section of this chapter will explore the idea of an 'emergent curriculum' and what an emergent music curriculum might involve in practice.

Emergent curriculum

The idea of the 'emergent curriculum' has gained credence in curriculum literature in recent years (Osberg and Beista 2008; Davis and Sumara 2006). While it is difficult to provide a comprehensive overview within the confines of this chapter, there are some key elements of emergent curriculum that resonate strongly with the previous discussion of curriculum as a lived experience and are worth exploring in more detail from a music curriculum perspective. These include that in an emergent curriculum:

- Knowledge emerges as 'human beings participate in the world' and therefore knowledge only exists 'in our participatory actions' (Osberg and Beista 2008: 313). In other words, knowledge only emerges through interactions, either with peers, teachers, resources or other influences.

- We should be 'concerned with the emergence of meaning [through these interactions] rather . . . than with the transfer of meaning from teacher to student'(Osberg and Beista 2008: 314). The purpose of the curriculum is therefore no longer to facilitate the acquisition of knowledge *about* a reality that is presented by someone else but for young people to find their own reality.
- The aim is not about 'bringing about the convergence of individual perspectives . . . by attempting to initiate or socialize [young people] into a common way of being', but about maintaining difference, enabling them 'to become more unique' (Osberg and Beista 2008: 324).
- We are less concerned with the content of a curriculum and how it is presented, with more concern placed on the idea 'that content is *engaged* with and *responded* to' [my italics]. 'The content that is engaged with is not pre-given, but emerges from the educative situation itself' (Osberg *et al.* 2008: 225).

Task 5.5 helps you to explore the implications of an emergent curriculum within a music education context.

Task 5.5 Identifying interactions that lead to emergence

Spend a few moments thinking about a music lesson you have observed or taught to answer the following questions:

1 What types of interaction (musical, non-musical) did the students have during the lesson?
2 Who or what (peers, teachers, ICT, musical instruments, paper-based resources, learning environment) were the interactions between?
3 On the following spectrum, mark where you feel the interactions best sit:

Transfer of someone else's   Emergence of students'
knowledge or meanings   own knowledge or meanings

4 How far did the interactions in the lesson seek out, share and encourage differences of opinion, approach and outcomes?
5 How far was the lesson evaluated in terms of whether content was 'covered'?

This view of curriculum as a constantly evolving framework within which to facilitate students' interactions, resulting in the emergence of their own knowledge and meanings, represents a significant shift in thinking from other conceptualisations of curriculum. In this view the curriculum is 'dynamic, self-renewing and [engaged with] creatively' (Osberg *et al.* 2008: 225). To achieve this involves an awareness as to how other conceptions of curriculum may limit such emergence, as Task 5.6 will help you to explore.

Task 5.6 Reviewing curriculum statements

Spend a few minutes reviewing the statements about curriculum in Box 5.1. In what ways would the views of curriculum in these statements limit students' interactions and limit the emergence of their own musical knowledge and meanings?

An emergent music curriculum

As Tasks 5.4 and 5.5 demonstrate, an emergent curriculum raises significant questions, but also opportunities for music teachers. These opportunities and challenges are examined below. The principles that underpin an emergent curriculum (in italics), their implications for an emergent music curriculum and practical examples (Boxes 5.2–5.6) allow us to consider what an emergent music curriculum might look and sound like.

Conceptualising 'curriculum' as a lived experience

As young people interact as musicians, both with each other and with the context, they will inevitably be drawing on their previous experiences, whether from the classroom, in school, in community groups or at home. Therefore the music curriculum as a lived experience cannot be considered as purely that which the young person participates in within class or school but something that embraces their musical experiences as a whole. This challenges the music teacher to understand the students' musicianship in all its manifestations in order to create interactions that build on but also provide alternative perspectives to this broad range of musical experiences. To do so effectively involves classes or individuals negotiating the next stages of the curriculum with the teacher, identifying what they want to explore, how they want to do it, what resources they will need and, most importantly, what experiences, connections and ideas they already have in relation to the unit.

Box 5.2 Curriculum as lived experience: an exemplar

Knowing that a GCSE student DJs at the weekends, the class teacher has been working with her to explore how that links to the minimalism unit. By making some initial connections, the student has started making all sorts of other links which are now coming through in her minimalist composition, which uses electronic samples and phasing. She has also become very interested in how the American minimalist composer Steve Reich's work has been used in dance music. Just learning about the techniques and composing a minimalist piece using a given formula would have had such a superficial impact compared to the deep, integrated learning that she has generated.

Curriculum as a contextually bound experience

An emergent curriculum will inevitably be contextually bound by the particular influences and interactions that are available and made within a class. Therefore, with students arriving with such varied musical identity, curriculum experiences will rarely be uniform. Every individual within a class will therefore respond to, interpret or take different things from the musical experiences. Equally, the particular mix of individuals within a class or group will create a unique set of interactions with the teacher, leading to a diverse range of musical outcomes. This challenges the objective- and outcome-led planning on which many curricula are based and provides greater scope for teachers and young people to explore and discover new learning together.

Box 5.3 Curriculum as context-bound experience: an exemplar

A medium-term planning document used to state that Year 9 students in the Blues unit would compose using the twelve-bar blues chord sequence, but the teachers recognised that it became a very mechanical exercise with them just following instructions. They have now changed it to 'working with musical features of the blues to compose their own piece', which means the young people can go in many different directions, including into rock 'n' roll and blues-based jazz. The range of possibilities has really engaged the young people and the teachers have enjoyed exploring a much wider range of music with the students to help them identify blues connections they might want to explore.

Interactions are core to curriculum decision making

In an emergent curriculum, decisions about the nature, direction and detail of the curriculum experience are negotiated. At the centre of these negotiations are the musical and non-musical interactions that occur between the young person, their peers, the resources, the environment and the teacher. It is through these interactions that new directions, opportunities and possibilities are opened up to be explored together. This presents a challenge to the teacher, as the direction of a particular unit with a particular class cannot be predicted, but can only be anticipated. Therefore the teacher has to be constantly open to alternatives and attentive to the musical decisions that the students are making. In many senses the curriculum decision-making process can be viewed as being a bit like improvising. There is a framework, but the young people and teacher are deciding together at every moment whether the framework is the right one, how it might be manipulated to help them do what they want musically, and together to make something creative and unique. To do this, it is necessary to create times where teachers and students reflect about the unit, the directions they have taken and whether they want to explore alternative routes. The teacher's role therefore is to guide students as to what alternatives they might like to try.

Box 5.4 Curriculum decision making

8D (12-13 year olds) started to compose a whole-class pop song, but the class quickly found themselves disagreeing as there were so many different ideas. In the end the teacher helped them to form four groups with compatible ideas, and set the same lyrics. The young people really enjoyed seeing the different results. Previously, the teachers would have made them stay together if that was on the unit plan and led them to compose a whole-class song. In the new scenario, it was completely owned by the young people, and the teachers reported that they learnt much more from the experiences.

Meaning, and therefore ultimately learning, emerges from interactions

If meaning and therefore learning emerges from interactions, it follows that musical meaning and musical learning emerge from musical interactions. Therefore young people need to act as musicians, responding to musical problems and opportunities. In this way, young people will engage in musical and verbal interactions that allow them to develop their own meanings and ultimately their own learning. To facilitate this, music teachers need to allow young people time to develop their own meanings, rather than imposing their own meanings onto musical experiences, something that is easier said than done in a time-pressured, outcome-orientated environment.

Box 5.5 Musical learning and musical interactions

A group of teachers analysed their use of questioning during their lessons and concluded that they needed to ask more questions to open up ideas and emerging understanding. After a few weeks, they shared their experiences. In one class, a young person had asked to use the drum kit when the teacher was setting up an African drumming unit. The teacher admitted that previously they would have told the youngster they were only using the African drums. Instead, the teacher asked why he wanted to use the drum kit. What musical effect was he imagining as a result? The teacher thought about what connections, parallels etc. could be made between the different drums. Opening up the questioning made the curriculum far more exploratory, and the teachers consequently opened up the planning to give space for this by rewording objectives, outcomes and activities to allow for multiple interpretations.

The curriculum develops with the young people's learning

As meaning emerges from interactions, the curriculum constantly evolves, moving with the young people's learning. Although the curriculum will have structures that allow young people to engage with a wide range of musical resources and experiences (and therefore interactions), music teachers will constantly be open to unexpected, creative meanings that lead young people in alternative directions. This involves expecting classes, groups and individuals to respond in different ways and ultimately shape their own curriculum experiences.

Box 5.6 Young people as shapers of curriculum experiences

A teacher asked his Year 7s to reflect on their children's songs unit and he was amazed by the results. The children came up with so many different explanations for what was taught, described the process of composing in so many ways and had interpreted the music so differently. For example, they used the unit to explore melody (returning to the tonic, using repetitive motifs and step motion within an easily singable range). However, when the young people described what they did, they were more concerned with the aesthetic outcomes, such as finding an attractive timbre and using rhythms that made the words memorable. Equally, when asked to describe examples of children's songs they knew, they had found all sorts of examples that were difficult to sing, didn't return to the tonic and had elaborate structures. The teacher felt he had learnt a lot about children's songs himself, but also crucially he learnt about what these young people had brought to the unit, and what they had taken away from it.

If the young people hadn't used key words in the past, the teacher admitted he would have taken this to be a lack of understanding about the key vocabulary of the unit, but now he viewed different responses as being about the meaning they had developed from the unit. This wasn't always expressed verbally and wasn't always what was anticipated.

Planning for an emergent view of a music curriculum does not provide a 'template' for teaching and is not particularly disposed to being supported by commercial curriculum packages. Rather it asks of teachers that they engage with fundamental *pedagogical* questions around musical knowledge and understanding (questions of epistemology), and how such knowledge is best taught and assessed (questions of pedagogy) with *their* young people in the particular context in which they teach, recognising that this context includes the music and musical learning that goes on beyond the school. Task 5.7 provides an opportunity to explore how you might plan for a lesson that allows for the principles of an emergent curriculum.

Task 5.7 Planning for an emergent curriculum

Choose a lesson you have taught or observed.

Using the existing lesson plan or your observation notes, imagine an alternative lesson using the principles of an emergent curriculum as identified above. What would the learning environment look and sound like? How would students be grouped?

(continued)

Task 5.7 *(continued)*

What sort of activities would they be involved in? What would your role be as the teacher and how could you best prepare for this? What resources would be needed? Would the routines of the lesson need to be altered?

Prepare a lesson plan to reflect this new lesson. If the lesson was being observed, what sort of phrases could you use on the plan or what sort of information could you provide with it to make clear the emergent nature of the curriculum experience?

Most importantly, however, emergent music curricula require of teachers a willingness to initiate and engage in pedagogical discourse with those they teach in the construction of knowledge. It also entails teachers reflecting critically both before and after a lesson and, perhaps, most especially 'in-action' (in the moment) in response to the outcomes of this discourse. In particular, an emergent curriculum challenges teachers to be more open to extemporising the curriculum (both musically and non-musically) with their students, allowing them to take the lead, follow the teacher's lead or go together to develop new and exciting understandings and meanings. This does not mean that teachers aren't responsible for what goes on in the classroom, but rather that they come to the classroom not with fixed ideas about what is to be learnt and how learning will be sequenced, but with what Smith describes as '. . . a proposal for action which sets out the essential features of the educational encounter' (Smith 2000: 15).

So what is a music curriculum? As we noted at the beginning of the chapter, as a (beginner) music teacher you may well be faced with a curriculum document, a series of comments about what it means to turn this document into practice and an expectation that the music curriculum as envisaged in this document will translate in similar ways between different teachers, classes and students. What we have outlined is a counter-argument to this common focus on reified content and product curriculum approaches. However, it is vital to highlight that an emergent music curriculum approach does not necessarily rely on changing a curriculum document or changing how others talk of curriculum. Instead, an emergent music curriculum relies on individual teachers developing pedagogies that enable them to work with young people in ways that allow the lived experience of the curriculum to be recognised as having the greatest importance. In this way, our argument for an emergent approach to music curricula empowers you (whether as a beginner teacher or a more experienced teacher) to develop an emergent approach within whatever setting, context or stage of career you are working.

In answer to the question 'What is a music curriculum?', we would argue that a music curriculum is a combination of how you as an individual facilitate young people (through appropriate use of pedagogy) to explore and co-create lived musical experiences from the 'proposal for action' which allows his/her musical knowledge to emerge.

Task 5.8 Reviewing your thinking about a music curriculum

In Task 5.1 part (b) you were asked to complete the following statements:

- 'An effective music curriculum for teachers should . . .'
- 'An effective music curriculum for young people should . . .'

(a) Revisit what you wrote and consider the extent to which what you have read either reflected what you thought or has caused you to rethink your understanding of what a curriculum is. How – if at all – would your statements need to be changed to reflect any changes in your thinking?
(b) Consider how you would now answer the question 'What is a music curriculum?'

Summary

This chapter has presented a variety of theoretical and philosophical positions around curriculum in order to argue that a music curriculum cannot be understood exclusively or even primarily through a reified conception of it as a document.

Rather, we suggest that a music curriculum is a dynamic phenomenon which is emergent from the (musical) interactions of teachers and students in the particular circumstances (context) of that music classroom. Whether working within an existing curriculum framework or embarking on creating one, this view of a music curriculum is one that empowers us to pay attention to what is happening moment by moment within our classrooms to enhance students' ability to lead their own 'lived' curriculum experience, which not only connects with young people's lives but *is integral* to their musical life.

Further reading

Smith, M.K. (2000) Curriculum theory and practice, in *The Encyclopedia of Informal Education*, www.infed.org/biblio/b-curric.htm.
Green, L. (2005) 'The music curriculum as lived experience: children's "natural" music learning processes', *Music Educators' Journal*, 91, 4: 27–32. (Can also be found at: http://eprints.ioe.ac.uk/1104.)
Regelski, T. (2005) Curriculum: implications of aesthetic versus praxial philosophies, in D. Elliott (ed.) *Praxial Music Education: Reflections and Dialogues*, Oxford: Oxford University Press.

These readings will help you gain additional perspectives on different conceptions of 'curriculum' and particularly ideas around informal learning and the curriculum as 'lived experience'.

6 An integrated approach to lesson planning

Gary Spruce

Introduction

Why plan?

An unproblematised and perhaps slightly technicist approach to planning might suggest that its primary purpose is to address two central and important questions:

1   *Learning outcomes.* What do I want young people (or different groups of young people) to learn by the end of the lesson (what should they understand and be able to do when they leave the music classroom that they did not understand or could not do when they entered it)?
2   *Teaching and learning strategies.* What musical experiences and activities do young people (or different groups of young people) need to have in order to ensure that this learning takes place and how can these experiences be managed and structured?

It is certainly the case that if these 'big' questions are not addressed through planning, lessons will almost inevitably be much less effective than they might be. Unplanned lessons may well be full of *activity*, but if these activities are not directed towards some kind of planned learning aims and outcomes, then learning (if it takes place at all) may be haphazard and you – and the young people – may not know what to do next in order to make progress.

Planning in music is, however, about much more than responding to these questions – important though they may be. It is also about planning for how one will afford openings, opportunities and departure points for young people's music making and hence musical learning – the kinds of musical learning that cannot necessarily be anticipated but that emerge from young people's responses to the musical stimuli, problems and ideas that they encounter in a lesson. It is often these unexpected and surprising moments of music making and musical learning that are the most valuable to a youngster and reveal to the teacher a young person's previously unrecognised musical understanding, knowledge and skills – sometimes even unrecognised by the youngster themselves.

The purpose of this chapter is to consider not only how these two 'big' questions might be addressed, but also how you might plan to create a flexible framework that allows for the ' unexpected' to happen and to flourish and for young people to develop as independent musicians. One way of doing this is through approaching planning in terms of three key principles:

1   recognising and taking account of different types of musical knowledge, skills and understanding, including those that young people bring into school;
2   teaching music *musically* through activities that *immerse* young people in musical activity and experience;
3   *integrating* the different aspects of musical experience: performing, composing/ improvising and listening.

In the first part of the chapter we explore the implications of these *principles*, while in the second part we consider the *process* of planning. There is a sense, of course, in which this entire book is about planning, and therefore some critically important issues, such as inclusion, which are dealt with in detail elsewhere, are only touched upon here. References to other chapters are made at appropriate points.

Objectives

By the end of this chapter you should be able to:

*   identify the key principles underpinning effective lesson planning;
*   understand the factors that need to be taken account of when planning;
*   know how to apply these principles and factors to your planning for young people's musical learning.

Three key principles in planning for music learning

1: Planning should take account of different kinds of musical knowledge, including the knowledge young people bring to their school music lessons

In Chapter 3, Philpott identifies three types of musical knowledge:

*   knowledge 'about' music – factual knowledge about the history, style and theoretical underpinning of music;
*   knowledge of the know 'how' of music – such as technical instrumental skills, aural perception skills and the ability to read musical notation;
*   knowledge 'of' music gained through a developing relationship with music performer, composer and responsive listener (see also Chapter 10).

Elliott (1995) offers a slightly different perspective, arguing that there are four types of musical knowledge which gradually converge during the process of moving from novice to expert musicianship:

- *formal* knowledge – which is closely related to Philpott's knowledge 'about' and 'how' of music;
- *informal* knowledge – the knowledge that young people bring into school resulting from their musical enculturation;
- *intuitive* – 'knowledge' of what feels musically right within a particular style, resulting from immersion in that style;
- *supervisory* knowledge – knowledge that enables young people to appraise music appropriately and make musical decisions based upon an understanding of the musical style within which they are working (a kind of conscious application of what was intuitive knowledge). (Elliott 1995)

These two sets of knowledge types are to a great extent complementary. Elliott's informal, intuitive and supervisory knowledge in a sense differentiates or subdivides Philpott/Reid's knowledge 'of' music. What is common to these knowledge types is a belief that a developing relationship and understanding of music can only take place through young people's *immersion* in music as audience, performer and composer/improviser, with these three roles bringing different but related perspectives to the relationship between the person and the phenomenon of music.

In the skeletal lesson outline in Figure 6.1, we demonstrate one way in which Elliott's knowledge types contribute to musical learning and understanding.

Task 6.1 Identifying different kinds of musical knowledge

Think about a lesson you have taught or observed, using Elliott's knowledge types. Consider whether any one type of knowledge predominated. If so, how might the lesson have been changed so that other types of knowledge might have been given greater focus? Consider the extent to which each type of knowledge contributed to young people's musical *understanding*.

2: Planning should ensure that learning is developed through immersion in music

The primary aim of planning is to ensure that young people develop their knowledge 'of' music and consequently form a deepening relationship with it. This can occur only if young people are given the opportunity to become immersed in music: being fully engaged in music as composers and performers underpinned by strong 'listenership' (Chapter 10). Immersion in music is fundamental to teaching music *musically*. Figure 6.1, as well as being an example of how different types of knowledge can be developed within a lesson, is also one example of how such immersion might be achieved.

Lesson Outline

Context: Parkville is an inner city school which draws most of its young people from the Afro-Caribbean community. There is a strong commitment by many families to the local Evangelical churches where there is a tradition of Gospel singing. Most children hear Gospel singing in the church and a number are involved in Gospel choirs.

Most young people bring to the lesson an '**informal**' knowledge of Gospel music. For those who sing in choirs this knowledge is intuitive - they know what sounds 'right' and wrong in Gospel singing and 'why' it does.

Module Overview.

To develop young people's understanding of the musical characteristics and social function of Gospel music through composing, performing and appraising. (Year 7)

Lesson 1: Setting the scene.

Ten-minute singing activity which involves initial 'call and response' activities followed by performance of the bass line and melody of 'Didn't my Lord Deliver Daniel'. Following this the teacher questions young people about their reactions to the music and whether they recognise the style.

This part of the lesson builds on many young people's *informal* knowledge of Gospel music gained outside of school.

The teacher revises learning of music terminology from previous lesson (melody and bass) relating this to what they have just sung.

Formal musical knowledge.

Bass and melody are performed by two young people. Class asked to listen and decide what is good about the performance and also whether it sounds 'complete'. A number suggest it feels 'bare' or 'thin'. Teacher asks why? One or two young people mention 'harmony' and 'chords' but most young people don't recognise these terms.

Intuitive knowledge of what sounds 'right' within a particular style.

Young people listen to a recorded performance of 'DMLDD' (harmony, melody and bass') and are asked to identify and describe the parts they have yet to sing.

Here the teacher is building on young people's *intuitive* knowledge to develop their *supervisory* knowledge (their ability to consciously listen out for, and appraise specific aspects of the music in the context of a particular style.

Teacher explains the principles and terminology relating to 'harmony' and 'chords'.

Formal knowledge.

Young people rehearse all parts of 'DMLDD' and then individual young people improvise 'scat' counter melody. Lesson concludes with appraisal of a recording of another Gospel number focusing on the style of singing.

The *informal* and *intuitive* knowledge young people brought to the lesson has been further developed through the lesson activities. *Formal* knowledge has helped young people articulate and externalise this knowledge and to share their ideas with others. This then provides the basis for development of *supervisory* and more developed *intuitive* knowledge which is applied both to the improvisation and, particularly, the appraising that takes place at the end of the lesson.

Figure 6.1 Lesson planning and musical knowledge

Task 6.2 Becoming immersed in music

Select an aspect of music with which you are relatively unfamiliar but feel you need to learn more about. Find out about characteristics of the style and immerse yourself in it musically, including, where possible, playing/singing and composing/improvising examples of it. Now develop two or three performing, composing and listening activities for young people which allow them to become immersed in that style.

If they are to have any value, learning about musical concepts, notations and the historical and social context of music should be rooted in, and proceed from, musical immersion. Attempting to learn 'about' music (developing formal musical knowledge) without immersion in music may lead to young people developing negative attitudes to music in the classroom, resulting in poor attainment.

Two aspects of music teaching that are particularly prone to an overemphasis on formal knowledge 'about' music are listening (particularly at examination level) and the teaching of harmony.

Listening is typically the least popular part of an examination course for young people, and is often the section of the examination in which they tend to do least well (see Chapter 10). Part of the problem is the sheer breadth of knowledge 'about' (the formal knowledge) music that is required in order to be able to recognise and identify the characteristics of different musical styles and genres from across half a millennium. Teachers are consequently forced into taking 'short cuts' in order to cover the ground. So, rather than young people gaining understanding of the music from the 'inside', through composing, performing and appraising it, they are, instead, drilled in the basic characteristics of musical styles and then required to apply these to listening tests – not surprisingly with limited success.

To be able to recognise style characteristics, particularly *within* musical sub-styles (for example, baroque music or be-bop), one needs to have immersed oneself in the music: to have listened to a range of examples of the music and, if possible, to have performed or composed some of it. Victoria Moore's description of the best way of acquiring wine-tasting skills could be applied equally well to recognising musical styles and genres, though she stops short of recommending immersion in vin rouge!

> It's not such a difficult skill as you might think, although the only way to acquire it is by tasting until you know a wine's signature as instinctively as you might recognise a footballer – not by matching in your brain the words you would use to describe him to someone else (for example 'heavy built but fast, with black hair'), but because his gait across the pitch, that very particular way he leaps to head the ball, is a pattern you just *know*.
> (Moore 2005: 65)

Harmony has also traditionally been taught in an abstract way, often unrelated to musical sound or experience. Young people learn the 'rules' of harmony and then apply these rules to harmony exercises, often without reference to any musical instrument or vocal realisation.

However, if we think of harmony not as an abstract intellectual exercise (where notes bear as much relationship to music as words in crosswords do to prose) but as an aspect of music that only makes sense in a *specific* musical context, then teaching it through musical immersion becomes both necessary and obvious – the only way that makes *musical* sense. In the exemplar in Box 6.1, we look at the way in which GCE A level students develop aural, improvising and performing (singing) skills and their understanding of harmony through both musical immersion and musical *integration*, the latter being the focus of the next section.

Box 6.1 Musical immersion

A suggested sequence of activities:

- The progression from Pachalbel's 'Kanon' (Figure 6.2) is played to the young people live and on a recording.
- They are asked to improvise vocally above the 'feel' of these chords, following a teacher model.
- They are then asked to sing/play one note from each chord, with and without accompaniment.
- They then sing/play one note from one chord and two from the next, then two notes from each chord.
- The young people then add linking or passing notes from each chord note.
- They freely improvise tunes together to create a contrapuntal texture.
- They then compose and notate their own melody.

Figure 6.2 Kanon

Task 6.3 Analysing the potential learning opportunities in a musical activity

Note down the musical learning that you think young people will gain through the activities in Box 6.1. You might want to structure your responses under the different kinds of knowledge headings discussed above. Compare your conclusions with the 'learning and teaching points' noted below.

The following 'learning and teaching' points emerge from the work in Box 6.1. Through these activities, young people develop an intuitive knowledge of harmony and harmonic progression in classical harmony. They begin to understand the way in which horizontal 'melodic' lines operate within, and emerge from, vertical harmonic progression. Consequently, for those young people who are, for example, rhythm or folk guitarists, their 'informal' knowledge of chord progressions is used as a foundation for learning and then built upon. Young people develop further their 'intuitive' understanding of harmony (what sounds right and what doesn't) within a particular musical context, which can then be used as the basis for the teaching of 'formal' knowledge, e.g. avoiding parallel fifths and octaves and the importance of composing singable lines. Formal knowledge is thus used to explain (externalise) intuitive knowledge. Young people instinctively 'feel' and begin to recognise intervals and chords, thus developing their aural skills in a musical context. All this occurs through musical immersion – learning through building a relationship with the music; a knowledge 'of' the music. As they consolidate this learning they develop their 'supervisory' knowledge, i.e. their ability to make appropriate musical decisions, having regard for the style and musical context within which they are working.

3: Planning should focus on the integration of musical activities

Integration can perhaps best be described as the bringing together of listening, composing/ improvising and performing activities to focus on common musical learning aims. A typical way in which integration might be employed is when teaching about musical concepts. For example, if a teacher wants the class to understand triple time, she may ask them to listen and respond to music in 3 time from a range of traditions and styles, perform simple triple time pieces, learn how 3 time can be represented in a range of notations and improvise and compose a waltz, perhaps using one of the notations explored earlier. The young people are conse-quently immersed in musical activity through the integration of the main areas of musical experience, with formal knowledge/knowledge about music emerging from this immersion.

Task 6.4 Beginning to integrate musical activities

Consider how you might teach the musical concept of ostinato. Note down the kinds of linked composing, performing and listening activities that you would ask young people to do in order to learn about this concept through immersing themselves in musical experience and activity. Plan the activities in detail (though not their sequencing) and identify specific tasks they will do and the examples of music you will use.

Lessons that integrate performing, composing and appraising have the potential to provide young people with a rich musical learning experience and break down the often artificial separation of performer, composer and audience. Indeed, it can be argued that an integrated approach is fundamental to good classroom music teaching and, within formal education, is what gives curriculum music its distinctiveness. Young people musically 'problem solve' by developing a *multifaceted* relationship with the music as composer, performer and appraiser.

Planning lessons that draw on and take account of different kinds of musical knowledge and ways of learning, that immerse young people in musical experience and that integrate musical activities requires, on the part of the teacher, a high level of intellectual and creative energy and presupposes a wide-ranging knowledge of music. It is a willingness and ability to make this creative and intellectual commitment that marks out the successful and innovative teacher from the one who is, perhaps, simply adequate. It is, moreover, what marks out the teacher as a *professional.*

The process of planning

The key principles of lesson planning are that planning should:

*   take account of different kinds of musical knowledge;
*   provide opportunities for musical immersion;
*   integrate performing, composing, and responding activities;
*   create a flexible framework within which unplanned and unexpected learning and music making can take place.

However, these principles are *preconditions for* but not the *guarantee of* effective teaching and learning. Effective teaching and learning can only be achieved through detailed and thought-through planning. In the second part of this chapter we explore the process of planning a lesson:

*   by presenting a framework for planning;
*   and analysing the implications of this framework for the process of planning.

Issues covered in other chapters are highly relevant to your planning of lessons and we make reference to these at appropriate points.

A framework for lesson planning

Figure 6.3 sets out a framework for planning lessons. It shows the sequence of planning and the way in which the various aspects of planning relate to each other.

Task 6.5 Analysing a framework for planning

Look at the framework for planning set out in Figure 6.3. For each central box, briefly annotate the main issues you think you need to consider for teaching and learning, drawing on your experience as a young person and observations you have made of teachers. Add to your responses as you work your way through the remainder of the chapter.

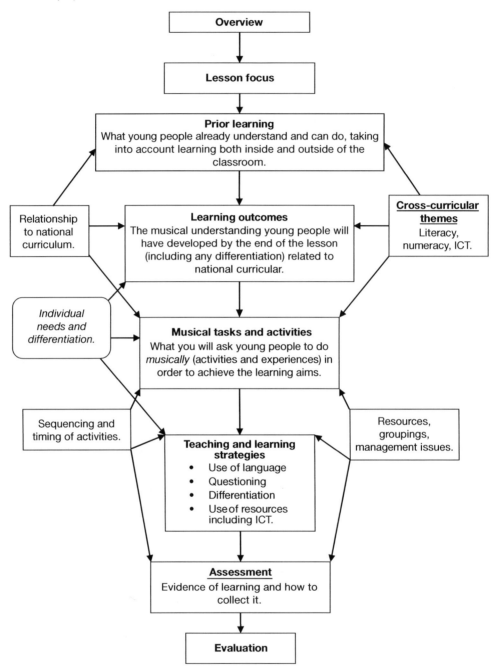

Figure 6.3 A framework for lesson planning

We now consider each of the 'central' boxes of the framework and explore the issues that you need to take into account at that point in the process of planning your lesson. Remember, however, that many of these issues are dealt with in much more detail in other chapters in the book.

Overview

A brief statement concerning the focus of the sequence of lessons of which the planned lesson is a part. This statement is the same (or similar) for all lessons in the sequence and reflects the overall learning aim for the sequence identified in the department's Scheme of Work.

Lesson focus

A short and precise statement setting out in broad terms the purpose of the lesson, including the broad learning aims and musical activities included within it. For example: exploring musical change and variation through cover versions; developing compositions based around features of the Javanese gamelan; exploring the influence of social context on the form of the blues.

Prior learning

Here is identified the learning that young people may bring to the lesson. Prior learning should take into account not only those things that have been learnt in the formal music curriculum but also the learning that takes place outside of school as part of young people's enculturation – what we referred to as 'informal learning'. Young people bring into the classroom what Piaget (1952) describes as a 'partial schemata' – a level of understanding based upon previous experience – which they then bring to bear upon their learning. Many young people play instruments or listen to music outside school, and this needs to be taken into account when planning lessons. There is therefore a whole range of prior learning within one class, with a consequential impact on the planning you need to do to address individual needs and interests.

As a beginner teacher planning to teach a class for the first time, you will need to gain as much information as possible about the young people's attainments and musical interests. This can be achieved in a number of ways:

- talking to young people themselves;
- talking to their regular teacher about what they have done and achieved;
- looking at the department's Scheme of Work and the intended learning outcomes for previous modules/sequences of lessons;
- scrutinising assessment information and pupil records (also useful for identifying any special needs).

Task 6.6 Taking account of prior learning

Note down the kind of prior learning and experience that you need to take account of when planning a lesson for a class you have taught or observed being taught.

Learning outcomes

These are what you might expect different groups of young people to have learnt by the end of the lesson. One learning outcome might be that young people understand what an ostinato is and are able to recognise one in a piece of music. It should be made clear how these learning outcomes fit into the overall sequence of lessons, proceeding from the previous lesson and leading on to the next one in the sequence.

There are two important issues to note about learning outcomes. First, it is critically important in the light of what we discussed in the first part of this chapter, that the learning tasks and outcomes are *musical*. 'To be able to write out a pentatonic scale' may be a learning outcome but it is not a *musical* one. To understand the way in which the pentatonic scale is used in a range of different musics, including Balinese gamelan, Appalachian folk music and by composers such as Debussy, and then compose music based on the pentatonic scale provides a whole set of musical learning outcomes. Writing out the scale *may* then be an *activity* (an example of 'formal knowledge') that supports progress towards these learning outcomes.

Second, there needs to be clarity about the distinction between a learning outcome and an activity. To identify performing 'On My Own' from *Les Miserables* as a learning outcome is to misunderstand this distinction. The teacher needs to have a clear idea why this song has been chosen in terms of the learning outcomes and experiences it might address (including the sheer pleasure of performing the song for its own sake). Learning occurs through using the song as the focus for a range of composing, appraising and performing activities, which may well *result* in learning about, for example, effective word setting, or how a particular emotion can be expressed musically.

Task 6.7 Ensuring learning outcomes are *musical*

Note down three examples of what you consider to be appropriate musical learning outcomes, as distinct from activities. Show how these learning aims are musical and relate to any National Curriculum or examination syllabi or specifications you are working with.

Musical tasks and activities

This section identifies the musical tasks and activities that young people undertake during the lesson in order to achieve the learning outcomes. It identifies the composing, appraising and performing they do and the musical repertoire in which they engage. Auditing a lesson's musical content ensures that the lesson is a musical experience. It is always worth asking the question: 'Would this activity be recognised as a musical activity outside the classroom?' If the answer is 'No', you need to reconsider what you are planning to do.

Task 6.8 Auditing the musical content of a lesson

Audit a lesson you have recently taught or observed in terms of the musical experiences and activities that young people gained from it. Ask yourself whether some activities were 'unmusical' and, if so, what might have been changed to ensure that this was not the case.

Teaching and learning strategies and their sequencing

Teaching and learning strategies are the ways you bring about learning, and the sequencing of these activities is the most appropriate order for them to take place.

Planning for teaching strategies draws heavily on your understanding of:

- musical learning and development (Chapter 3);
- meeting individual needs (Chapter 12);
- language and learning (Chapter 4).

Assessment

Assessment is discussed in detail in Chapter 13 and involves recognising and identifying evidence of learning, and knowing how to collect and record it. Planning for assessment involves:

- identifying opportunities for assessment (assessment points);
- strategies for assessment (e.g. questioning, peer-assessment);
- considering the appropriateness of different types and purposes of assessment (e.g. formative and summative assessment).

Effective assessment will enable you to carry out lesson evaluations.

Lesson evaluations

Lesson evaluations involve evaluating the effectiveness of your teaching through evaluating its impact on young people's learning. Evaluations address key questions such as:

- Did the young people learn what I had planned they should learn?
- If yes, how do I know? What is the musical evidence?
- If learning didn't happen, what was the problem – the outcomes, the tasks, the strategies used, the approaches to assessment?
- Did they learn things other than what I planned they should learn? Were these things of musical value? If so, how do I know? What is the musical evidence?
- What can I change/try in the next lesson to better support musical learning and young people's musical experiences?
- How can I improve this lesson the next time I teach it?
- How will my evaluation impact upon my teaching of *this* class?

Task 6.9 Evaluating a lesson

Evaluate a lesson you have taught, using the questions set out above. Identify those aspects of the lesson you would change if you taught it again.

Bringing planning to life in the classroom

Thorough and creative planning is a fundamental precursor to a lesson in which young people learn of music through music. However, plans only become a reality in the classroom through the actions of teachers and responses of young people. Effective teaching - the bringing of plans into action - is key to successful and musical teaching and learning. Plans need to be brought to fruition through teaching that:

- has a sense of purpose and good pace;
- has high expectations of young people's behaviour and achievement;
- provides opportunities for young people to organise some of their own learning, including problem solving, and creativity;
- elicits and sustains interest;
- has relevance and challenge;
- is matched to the ability and needs of the young people;
- includes a variety of strategies and activities;
- is well organised;
- allows young people to understand the nature of their involvement and the nature of the assessment procedures. (Adapted from Kyriacou 1991)

Good teaching is also about being able to identify, accommodate, celebrate and build upon those unanticipated instances of musical learning and manifestations of music understanding that provide evidence of the young person as an individual and independent musician.

As a beginner teacher, you will only be able to meet these challenges, as well as create a framework for and react intelligently to unexpected occurrences in lessons, if you have thought about and planned lessons thoroughly and creatively. This is why planning is so important.

Task 6.10 Planning a lesson

Create or adapt a lesson plan pro-forma that addresses the issues and processes outlined in this chapter. Following on from this, plan a lesson, for a class that you know well, that reflects the principles of effective planning we have discussed. Finally, write a short commentary to the lesson that shows how the planning, lesson content and proposed teaching strategies will enable you to meet Kyriacou's characteristics of good teaching as outlined above.

Summary

In this chapter you have developed your understanding of the principles that underpin effective lesson planning, including:

- the need to take account of different kinds of musical knowledge;
- that musical learning must be underpinned by immersion in musical activity and experience;
- the importance of integrating performing, composing and listening activities.

We have also examined:

- the process of planning; and
- the factors that need to be taken into account when planning a lesson.

Further reading

Mills, J. (2005) *Music in the School*, Oxford: Oxford University Press (Chapter 11: 'Making progress in music').

Swanwick, K. (1999) *Teaching Music Musically*, London: Routledge.

These two books will allow you to engage with the issues surrounding what it means to plan 'musical' lessons.

Fautley, M. and Savage, J. (2014) *Lesson Planning for Effective Learning*, Maidenhead: The Open University.

This generic book has some important material to help you think through key issues in planning lessons.

7 Behaviour for musical learning

Carolyn Cooke

Introduction

Students' behaviour is often cited as one the main concerns of beginner and newly qualified teachers (Welsh *et al.* 2011), and poor behaviour is also often referred to as a reason many leave the profession. But do we have a common shared understanding of what we mean by learning behaviour in a music classroom, and how can beginning music teachers take a proactive approach to developing a positive learning environment? In many contexts, managing behaviour concerns itself with how a teacher reacts to negative behaviour in the classroom. There is often an attempt to link it to how teachers plan and facilitate learning in order to maximise engagement and reduce opportunities for disruptive behaviour to occur (proactive steps) and to school-wide policies for rewards and sanctions (reactive steps).

However, this chapter will argue that this misses a vital step in learning about behaviour in the music classroom. While it is relatively easy to think of examples of 'bad' behaviour (e.g. throwing a chair, pushing another child, breaking an instrument) and possible responses to these, it is far less common to consider the issue from the other perspective: 'What behaviours do we want students to demonstrate in order to learn effectively, and how can we create a learning environment in which they will do so?'

Understanding this alternative way of thinking about behaviour has led to a number of initiatives, such as Behaviour for Learning (B4L) in England. These initiatives have often adopted cross-curricular or whole-school approaches to thinking about learning behaviours. However, within the music education context, very little has been written to address specifically the question of what behaviours we want to promote in a music context and how to do this. Although generic learning behaviours (developed through a pastoral or cross-curricular programme) will, of course, complement and support musical learning, it is possible to argue that musical learning requires music-specific learning behaviours that may not be developed in other areas of the curriculum. Therefore we need to be able to articulate what these musical learning behaviours might be and consider how to develop them effectively.

This chapter will argue that facilitating learning behaviours in the music classroom requires us to:

• understand the complex relationships that underpin students' learning behaviours in a music context;

- explore what it means to demonstrate learning behaviours in a music context and, as teachers, be able to recognise them;
- understand how to actively plan and facilitate musical learning behaviour.

It is through doing this that we can ensure all students in our classrooms are engaged and motivated to learn, as they will have the learning behaviours to be able to access and influence the curriculum successfully.

Objectives

By the end of the chapter you should be able to:

- justify why learning behaviour needs to be considered within a music-specific context;
- understand how developing learning behaviours underpins the students' relationship with the curriculum, with other people and with themselves as learners;
- understand what musical learning behaviours are and how they might be facilitated in the music classroom.

What do we mean by learning behaviours?

Ask two different teachers or schools what they consider to be learning behaviours and you may be surprised by the differences in their answers. Some may talk of skills such as teamwork, others may talk of organisation and independent learning, while some argue that learning behaviours should be about young people challenging assumptions or questioning their own learning process. The Teacher Effectiveness Enhancement Programme (TEEP) developed a model in which effective learner behaviour explored areas such as collaboration, thinking and metacognition and communication (TEEP 2009). The PEEL project (Project for Enhancing Effective Learning) developed a set of twelve good learning behaviours (Box 7.1).

Box 7.1 Good learning behaviours (PEEL 2009)

1 Checks personal comprehension . . . requests further information . . . tells the teacher what they don't understand.
2 Seeks reasons for aspects of the work at hand.
3 Plans a general strategy before starting.
4 Anticipates and predicts possible outcomes.
5 Checks teacher's work for errors; offers corrections.
6 Offers and seeks links between different activities and ideas, topics or subjects or between school and personal life.

(continued)

Box 7.1 *(continued)*

7   Searches for weaknesses in own understanding.

8   Suggests new activities and alternative procedures.

9   Challenges the text or an answer the teacher sanctions as correct.

10 Offers ideas, new insights and alternative explanations.

11 Justifies opinions.

12 Reacts and refers to comments of other students.

These differences in definition and perception of what learning behaviour is about can be seen in practice. As highlighted in Didau's article 'Children are at school to learn, not to behave', there is a risk that the term 'learning behaviour' can get reduced at a practical level in schools to young people 'being quiet and listening', which he argues gets distilled into or used to justify a set of classroom rules such as the ones listed in Box 7.2 (Didau 2012).

Box 7.2 Classroom rules (Didau 2012)

1   Listen when others are talking.

2   Follow directions.

3   Keep hands, feet and objects to yourself.

4   Work quietly and do not disturb others.

5   Show respect for school and personal property.

6   Work and play in a safe manner.

As Didau goes on to argue, 'These are great rules for instilling "good" behaviour . . . But they've got nothing at all to do with the types of behaviour required for learning' (Didau 2012). Didau is arguing here that although some of the above rules might enable all students in the room to engage and concentrate on learning, they don't in themselves help young people to understand *how* to learn. In fact, you could argue that some of the rules listed in Box 7. 2 transmit messages about the type of learning that will occur which could be contrary to the type of behaviour needed for learning musically, as you are asked to explore in Task 7.1.

Task 7.1 Identifying musical learning behaviours

Consider the learning behaviours in Box 7.1 and the list of classroom rules in Box 7.2. Think critically about the type of learning that they promote and whether they work within a music context.

- Are there some that are inappropriate to a music context or would need rewording?
- Which do you feel are vital for effective *musical* learning?
- Are there any you would add?

School-wide rules or agreements and generic ideas about learning behaviours have their place, but, as has been demonstrated, learning behaviour will be influenced by a range of factors, including the subject and pedagogy. For example, a 1950s history lesson delivered in a lecture style required students to learn and therefore behave in a very different way from a group composition and performance in a music classroom today. It is therefore crucial to consider what learning behaviour means within today's music context.

Based on a systematic review into learning behaviour, Powell and Tod (2004) developed a model (Figure 7.1) to demonstrate that learning behaviours underpin, and in turn are a result of, a young person's relationship with three critical elements of education; the curriculum (cognitive wellbeing), other people (social wellbeing) and with themselves as learners (emotional wellbeing) (Powell and Tod 2004). This model acknowledges the complexity of external influences on an individual's behaviour (i.e. how the learning behaviour environment can impact on their effectiveness as a learner) and the interdependent relationship between learning behaviours and a young person's relationships with curriculum, others and self. Put another way, it recognises that to learn effectively and to build effective relationships (whether cognitive, social or self) requires young people to be able to behave in appropriate ways.

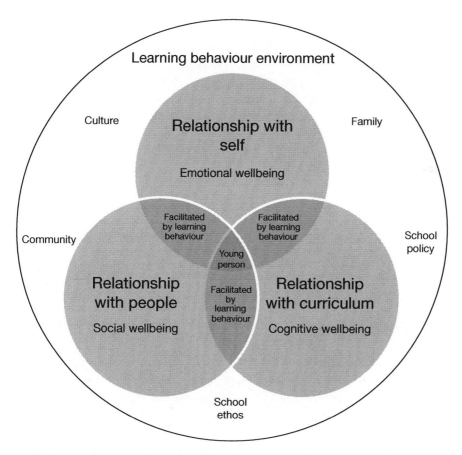

Figure 7.1 Learning behaviour conceptual framework

Task 7.2 Reflecting on Powell and Tod's model

(a) Using your own experience as a learner at school, consider how the model reflects your own experience of developing your learning behaviours as a musician.

(b) If possible, discuss with other (beginner) music teachers the implications of this model for developing musical learning behaviours in the classroom.

Justifying a music-specific approach

Although it wasn't designed for this purpose, the model gives us a way of thinking critically about the relationships between the students we teach and their cognitive, social and emotional wellbeing within a music-specific context. It is by doing this that we can consider how these relationships may raise particular issues with, or circumstances concerning, how students learn in music. Fundamentally, we can use it to justify why learning behaviour needs to be considered within a music-specific context, as the next sections will argue by considering each of the three relationships in turn.

Musical learning behaviour and relationship with the curriculum

As has been discussed in Chapter 5, the concept of a music curriculum is complex. Part of this complexity is the range of prior music curriculum experiences the students in a class bring with them and the relationships with music all young people have before they enter the classroom, whether as listeners, producers, composers or performers. This might be most obvious at points of transfer between schools, where students within one class may have had very different experiences, but equally might occur at transitions between different year groups, whch may highlight dissonances between different teachers' expectations and those of the young people. These previous experiences, if considered carefully during planning, may enhance students' cognitive wellbeing as they are asked to draw on and extend learning behaviours that they have already begun to develop. For example, a class that has developed behaviours around effective group rehearsal (e.g. identifying for the teacher small sections that need rehearsing by themselves) are asked to develop this further during a small-group project where they are expected to rehearse independently from the teacher and negotiate how best to rehearse as a group.

It is also important to consider that many students will have developed musical learning behaviours independent from the school environment. Thinking about the range of musicians in a classroom demonstrates just how varied their learning behaviours might be: the student who composes in their own bedroom; the group of friends who have formed a band; a young person who plays in the local orchestra; someone who learnt in a whole-class instrumental group at primary school; a student who sings Karaoke using her games console.

All of these young people will have developed quite different learning behaviours in relation to their experience, whether it be a high level of independent creative decision making, carefully following instructions and etiquettes around particular types of group performance, questioning what is happening while playing or getting feedback on their performance or composition from virtual sources. Thus, asking students to learn (and therefore behave) in a particular way may cause dissonance between what they know as musical learning behaviours and what is being promoted. For example, a student has taught herself a complex guitar accompaniment to a song aurally by listening, singing the bass note and then finding the chord through experimentation. In a project about pop songs the student is then encouraged to read notated chord sequences (using only three chords) as the way of achieving the highest marks, therefore undermining the more musical learning behaviour that she has developed.

Of course, no teacher would deliberately set out to cause such a stark dissonance between previously developed learning behaviours and the curriculum, but it is surprisingly easy to transmit a particular set of values about learning behaviours and what teachers consider valued knowledge – and difficult to identify students' previous learning behaviours if they aren't given the opportunity to demonstrate and share them.

As well as students having developed their own musical learning behaviours from the range of experiences they bring to the classroom, there is also the issue of learning behaviours associated with different musical genres, cultures and types of activity. A quick glance at how musicians learn in different musical cultures highlights the diversity of approaches to musical learning and therefore expectations of behaviour (e.g. master apprenticeship model, within a community group, through structured and progressive technical exams). In developing a music curriculum, teachers draw on this variety of cultural practices and learning approaches to develop a young person's musicianship, skills and understanding. However, in the context of cognitive wellbeing it does raise some important questions. First, do we as teachers prepare ourselves for the differences in learning behaviour associated with different musical cultures, genres or activities (i.e. do we expect students to behave similarly when engaging in a western art composition and an Indian Raga improvisation and is this alright)? Second, do we prepare students by helping them understand different musical learning behaviours or do we expect this to happen intuitively?

Musical learning behaviour and relationship with people

Powell and Tod, in their systematic review of research into learning behaviours, identified that 'Social interaction is pivotal to cognitive development and influences the development of learning behaviours' (Powell and Tod 2004: 81). At a whole-school level, strategies to support young people's social wellbeing, such as mentoring, tutoring and social education sessions, all contribute to ensuring that students are able to be effective learners. In this way, learning behaviours to ensure social wellbeing involve helping young people work confidently in groups, communicate their ideas and present information. However, just as with cognitive wellbeing, there are some particular issues within a music learning context that may affect how young people behave as learners.

First, it is well established that musical engagement and choice is a core part of some students' developing personal identity. This may come in the form of membership of a particular social group (including peer group) or community, or may be more individualistic.

This can often be seen in practice during small-group work where the task requires negotiation about the direction the task should take, the way it should be undertaken and the outcome they are aiming for. It is in these circumstances that dominant views about musical styles and genres, processes or products might override valid and important minority views and musical learning behaviours.

Dominant voices or opinions can be related to students' perception of hierarchies among the peer group. It is easy to bring to mind circumstances in which students may feel that hierarchies exist within a group. The most commonly referred to is the perception of students who have instrumental or vocal tuition beyond the curriculum, their musicianship in relation to others in the class and their ability to succeed in curriculum music. Other hierarchies may also exist around perceived intelligence or resources to which students have access beyond the classroom. These perceived hierarchies influence social wellbeing within music learning contexts and therefore the learning behaviours that students demonstrate and perceive to be valued.

Finally, another influence on social wellbeing is the interactions that students have with their teacher and the values and beliefs they promote (whether consciously or subconsciously). As has already been stated, it is surprisingly easy for teachers to promote particular beliefs and values about music, musicianship or learning music through what they do or how they phrase something, which can have ramifications for social wellbeing.

Being aware of these issues and their potential effect on how students behave as learners within the classroom is key to establishing a socially supportive learning environment.

Musical learning behaviours and relationship with self

It is clear to anyone who has worked with learners within a music context that they will either have or will develop their own personal relationship with the music, musical activities or ways of learning. Of course, it is possible to argue that emotional wellbeing stems from cognitive and social wellbeing; however, there are a few more personal issues to consider within a music context. These include considering issues such as the students' reactions to the learning environment, their individual learning needs and the ability of individuals to manage their own learning and influence their experience within the music classroom.

The learning environment is a powerful, yet often underestimated ingredient in facilitating students' learning. The layout, displays, accessibility of resources and instruments all send messages to young people about how they are expected to behave and learn. For example, a new class faced with lines of desks with computers and keyboards are likely to deduce a different message about learning from those faced with a circle of chairs and a variety of percussion and acoustic instruments around the edge of the classroom. Equally, a classroom filled with displays of photographs of students working in groups on a variety of projects, with quotes, key words and reviews of the project, gives strong clues as to what the teacher considers to be valued ways of working as compared to a music history timeline display. The impact of the learning environment on individual student's relationship with self cannot be underestimated. In an ideal situation it should make them feel safe to learn and experiment, supported in making musical decisions and choices and included as part of the classroom or even department community. At its worst, it may turn students off, making them feel that learning within school music bears no relationship to themselves as individuals and removing any sense of empowerment to influence how they learn.

As with any discussion of learning, the learning behaviours that need to be facilitated and supported by the teacher will vary from student to student. This is not just associated with the identifiable learning needs of certain students, but the individual learning needs of *all* young people, depending on their particular interests, background, ambitions and learning approaches. This requires of teachers a great deal of individual knowledge of students and a commitment to all young people as individuals at every opportunity.

Finally, enabling students to influence their own learning approach is highly likely to increase emotional wellbeing, as it is through this process (often referred to as pupil voice) that all students can feel the curriculum is theirs, rather than something that is being done to them. Of course, running a busy department within the context of a school institution poses many challenges to the concept of a personalised, individualised curriculum experience. However, musical learning is characterised by personal interactions and experiences of music and a plethora of musical decision-making moments, all of which provide opportunity for students to shape their experiences. At a larger scale, student involvement in curriculum design and development, or developing students' ability and confidence to take their learning in an alternative direction, gives greater scope for truly personalised experiences that may contribute to emotional wellbeing. Task 7.3 asks you to consider these issues in light of your own experiences.

Task 7.3 Young people's learning behaviours

Think of two young people you are working with, who were not learning effectively in a music context (remember this may not be that they were 'misbehaving', but demonstrating little progress). Looking at the issues that have been raised in relation to cognitive, social and emotional wellbeing, which do you feel may impact (positively or negatively) on these young people's learning behaviour in a music context?

Musical learning behaviours

So far we have discussed issues that impact on students' learning behaviours within a music context and the justification as to why musical learning behaviours might need specific consideration. So what do we mean by musical learning behaviours? Of course, the answer to this question will depend on the nature of the learning activity, the students involved and the expected learning outcomes. However, we can start by considering what we mean by using three examples of learning behaviours during group composition tasks (Box 7.3).

In establishing what evidence there is of learning *behaviours* within these three vignettes, it is easy to slip into identifying learning styles, preferences or strategies. A useful tool to help distinguish learning behaviours is Claxton's research into learning power (Claxton 2002). He argues that a supple learning mind, and therefore a powerful one, requires young

Box 7.3 Examples of learning behaviours

Vignette 1

Jack was asked to compose a pop song as part of a group of five. The group have already performed a range of pop songs, negotiating how different people in the group would contribute. This included some working aurally from a downloaded copy of the song, some teaching others in the group using imitation and call and response and some using a tab score. When it came to composing, the group decided that they would use a sequencing program to record their initial ideas in case they came up with something they couldn't then replicate. Two of the five also made some written notes about the chords. By the end of the first lesson they had recorded a lot of material for a possible chorus. Jack, who was used to composing using a software package at home, volunteered to produce a draft version. In the next lesson they listened to the track and replicated it, although they found a more suitable drum beat. They then repeated the process for composing the verse.

Vignette 2

During the first term in the secondary school Siobhan completed a unit of work on programme music, focusing specifically on writing melodies and using the musical elements to provide contrast. The unit was based around a children's story. When composing and refining their group composition, Siobhan was able to describe the composition process using phrases such as 'we used the first bit of the melody each time the main character came in' and 'we thought the music for this bit of the story needed to be more dancy and so we used some drums'. In performance, the teacher identified that Siobhan was noticing when others in the group were out of time, out of tune or out of balance. Siobhan was able to negotiate with the others in the group how to stand in the space to make sure they could all see each other to improve the timing and balance.

Vignette 3

Ali knew that he didn't cope well with the hustle and bustle of a noisy music classroom when there was group work going on. He had an understanding with his teacher that his group would work in the corridor during group work or in the adjacent classroom if it was free. He was also aware that he was good at working on a specific problem or part of the composition independently rather than participating in group decision making. This often meant that he found himself resources and asked for advice when he felt he needed it. This rarely involved the class teacher as he often involved his guitar teacher, who was usually in the music office during Ali's music lesson. Although the class teacher was fully aware that Ali asked the guitar teacher to listen to things during her lesson, she wasn't aware that these conversations and musical starting points continued during Ali's guitar lessons. Drawing on two different adult perspectives led to Ali having to make decisions about which opinions and ideas to take on board.

Resilience	Resourcefulness	Reciprocity	Reflectiveness
Perseverance Staying with it. Dealing with uncertainty and disappointment.	**Making links** Seeing connections. Building patterns. Making meaning.	**Interdependence** Balancing self-reliance and sociability.	**Meta-learning** Knowing yourself as a learner [and] assessing possible learning gains.
Managing distractions Recognise, tolerate and reduce distractions.	**Questioning** Being curious. Asking questions. Playing with ideas.	**Collaboration** Sharing. Communicating effectively. Using appropriate roles.	**Planning** Planning ahead. Knowing what action to take. Using time well. Anticipating problems.
Absorption Being enrapt in learning.	**Capitalising** Looking out for and using materials / resources to support learning.	**Empathy and listening** Listening to understand. Putting yourself in others shoes.	**Distilling** Drawing out points from a learning experience [and] applying them to further learning.
Noticing Perceiving and sensing the details in experience.	**Imagining** Seeing how things might be. Visualisation. Creative intuition.	**Imitation** Picking up habits, traits and values from those you admire.	**Revising** Adapting. Thinking on your feet. Flexibility. Monitoring progress. Reviewing the situation.
	Reasoning Being logical and analytical.		

Figure 7.2 Learning capabilities (adapted from Ellis and Tod 2009: 76)

people to develop four types of learning disposition: resilience, resourcefulness, reciprocity and reflectiveness. These four dispositions each have a number of capabilities, as set out in Figure 7.2.

Although many of these capabilities and their definitions are easily transferable to a music context, a few can be changed to make them subject relevant. For example, *Imagining* talks of visualisation. Although there may be an element of visualisation, or seeing in your mind's eye, during a music task (e.g. the visual effect during performance or visualising a melodic shape), it may be helpful to add internalisation of musical sound to the definition. Equally, *Listening* is defined as 'listening for understanding' under the disposition of Reciprocity. In a music context, listening has a far broader role and could therefore arguably sit across the dispositions of Reciprocity, Reflectiveness and Resourcefulness. Finally, *Noticing* within a music learning context could also be broader than Claxton's definition. Noticing details of experiences could arguably straddle Resilience, Resourcefulness, Reflectiveness and Reciprocity.

Task 7.4 Identifying learning dispositions

- Using the four dispositions from Figure 7.2 as sentence starters, note down what learning behaviours are evident in the vignettes. You may feel that some dispositions are not explicitly mentioned, but must have existed in order for the students to be learning effectively.

(continued)

Task 7.4 *(continued)*

- Using a table like the one below, revisit the Powell and Tod model. Under the headings of cognitive, social and emotional wellbeing, note down the Claxton dispositions that can be associated with each; for example, 'perseverance' could be associated with emotional wellbeing.
- For each of Claxton's dispositions, write down an example of how music teachers might facilitate students' use of the disposition.

Cognitive wellbeing	Social wellbeing	Emotional wellbeing
		Perseverance, e.g. give praise for persevering with a composition problem until a solution is found.

It is possible, looking at Claxton's four dispositions and the three relationships (cognitive, emotional and social) that underpin effective learning behaviours, to identify a correlation. Very broadly, it is possible to argue that cognitive wellbeing is supported by the development of Resourcefulness and Reflectiveness, social wellbeing is supported by Reciprocity, while emotional wellbeing is supported by developing a student's Resilience. This correlation allows us to identify more clearly what we can do to support and develop learning behaviours in a music context.

Facilitating effective learning behaviours

Throughout this chapter we have identified ways in which thinking about developing learning behaviours, instead of managing behaviour, can be used as an alternative, more proactive way to promote effective learning in the music classroom. It has argued that through supporting young people's cognitive, social and emotional wellbeing and by being aware of exactly what learning behaviour looks and sounds like in a music classroom, we are more equipped to develop effective learners. However, it is arguably the teacher in the classroom who can make the most substantial contribution to ensuring this can happen. The question is how.

To answer this, the final sections of this chapter suggest there are four factors which can be considered key to developing students' ability to be effective learners in a music classroom: knowledge of students as musicians and learners, planning for the development of musical learning behaviours, creating a musical learning environment and interactions.

Students as musicians and learners

Ensuring young people's social, emotional and cognitive wellbeing can only happen if we know the students well. However, helping them to use and develop their learning behaviour in a music context requires us to know them, their generic needs and personalities, as musicians with their previous experiences, skills and understanding and as musical learners. This is daunting for any music teacher who may see hundreds of students each week; however, much can be gained from ensuring that the following conditions exist:

- Students have the opportunity to express and demonstrate how they learn best by influencing their approach to tasks and activities. This may be through choice of resources such as instrument or choosing how they approach a task rather than following a pre-set structure (i.e. allowing students to choose a different path to the end result rather than following what you would choose).
- Opportunities are provided to establish what previous musical learning the student has experienced and to demonstrate and draw on the learning behaviours that have been developed.
- Students are made explicitly aware that they are part of the planning process and that you, with their help, will try to find ways for them to learn effectively. It is through this partnership (using pupil voice) that you can begin to develop an understanding of them as individual learners.

Planning to develop musical learning behaviours

As with any learning, the question must be asked as to how we expect students to know what we value as teachers. As has been argued, this is particularly important in a music context where the type of learning, and therefore learning behaviours, may be different from those they experience in other subjects. Planning for the development of this understanding and associated skills is not straightforward. For example, it is quite possible that a student may demonstrate more advanced noticing skills than an older pupil. However, there are a number of points to consider in developing a student's ability to learn effectively:

- They will need a range of opportunities to develop the learning behaviours that will help them. You may, for example, audit your units of work to see what learning behaviours you are expecting students to demonstrate, and think about whether you are making this explicit to them.
- Being aware of the perceived hierarchies that may impact on learning behaviour, you may need to explicitly plan ways of demonstrating and sharing the contributions that all students can make. This may include suggesting alternative ways of tackling a task, being prepared to try something new, noticing connections between their musical learning and other experiences or reflecting on their learning process.
- Collaboration is key to effective musical learning. Planning how collaborative group work is introduced, and how students know what effective group learning can be like, is critical. This may involve modelling effective group work and decision making (possibly in a whole-class activity) through to praising groups who demonstrate effective group learning and sharing their experiences with others in the class.
- Different students will react to working in groups in different ways.

A musical learning environment

As highlighted by Claxton's research, resourcefulness is a key disposition to learning effectively (Claxton 2002). In a music classroom, this will often involve accessing a wide range of musical instruments and technologies, but will also include having access to other people (the teacher, other students). This is critical to planning the learning environment. How can you arrange the space and the resources within it to allow students to learn most effectively? Will you need to change the arrangement of the space for different types of learning? How can you plan spaces and time for students to be able to work both independently and collaboratively?

As was highlighted in Vignette 3 about Ali and Claxton's capabilities, managing distractions is also critical to successful musical learning. Thinking about other learning environments that young people might experience, there are very few that require this capability to such an extent. Discussing this issue openly with students, noticing who finds it particularly difficult and organising spaces and groups to maximise their ability to learn effectively will all help. This could be as simple as allowing students to express when distractions are making learning difficult, organising resources to create enclosed circular working areas within the room or allowing students to move into different spaces to complete certain parts of tasks (e.g. two boys want to listen carefully to a backing track they have composed and are allowed to listen to it in a practice room so that they can listen for the balance and timing accurately). In other words, it is imperative that the learning environment is a *musical* learning environment.

Interactions with young people

Developing behaviours for musical learning requires us as teachers to explicitly think about, plan for, model and discuss the behaviours we value. To this end, the interactions we have with individuals and classes will underpin how students understand what we expect and what is effective in helping them to learn. These interactions may be verbal but may also often be musical as students begin to understand you as a musician and how you would approach musical learning tasks. This is, of course, a form of modelling, and provides a strong argument for modelling musical learning processes (i.e. different approaches to a task, or musical problem solving) rather than just modelling the final musical outcome.

If the interactions are verbal, then using Claxton's research we can argue that open-ended, exploratory, questioning, reflective interactions are more likely to support the development of the behaviours we want young people to draw on (Claxton 2002). These might include 'what happens if . . .' or 'what other options did you experiment with . . .' or 'why did you decide that was the best option . . .'.

Finally, viewing interactions from a learning behaviour standpoint may make us think about how we use praise to support the development of musical learning behaviours. Instead of praising musical outcomes (although this is of course vital), learning behaviours give us another reason to praise a student (e.g. for noticing links between different units of work or persevering with a musical problem until a solution was found). This is important, not only for ensuring young people's cognitive, social and emotional wellbeing but also to reinforce, to the student and others in the class, what is valued behaviour.

The above factors support us in planning and facilitating music lessons in which we can promote and develop musical learning behaviours. In other words, *musical learning behaviours* can only occur and develop through *musical lessons* in which both teacher and student are *acting musically*. Task 7.5 will help you consider how a music teacher's own behaviours can promote effective musical learning behaviours in young people.

Task 7.5 Promoting effective learning behaviours

(a) Review the chapter (particularly the two models) and create a bullet point list of teacher behaviours that will support students in developing appropriate and effective learning behaviours in the music classroom.

(b) Observe a lesson taught by another music teacher. With their prior permission, focus on the following features:
   - What messages (either explicit through discussion or action, or implicit through the environment or activities) do students receive about what learning behaviours are expected during the lesson?
   - Is there evidence of students' learning behaviours being developed during the lesson? You may want to refer to the Claxton model.
   - Was there opportunity to plan for, or respond to, situations in a way that would have developed students' learning behaviours?

(c) Plan a lesson for a new class starting at the school. Think about how you could plan the learning environment, your dialogue with them and the activities to promote the learning behaviours you feel are most important when introducing them to what it means to learn in music.

Summary

This chapter has:

- discussed the importance of considering what learning behaviours we value and want to develop in our young people;
- argued that to do this we must consider learning behaviours within a musical learning context, as the cognitive, social and emotional wellbeing of young people is underpinned by a number of music-specific issues.

It is in this complex web of factors, as demonstrated by Powell and Tod's model, that we as music teachers need to be able to articulate and facilitate the development of musical learning behaviours.

Further reading

Building Learning Power, *www.buildinglearningpower.co.uk* (accessed 30 July 2015).

This website gives a comprehensive introduction to the principles and research underpinning Building Learning Power, including links to further publications.

Capel, S., Leask, M. and Turner, T. (2013) *Learning to Teach in the Secondary School: A Companion to School Experience*, 6th edn, London: Routledge, Chapter 3.

Although this chapter has argued strongly for a music-specific approach to learning behaviours, there are many generic skills and considerations which are common to all teachers in the secondary school. This chapter deals with these issues systematically.

8 Creativity and music education

Chris Philpott with Keith Evans

Introduction

Creativity is an important educational theme which has moved in and out of focus several times in recent history, during which time it has been through various ideological conceptions. For example, creativity in the 1960s and 70s was at the core of a progressive ideology that championed a child-centred approach to learning and *personal* development. Following publication of the influential *All Our Futures* (NACCCE 1999) report into creativity at the turn of the century, the championing of creativity has taken a more 'instrumental' turn, i.e. by focusing on the need for education to develop creative individuals who are able to adapt flexibly to an ever-changing world and thereby contribute to society and the economy. However, throughout this time, creativity has been consistently embraced by music and the arts in education. While accepting the personal and instrumental arguments, arts educators have also maintained the importance of creativity as an essential dimension to artistic disciplines, i.e. in our case the need for young people to develop their musical creativity.

Task 8.1 Creativity and education

When justifying creativity in the music classroom, what do you feel is the relative balance between the personal, instrumental and musical arguments? What, if any, is the relationship between these three manifestations of creativity? Discuss your ideas with other music and/or arts teachers, either face to face or on social media.

The arts do not have any particular monopoly on creativity, even if this is sometimes assumed to be the case. The populist notion of the 'two cultures' tends to conceptualise the sciences as rational and objective and the arts as being essentially creative and subjective. However, music, as with any human discipline, has creativity woven into its essential fabric and thus has an important role to play in developing both general and musically specific creativity.

Objectives

By the end of this chapter you should be able to:

- understand a variety issues that surround the nature of creativity;
- begin to develop a well-reasoned concept of creativity to underpin your classroom practice;
- understand how it is possible to facilitate creativity in the classroom;
- understand some practical strategies for stimulating creativity in the classroom;
- show your own creativity when planning for the classroom.

Creativity and the curriculum for music

Various iterations of the National Curriculum for Music in England have emphasised the importance of creativity, with the 'Purpose of Study' statement in the current manifestation noting that:

> Music . . . embodies one of the highest forms of creativity. A high-quality music education should engage and inspire pupils to develop a love of music and their talent as musicians, and so increase their self-confidence, creativity and sense of achievement.
>
> (DfE 2013b)

In the 2007 iteration of the National Curriculum, creativity featured as one of five 'Key Concepts' in music and was defined as: 'a) using existing musical knowledge, skills and understanding for new purposes and in new contexts; b) exploring ways music can be combined with other art forms and other subject disciplines' (QCDA 2007).

In music, the concept of creativity is commonly associated with the acts of composing, improvising and arranging. However, young people are also required to behave creatively when they perform and re-create music where there is always an act of interpretation and imagination. There is also a creative act involved when responding to a piece of music in audience and when communicating ideas and feelings about music. These dimensions to creativity are explored more fully elsewhere in this book. Having said these things, we must acknowledge that creativity is a slippery concept, and there is little by way of common consent about its nature or processes. For example, is creativity a gift or something that we can all engage with? Most might agree that some level of creativity is needed to solve a problem (composers and performers are problem solvers), and that the imagination needs to be applied in order for this to happen.

What is clear is that music and arts teachers need to develop their understanding of creativity in order to inform their work in the classroom, and this is where we begin.

What is creativity?

Box 8.1 contains some statements made about the nature of creativity, which exhibit a wide range of views. Read these quotations and then carry out Task 8.2 to explore your own views about creativity in music education.

Box 8.1 Creativity and music education

What possible virtue can there be in pretending that creativity, an attribute not possessed by towering geniuses until childhood is past, can and should be generated in the youngsters of primary schools . . . re-creation, that's the thing. But re-creation is surely also the apposite term for so many of the activities of that highly imitative being, the human child.

(Sherratt 1977: 34)

There is a continuum in the creative act which moves from the ordinary to the extraordinary, from daily perceptual vision to deep anological vision, to the rhythmic babblings and repetitions of the pre verbal utterance to the regular beat and syntactic echoing of epic poetry.

(Abbs 1989b: 8)

In contrast, on this approach (i.e. creativity = novelty), 'true' creativity arrives when individuals break rules or invent new ones.

(Pateman 1991: 33–35)

[A]rtistic activities which offer the greatest scope for the majority of youngsters to develop their innate sensitivity, inventiveness and imagination might have a strong claim for a place of importance in the curriculum.

(Paynter 1977: 5)

[C]omposing is one of the most difficult things it is possible to undertake: there have been less than thirty composers over the past two hundred and fifty years in Europe who are generally remembered with any deep sense of gratitude now.

(Fletcher 1987: 41)

Marx maintained that all making was creative.

[T]he text is a tissue of quotations drawn from innumerable centres of culture.

(Pateman 1991: 40)

(continued)

Box 8.1 *(continued)*

Martha Graham once said that it takes at least five years of training in the discipline to be spontaneous in dance, which brings out how misconceived is the notion that creativity is inhibited by learned technique. On the contrary, although of course technical competence does not necessarily give creative flair, it is a necessary precondition for such flair, in any subject discipline or activity.

(Best 1992: 96)

'When people ask me what comes first, the tune or the lyrics', said the well-known popular songwriter Sammy Cahn, 'I say the thing that comes first is the phone call . . .'

(Hargreaves 1986: 146)

When the muse is upon him, he works frantically, without food or sleep, until the work has been produced. According to this view, creativity is mysterious, unconscious, irrational, and anything but ordinary.

(Hargreaves 1986: 147)

The painter Max Ernst claimed to exert no conscious control over his work . . . whereas the writer Edgar Allen Poe insisted that the creative involves no more than conscious planning and rational decision making.

(Hargreaves 1986: 147)

Task 8.2 What is creativity?

Use the ideas in Box 8.1 and any others from your reading or experience to answer the following questions:

* What have you witnessed in the music classroom thus far (as teacher or pupil) that you consider to be evidence of creativity (during listening and responding to music, composition, improvisation and performance)?
* Which of the views discussed above have most resonance for you?
* Can 4 year olds compose music?
* What is the relationship of composing to technique?
* Attempt a definition of creativity for yourself, or with a fellow beginner teacher.

Out of these quotations certain tensions arise in relation to the concept of creativity. These tensions are identified in Figure 8.1 and represent differing attitudes to the possibility of creativity and the conditions under which it can take place. It is important for you to explore the tensions shown in Figure 8.1, for your attitudes to these determine the extent to which you believe creativity to be a possibility in the classroom.

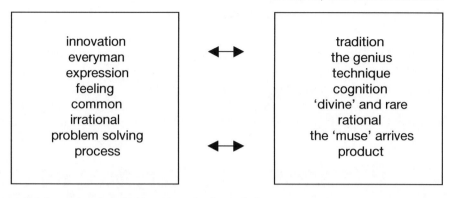

Figure 8.1 Some tensions in the concept of creativity

For example, an important issue that arises out of studying creativity is the relationship of technique to creativity. Is it necessary to develop technique before we can become creative? If so, is it that creativity is a state only achieved after a technical 'apprenticeship'? Is it possible for technique to develop alongside the creative use of imagination? Can technique develop out of the problems posed by the creative process itself, where new technique becomes a means to solving the problem? The widespread use of music technology has introduced an interesting perspective here and, arguably, 'technique' in the traditional sense is no longer required *at all* for young people to be musically creative.

In relation to such developments, Pamela Burnard argues that it makes more sense to talk of 'musical creativities' as opposed to creativity in the singular, and that in any case 'technique' is always being reinvented as a result of the interplay between music, society and technology. Burnard maintains that:

> The notion of equally valued musical creativities is pertinent to the radical changes in the production and experience of music across the past 20 years . . . The creativity from which music originates is evident in the interplay of myriad social and technological practices . . .
>
> (Burnard 2012: 16)

Having briefly examined some of the issues surrounding the concept of creativity, we must also explore ideas on how it takes place; in other words, the *process* of creativity. Understanding the creative process also further enhances our understanding of the concept of creativity itself.

What is the process of creativity?

Three models of the creative process are presented in Figure 8.2. These are not designed to be definitive, but are introduced to illustrate a range of thinking to stimulate your own reflections on the creative process. Having read these models, carry out Task 8.3 to explore your own experiences of creative processes.

Model A

Wallas (1926) suggests that the creative process has four stages:

- *Preparation:* researching the problem

- *Incubation:* conscious attention is turned away from the problem and unconscious processes dominate, imagination plays a large role.

- *Illumination:* the 'eureka' experience when a creative solution is defined.

- *Verification:* formalisation of the solution, refined and adapted to meet practical constraints.

Model B

Ross (1980) proposes four stages to creativity:

- *Initiating* the creative impulse by exploring, doodling and playing.

- *Acquainting* oneself with a particular medium, with the potential and possibilities of sounds for particular purposes; further playing around with ideas.

- *Controlling* the medium through the mastery of basic skills and techniques; understanding constraints and limitations.

- *Structuring* the ideas into a satisfying and comprehensible whole; can also involve reviewing.

Model C

Abbs' model of the creative process has many elements contained in the above (Abbs 1989):

- The release of impulse; a stirring of the psyche.

- Working in a medium; representative embodiment.

- Critical judgement moves towards a realisation of final form.

- Presentation and performance; taking the work into the community.

- Responses and evaluation by the community.

Figure 8.2 The creative process

Task 8.3 The process of creativity

After examining the three models outlined in Figure 8.2, answer the following questions:

- What evidence have you seen of these processes at work in relation to composing, performing and responding in your placement school?
- Consider your own creativity in relation to music making. Do you recognise any features of the creative process in your own work as composer, improviser, listener or performer? Illustrate any comments you make.

It is important that as a music teacher you develop for yourself a concept of creativity. This concept will define what counts as creativity in your classroom and how you will plan for an environment that promotes its development. Through understanding something of the concept of creativity and the creative process, you will be in a better position to plan for the emergence and development of creativity in your lessons.

How can we facilitate the development of creativity in the music classroom?

It is possible for you to create the conditions under which creativity can flourish, although like any flower you cannot guarantee that it will grow. Despite producing a suitable environment for creativity, we have to accept that sometimes little creative activity emerges and that there will be failures for student and teacher alike. However, despite the necessary risks, it is only by making music in many different ways that opportunities for creativity appear. In other words, a young person's entitlement to music is also an entitlement to be creative.

Here are some points for consideration when facilitating creativity in the classroom:

- *Resources:* You can enhance the potential for creativity by building up rich and stimulating resources which can be used to both initiate and support the creative process. These resources can be both musical (e.g. a variety of recordings) and extra-musical (e.g. images and video).
- *Levels of structure:* It is appropriate to include various levels of structure when promoting creativity, depending on the students, the task and the desired musical learning. For example, teachers might set their students:
  - a free choice about which problems to solve and how to solve them (self-directed creativity);
  - open-ended tasks which channel responses through particular stimuli, e.g. a verse/chorus song;
  - structured problem solving in which the expressive and structural ingredients are limited to a specific set of conventions, for example when creating a minimalist composition or harmonising a Bach chorale.

- *Challenge:* As a teacher you can plan suitable challenges in relation to the students' developmental stage; in other words, challenges that stimulate them and set a problem that they have a realistic chance of solving.
- *Modelling:* As a music teacher you need to be a role model and set up opportunities for other role models to be seen and heard, for example peers and external musicians. This requires you to show your creativity by, for example, 'jamming' with the class or composing for them yourself.
- *Space and time:* When solving problems, students need 'space' in which to demonstrate and develop their creativity. You need to be sensitive to this and flexibly adapt your expectations as the lesson or unit of work progresses.
- *Support and intervention:* You should be prepared to give the type of support your students need in order to complete tasks, such as help with the technical skills that can enhance the work in progress. This support can also come in the form of feedback, questioning, prompting and modelling (assessment for learning).
- *Creating a safe environment:* You should aim to establish an environment in which students feel able to take risks, in which all contributions are valued and mutually respected by all. This attitude can be modelled and encouraged by the teacher through their exchanges with the class or group.

Task 8.4 Creating the conditions for creativity

Can you think of any other conditions that will enhance creativity in the classroom? Share an example of your planning (or an observation) in which you feel that creativity has been promoted. How were the students stimulated? What support was given to them? Describe the outcomes of the lesson and your reflections on them.

CONTENT OPEN

Informal lessons

FOCUSING   FREEWHEELING

Convergent thinking on   Divergent thinking promoting
rules and conventions   discovery and creativity

CONTENT CLOSED

Formal lessons

Figure 8.3 A pedagogy for creativity

Source: adapted from Berkley (2004)

These strategies are part of a *pedagogy* for creativity. Berkley (2004) has suggested a pedagogical framework for teaching composing as problem solving, which could also be adapted to include our broader concept of creativity to include improvisation, performance, listening and responding to music. The outline of her model can be seen in Figure 8.3.

It is most likely that a pedagogy for creativity would freely move between different aspects of the model as the teacher responds to the ongoing needs of individuals. For example, it might be appropriate to offer input on conventions to one group or individual, whereas others might need to be challenged to 'freewheel'. Here the teacher flexibly adapts the pedagogy during the lesson or workshop, and this is most easily done where a rich set of resources and media, e.g. instruments, technology, recordings etc., are available to support the learning and teaching process.

Task 8.5 A pedagogy for creativity

Where do the various strategies we have noted thus far (and any others you have observed in the classroom) fit into Berkley's model? Choices about balancing the various aspects of the model inevitably relate to an individual teacher's ideology. Are you drawn to a particular approach for facilitating creativity above others, and, if so, where does it fit in the model?

Some practical strategies for stimulating and developing creativity in the classroom

There are many potential approaches and starting points for creativity in the music class-room, and what follows are *some* suggestions which may stimulate your own. While teaching in a way that promotes creativity and teaching creatively are not the same thing, it is the case that in order to facilitate creativity in the classroom, teachers must themselves be creative in their musicianship and the pedagogical strategies they employ.

Teaching and learning based around 'expressive problems'

In this approach the expressive problem is seen as the essence of musical activity and a strategy for musical learning. The composer confronts herself with expressive problems and must solve the problem of how the piece can be put together successfully. The performer needs to solve the problem of presenting the music coherently and address how the composer has solved a particular compositional problem. The listener is constantly interpreting in response to how the composer-performer (they might be the same person) have solved expressive problems. In all musical behaviours there is always, at the very least, an intuitive interpretation of particular solutions to particular expressive problems.

The expressive problems approach may emerge from almost any starting point. If the expressive problem is framed around the fundamental activities of music making, it is possible to turn even the driest and dustiest piece of 'knowledge about' into a meaningful musical experience (see Chapter 3 for a discussion of knowledge types). Any starting point may lead us into the realm of solving musical problems, as we search for a means to express ourselves in the context of the traditions and styles that surround us (see Box 8.2).

Box 8.2 Expressive problems

Factual notes on the history of the blues (knowledge about)

How does the music reflect the history? How did/do blues performers/composers solve the problems of creating meaningful music in this context? What expressive features and structures that reflect its history are to be found in the blues? Can we perform a blues piece? How can we compose a blues piece?

Learning three chords on a ukulele (know how)

How can we effectively accomplish this skill in order to perform with confidence? Can we recognise the chords in different orders? What tunes can we now accompany? What are the expressive possibilities of these chords? Can we compose with them?

Learning about the concept of the semitone (knowledge about)

What is a semitone? How are tones structured on the keyboard? How can we play chromatic notes effectively and with confidence? How have composers used them? What would happen if . . .? How can we use them in our compositions? What expressive effects are possible?

In this approach, starting points can be concepts, skills, features, factual knowledge, the so-called 'elements' of music or activities. Each of these can be viewed in terms of expressive problems, providing we have a commitment to immerse young people in creative music making. All music making can be viewed in terms of problem solving, whether creative, re-creative or in audience, and all musical 'knowledge' can be used to set, solve or seek solutions to problems. By setting expressive problems from a variety of starting points, we maintain direct contact with real music and maximise the chance of the students' creative engagement with musical understanding.

Task 8.6 Using expressive problems to design a teaching activity

Take any starting point (e.g. a specific example of any knowledge type and develop a range of strategies based on the expressive problems thrown up. Is it possible to cover all of the knowledge types? Design an outline unit of work to show your thinking.

Musical 'features' as a stimulus for creativity

Swanwick (1988) suggests a different approach and argues that unless we plan for musical understanding and knowledge 'of' music, we cannot expect it to happen except by accident. He suggests that one route to ensuring genuine musical experience is through a creative engagement with real musical ideas in specific musical contexts, with what he calls *features*. For example, the opening four notes of Beethoven's Fifth Symphony are an expressive feature.

Using features as a stimulus for creativity might work in the following way. Taking the figure from the opening of Siegfried's 'Trauermusik' from *Gotterdamerung* by Wagner (see Figure 8.4), you can make this the basis for improvising, composing, performing, listening and responding. You could explore the expressive and structural potential of this 'feature' and possible transformations of it, by asking the question, what would happen if? For example:

- What would happen if it is played lightly like a whisper?
- What would happen if it is speeded up and made into a more nervous 'feature'?
- Can we experiment with playing the rhythm as an ostinato or riff?
- Can we use the rhythm as an accompaniment feature to a song such as the round 'Old Ab'ram Brown'?
- Can we compose death music of our own by adding episodes to the Wagnerian 'feature'?
- Can we base a class improvisation around the same process?
- Can we respond to the original music and talk or write about its expressive and structural qualities?
- Can we ask: what expressive features do other examples of funeral music have?

The point is that the primary emphasis is on 'playing' creatively with the expressive qualities and possibilities of the musical feature. Swanwick is concerned that unless we engage with these qualities, musical experience and learning can become a barren and reductive experience.

Figure 8.4 A musical 'feature': Wagner's 'Trauermusik'

Task 8.7 Musical features

Extract some 'features' from a variety of different pieces of music. Choose one feature and suggest how you might use it to stimulate creativity. Design an outline for an integrated unit of work from this starting point and share with other music teachers and/or your mentor.

It is often the case that a particular expressive problem is set for composers and performers based on ideas that are not musical at all, for example the composer of film music. We now turn our attention to extra-musical ideas as important ways of stimulating creativity.

Musical creativity stimulated by extra-musical ideas

Music is by its very nature an abstract art in which meaning is notoriously difficult to pin down. It is common for us to attach feelings, emotions and ideas to the music we are listening to, and this is an important way in which we can hold our knowledge 'of' music. Extra-musical ideas are one way in which music can be 'held', known and also a stimulus for creativity.

The following strategies might be employed when using extra-musical ideas in the teaching and learning of music:

1   Many composers have been inspired by extra-musical themes; they have often been a part of their expressive problem. Given that this is the stuff of real composers, the use of a 'programme' as an expressive problem is a perfectly valid way of stimulating creativity.

2   It is possible to use extra-musical ideas as ways of teaching and learning the expressive shape and structure of music. One of the reasons that music is significant for us is that its shapes and structures are congruent with other aspects of our life. For example, the rise and fall of tension, ebb and flow, birth and death. We can use these extra-musical ideas as props and supports to our understanding of music. These props are important when we stimulate talk in response to music and when we stimulate composition.

3   Another approach to extra-musical ideas as a stimulus for creativity is the use of artefacts, styles and traditions from other art forms. For example, sculpture can be used as starting point for composition. Poems, pictures, plays and film footage can be used in a similar way. Youngsters can also respond to music through drawing or painting and can use a common set of 'concepts' to discuss the work, e.g. line, texture, colour, form (although this approach can also highlight the different meanings of these concepts in each discipline).

While music can never definitively describe extra-musical ideas, these ideas clearly have an important role to play with professional musicians and thus inevitably for the music classroom. In the 'real world', media are constantly being combined and used to mutually stimulate each other. As a music teacher you need to be sensitive to the ways in which extra-musical ideas can be used as a tool for learning, teaching and creativity.

> **Task 8.8 Extra-musical ideas**
>
> Make two lists:
>
> - a list of pieces that have an explicit programme or have been inspired by something extra-musical;
> - pieces (or parts of pieces) that have a 'likeness' to something external to music, for example an arch or other shapes.
>
> Discuss with other beginner teachers how these can be used to stimulate creativity.

We now turn our attention to strategies for stimulating and developing creativity during improvisation.

Creativity and improvisation

It is not always possible to distinguish between composition and improvisation. Improvisation is generally understood to mean: '. . . playing or singing with little or no preparation, inventing the music in whole or in part as it progresses' (NAME, 2000: 8). While composing is understood to mean: '. . . greater preparation . . . the fixing of ideas, refining, changing and thinking through ideas . . .' (NAME, 2000: 8).

However, composition might include improvisation in its process or as part of its performance. Furthermore, it is also the case that improvisation works within set parameters which allow us to prepare for it. Eddie Harvey suggests that we develop a wide series of musical ideas which we internalise through experience and draw upon when composing and improvising. He calls these musical ideas a 'dynamic library' (NAME 2000: 9), and the role of education could be seen as developing the 'dynamic library' in each of our students.

Improvisation is an important outlet for creativity, and for the reasons above it needs to be carefully and progressively developed in the classroom. All strategies for composition noted thus far can also be used to facilitate improvisation. The strategies noted below are intended to show how a young person's confidence and skills can be developed in improvisation and can be undertaken vocally, instrumentally or by using digital technology.

1   First attempts at improvisation can be approached through two-bar questions and answers, which at first can be practised with the teacher through clapping. Books such as Eddie Harvey's *Jazz in the Classroom* (1988) offer some useful advice on question and answer technique, and he encourages students to intuitively 'feel' the two-bar structure as opposed to reading it (see Figure 8.5).

Figure 8.5 Question and answer

2   One of the main tasks of the music teacher, when encouraging first attempts at improvisation with students, is to clear away some of the 'technical' barriers. One way of approaching early attempts at melodic improvisation is to take away the issue of 'wrong notes', that is, where any note chosen will 'work'. This strategy *does* engage students with note selection and constructing melodic shape, yet provides them with the safety net of knowing that all notes 'fit'. For example, in a blues in the key of D, melodic instruments can be set up for an F pentatonic (with Es and Bs taken off tuned percussion instruments, 'marked' on keyboard or selected in software) such that any improvisation 'works' with the blues chord sequence played (see Figure 8.6).

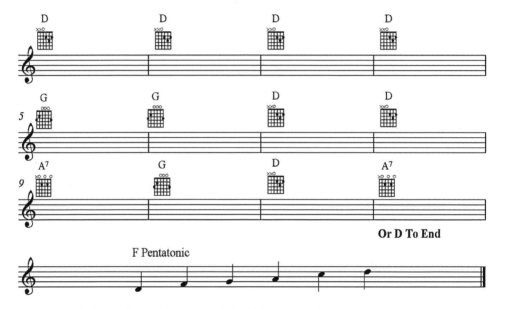

Figure 8.6 The blues in D with an F pentatonic improvisation

3   Improvisation can also take place within the context of notated classroom ensemble pieces; for example, in the 'blues' shown in Figure 8.6 you could model a simple riff in F pentatonic to be learnt by the whole class (see Figure 8.7). This could be interleaved with improvisations in the form of twelve-bar breaks (which might involve three questions and answers) or a two-bar answer to the riff itself. Other 'white note' approaches can work in the same way and initially preclude the need for using chromatic instruments (see other examples in Figure 8.8). Each of these can provide easy access to improvisation in the whole-class situation, in groups and as an individual.

Figure 8.7 Riff and break

Figure 8.8 Some other ideas for improvisation

4   A more structured approach to improvisation can be made by paying attention to the underlying chord structures, by playing with motifs or by using the conventions of different styles, genres and traditions. Improvisation can also take a musical concept as a starting point, such as 3 time.

5   Other forms of improvisation can begin with extra-musical themes or ideas, for example 'storm', 'machines' or 'the arch'.

6   Improvisations can be set in a strict pulse or 'free' time depending upon the learning at stake. Much Indian music, for example, has both a 'free' section (called alap) and a more metrical section of possible improvisation over the 'tala' rhythm.

Above all, it is important to give youngsters the confidence to take part, for making up music on the spur of the moment can be very daunting. Clearing away as many of the technical barriers as possible is one way of addressing this problem. However, we should also be concerned with developing their dynamic library such that they can increasingly engage in musical dialogue when improvising.

Task 8.9 Developing and using improvisation

Beginner teachers need to build their own confidence in improvisation before trying it out in class. Take one of the ideas suggested above, such as using the two-bar question and answer technique or an extra-musical idea, and build up an improvisation either vocally or on your instrument. Try this exercise with a partner or small group of musicians. Finally, try this with a small group of students by building their own confidence as suggested above.

Continuity and progression in creativity

The concept of musical progression implies that knowledge, skills and understanding develop over time from lesson to lesson, from week to week and from year to year. How, for example, can we build in continuity and progression when stimulating creativity around the notion of variation? Lessons might be based around how composers have solved the problem of variation (there will be many solutions), how musical ideas have been employed and transformed, how we might employ successful variation techniques in our own compositions and how to put these over most effectively in performance. Continuity can then be achieved by formally revisiting the notion of variation over time. Bruner (1966) has suggested that all 'ideas' can be addressed at any age and that the nature of the engagement changes depending on developmental stage. The examples in Box 8.3 explore how Bruner's principles of continuity and progression might be managed over time in relation to a creative engagement with 'variation'.

Box 8.3 An illustration of continuity and progression in the concept of 'variation'

Year 7

With some of your songs, ask what would happen if we . . .? How can we make a single repetitive beat more interesting? Initiate compositions called 'variations on one note' (or a simple tune such as *Twinkle, Twinkle*). Listen to Charles Ives' 'America' variations; appraise the changes to the tune (the British National Anthem!). How can musical ideas be changed?

Year 8

Play a recording of 'Variations on *Frere Jacques*' (John Iveson). How is the tune changed? Sing the tune and ask, what would happen if . . .? to explore how variation can be achieved. Begin to learn the tune vocally or on instruments and then ask groups to compose variations, which might be performed and recorded in a class 'set'.

Year 9

Discuss the concept of 'cover' versions while appraising various examples. How do cover versions work? Use motifs, phrases or the whole tune (provided by the teacher or chosen by students) as basis for a group arrangement and performance of a 'cover'.

Years 10 and 11

Compare more extended 'sets' of variations, such as the Rachmaninov and Lloyd-Webber *Paganini* variations, and use these as the basis for composition, improvisation and performance. For example, the underlying chord structure of the main theme can be used for individuals to put together their own variations.

Creativity in the music classroom can be and should be at the heart of progression, and creative music making as a pedagogical strategy can be central to musical learning at all levels of study. For example, when studying set works for post-16 examination syllabi, composition, improvisation and performance can be key to developing a rich musical understanding. This is modelled in Box 8.4 and Figures 8.9 and 8.10.

Box 8.4 *The Rite of Spring*

Composition stimulated by studying The Rite of Spring (1913)
by Igor Stravinsky

Composition can bring about many gains in understanding through knowledge 'of' the musical resources used in a particular expressive context.

1   Listen to Auguries of Spring from part 1 of *The Rite of Spring* (although this could be saved until the end of the exercise).
2   This music has a ritornello of a pounding, percussive rhythmic section (see Figure 8.9), followed by a series of episodes.
3   From the episodes the following chord structure can be found (see Figure 8.10).
4   Teach the group the ritornello section (orally and aurally) and ask them to compose/improvise their own episodes based on the chords provided (the notes of each chord could simply be listed).

Teaching points: the emancipation of dissonance, polytonality, expansion of tonality, primitivism, elemental pounding, dark register of strings, percussive chords hurled out by the horns on the rhythmically dislocated accent, hypnotic insistence of ostinati: a favoured 'folk' device for Stravinsky, and so on.

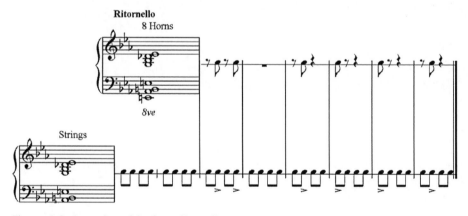

Figure 8.9 Auguries of Spring: ritornello

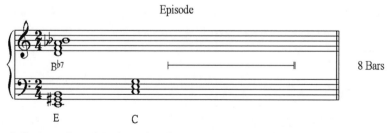

Figure 8.10 Auguries of Spring: chord structure of episodes

> ### Task 8.10 Musical approaches to teaching post-16
>
> From a post-16 syllabus, choose a specific aspect of a set work or an area of study or a style or tradition. How can this be taught through creative approaches to singing, performing, composing and improvising as a *basis* for any analytical and technical understanding that is required? Devise a lesson using this approach and share with colleague and/or a mentor for comment.

In the examples above, we have tried to establish some principles of working that encourage you to look for creative approaches to musical learning, even where the 'syllabi' or curriculum does not explicitly require you to do so. As we have said, creativity is at the heart of what it means to behave musically and so should also be at the heart of a pedagogy for developing a rich musical understanding.

Summary

In this chapter we have seen that:

- creativity is an important theme in music education, and that creativity underpins many of the expectations in music curricula and syllabi;
- it is important for teachers to have a well-reasoned concept of creativity and the creative process to underpin their practice;
- creativity is complex and there are many ideological issues surrounding the conditions under which it is assumed that it can manifest itself;
- whatever the rationale for creativity in the classroom, the teacher needs much sensitivity to create the pedagogical conditions for it to flourish;
- this requires that the teacher exercise their own creativity when designing musical strategies for responding, performance, improvisation and composition;
- finally, continuity and progression in creativity can be achieved by carefully sequencing the depth and demand in the tasks and strategies used, and should be underpinned by a 'musical' pedagogy.

The ideas and principles outlined in this chapter apply equally to all phases and ages of music education from the National Curriculum at Key Stage 3 through the teaching of examination syllabi such as GCSE, AS, A level and BTEC. Music lessons across the secondary age range *can* be conducted with little or no creativity, and yet such lessons deny the essential nature of music itself.

Further reading

Burnard, P. (2012) *Musical Creativities in Practice*, Oxford: Oxford University Press.
Harris, R. and Hawksley, E. (1989) *Composing in the Classroom*, Cambridge: Cambridge University Press.

Odena, O. (ed.) (2012) *Musical Creativity: Insights from Music Education Research*, Farnham: Ashgate.

Savage, J. and Fautley, M. (2007) *Creativity in Secondary Education*, Exeter: Learning Matters.

Shirley, I. (2009) Teaching creatively, in J. Evans and C. Philpott (eds) *A Practical Guide to Teaching Music in the Secondary School*, London: Routledge, pp. 45–53.

These publications are full of ideas for stimulating and managing creativity in the classroom.

9 Performing for musical understanding

Keith Evans

Introduction

On the face of it, performing is what musicians do. In the same way that one assumes that students in an art lesson engage with art, it might be expected that music lessons involve some musical activity. Entering a music department in a school, it would seem odd if there were no music coming from the classrooms, in much the same way that you might question what was happening in a cookery class if you could not smell the baking. But while sound might be a defining characteristic of music, it does not mean that music education is solely about *making* sound. There are various ways in which we can build a relationship with and get to know music, including through performing, but, equally, it is possible to perform music and not move on very far in terms of musical understanding.

While some people might regard performing as a clear and quite distinct aspect of being a musician, this chapter takes the view that developing young people's understanding of music in an educational context is about coming to know music in different ways, one of which is in the role of performer. This chapter starts by considering what we are trying to do in promoting performing as a classroom activity, and then goes on to explore different approaches that might best promote musical learning. The reader is encouraged to reflect on the benefits of different-sized ensembles for particular musical goals as well as to consider when and how it might be appropriate to give students more responsibility for the outcome. Similarly, enabling all young people to feel they have something to contribute as a performer is an important principle of inclusive practice; therefore there are some important reminders here for giving access to the less confident as well as appropriately integrating those who are more experienced performers.

Objectives

By the end of the chapter you should be able to:

- define your own beliefs about the value and purpose of performing in the classroom;

(continued)

(continued)

- appreciate how students' performance contributes to their wider musical understanding;
- understand different pedagogies and strategies for performing as part of an integrated music curriculum.

Performer and musician

This might not be your view, but, for the general public at large, being a musician and being a performer are virtually synonymous. This is perhaps not surprising given that in most musical traditions creator and performer are predominantly the same person. Even in the western classical tradition, the notion of a composer who creates music for others to perform is not quite as pervasive as we might like to think, and composers such as Bach, Mozart and Bartók were of course renowned performers writing and showcasing their own work. This conflation of musician and performer is also recognised when you meet someone for the first time and they ask about your job, and you reply that you are a musician or a music teacher. The next question is invariably, 'What instrument do you play?' In society at large, there is a tendency to identify being a musician with a narrow range of attributes around technical competence and fluency as a performer. This is supported by research on conceptions of musical ability, where 71 per cent of respondents defined a musical person as one who was able to play an instrument or sing, compared with figures between 20-30 per cent for other attributes such as having aural skills or an appreciation of music (Hallam 2006). It seems that many people find it difficult to conceive of musical ability in ways other than the formally trained musician achieving performing perfection after hours of practice.

Personal convictions about musicianship and what it means to be a musician also influence music teachers in schools. Long-held assumptions, prior experience and personal biography are powerful drivers for the way teachers approach their work. The choices about what students do in their music lessons reflect the personal philosophy and vision of the teacher, and, even when a nationally determined curriculum is introduced, there is often sufficient flexibility around what has been prescribed to accommodate a range of content and approaches. Therefore we need to be clear about what we are seeking to achieve and how we intend to go about it. This is nowhere more important than in the area of musical performing, as Task 9.1 asks you to consider.

Task 9.1 Why perform in the classroom?

The following are all valid reasons why you might wish to include performing activities in a music lesson:

- to develop technical skills;
- to develop students' ability to perform together;

(continued)

Task 9.1 *(continued)*

- to allow students to explore a range of sound sources for expressive purposes;
- to give students the means to realise their composing ambitions;
- to give students the skills to faithfully interpret an existing piece of music.

It is easy to say that they are all important, but which do you *really* value?

Do you think that some reasons here have to precede others, or do you think that some reasons have greater importance at different stages in the curriculum?

Would you prioritise, for example, mastery of an instrument over practical exploration in composing work?

What has been the purpose of performing tasks in your lessons recently and how does this reflect your personal beliefs?

It is clear that performing is an important aspect of developing musicianship and a fundamental means not only of engaging with music but also, in the process, of demonstrating musical understanding. The nature of this knowledge and understanding in music is explored in this book and elsewhere with reference to a range of authors and interpretations (Swanwick 1979; Elliott 1995; Fautley, 2010). Swanwick makes the distinction between three knowledge types in understanding music: propositional knowledge (knowing 'about'), skills (knowing 'how') and knowledge by acquaintance (knowing and instinctively understanding the expressive gestures and workings of different styles). He regards the latter as the ultimate goal of music education, which is best achieved by giving young people 'multiple opportunities for meeting up with music, homing in from different angles in order to become aware of its richness of possibilities' (Swanwick 1979: 42). This is a vision that emphasises the relationship between listening, composing and performing, and has become the basis of most music in the curriculum for the past quarter of a century. For Elliott, thinking and knowing in music is not about words but is shown in action. Musicianship is *procedural* knowledge, made explicit through the *process* of making music. In his view, 'Making music through performing and improvising takes learners to the heart of musical practice' (Elliott 1995: 179). Such interpretations emphasise that students come to understand the workings of music best through direct participation in musical activities.

While a curriculum that promotes musicianship through the interrelated skills of performing, composing and listening has been the common understanding of music education in the UK for over thirty years, your responses to Task 9.1 above might still reveal a view that students would have a far better chance of becoming effective composers and creators of music if they first developed the skills and related confidence as performers. This was certainly the view of Fletcher (1987), who took Swanwick to task for suggesting that purposeful composition and performance could take place without first acquiring basic technical control on an instrument, and for him the notion that technique could be acquired *in the process* of doing practical creative work seemed to make no sense. For Fletcher, who saw music education as solely about pursuing the highest standards in performance, there was no possible way to reconcile this with a desire to encourage instrumental activity in composing for all within the curriculum context. This belief in 'technique first' is still manifest in music departments with units of work that focus exclusively on instrumental fluency. You may have seen it in a unit of work on 'keyboard skills', where the entire focus for a class for a number of weeks is on learning the layout of the keyboard and individually mastering a performance of a set melody.

There are some who question why we still maintain such an emphasis on students as performers at all, given that so few are likely to continue actively making music into their adult lives. Walker (2005) recognises that most people in contemporary society engage with music as listeners. Although there are some societies where everyone participates in music making through singing and dancing, in most cultures music is performed by a small elite for the pleasure and enjoyment of the majority. Logically, therefore, music in education should acknowledge that listening is the musical involvement of the majority and focus on developing intelligent and informed consumers.

Notwithstanding such views, there is ample evidence to suggest that students' confidence and expertise as performers can develop as an integral part of the music learning process rather than independently of it. After all, the notion of having instruction to reach a certain standard of performing proficiency in order to then take part in a musical performance is specific to certain contexts. Many aspiring musicians hone their performing skills in less formal ways as well as in more integrated ways. For many, the notion of 'doing music' is a seamless integration of composing, improvising and performing. This might include jamming with friends to reproduce music by a favourite artist, participating in church in a worship context, or making music within a folk culture almost anywhere around the world (Green 2001; Jaffurs 2004). The key point is that through performing, youngsters not only develop their expertise in controlling sound with their voice, an instrument, or through technology, they also get to know the processes and inner workings of music. This is surely then what Swanwick means when he promotes 'knowledge of' music (acquaintance knowledge) as the ultimate aim of music education, to which technical mastery of an instrument or the voice (know 'how') could be seen as merely a means to an end. It is suggested, therefore, that we regard performing in the classroom as not solely about skill development but as an important way to help students more broadly 'get to know' music. For as Swanwick cautions (1994: 17), 'Skills allow us to find our way into music but they can also divert us from further musical understanding if they become ends in themselves'. Task 9.2 provides an opportunity for you to consider the broader musical understanding that might arise from a range of performance scenarios.

Task 9.2 Performing and musical understanding

Consider the following performing scenarios from secondary school music lessons. It is relatively easy to identify performing skills that students might be developing (e.g. specific techniques, ensemble skills etc.), but in the process of making music here, in what ways are they more widely *getting to know* music and developing musical understanding?

(continued)

Task 9.2 *(continued)*

Activity/scenario	Performing skills?	Musical understanding?
Example: making a vocal arrangement of *Wade in the water* in a small group	Example: building confidence as a singer. Maintaining a part within an ensemble.	Example: the emotive power of the spiritual/songs of freedom. Blues inflections. Effects of textural and structural changes.
Whole-class drumming activity, e.g. samba band, djembe drumming		
Creating music at a computer to accompany a short video		
In a small band creating a cover version of a rock classic		
Learning the James Bond theme on a keyboard		
As a class, learning chords on the ukulele and then in groups creating their own song over the chord pattern C-G-Am-F		

Performing with others

If we accept the premise that music lessons in the curriculum are about developing students' musical understanding, performing becomes a vital part of the learning process. What and how students perform may be linked to overarching learning objectives, but decisions still need to be made over matters such as the size of the performing group, the roles individuals have within it and the degree of flexibility and choice they have in determining the outcome. By taking the size of the group as the starting point, we explore some of these implications below.

Whole-class performing

It is quite surprising how little performing takes place as a whole-class activity in many schools. If this is the case, is it a considered pedagogical decision or simply pragmatism in the face of the perceived organisational challenges? In the past, whole-class singing was virtually the sum total of the music curriculum in many schools and, certainly before the arrival of electronic keyboards on the secondary music scene in the late 1980s, the idea of a whole-class band comprising an eclectic mix of tuned percussion, recorders, guitars, and whatever instruments individual students happened to play was quite commonplace. As likely as not, the whole ensemble would be held together by the teacher at the piano. The teacher would have been able to draw on a wealth of published 'mixed ensemble' arrangements of themes from the classics, popular TV themes and the like and, although generic parts 'in C', 'in B flat', 'in E flat' took little account of idiomatic writing for the instruments likely to be playing them, by careful allocation of parts to students and students to instruments it was possible to offer an inclusive performing experience. More enterprising teachers might take the trouble to arrange music for their classes, and this at least allowed the opportunity to tailor a particular part to individual capabilities.

A more contemporary example of the whole-class performing ensemble capitalises on the popularity of the ukulele as a classroom instrument. Typically, students learn three or four chords and then the teacher leads them in a class performance of a song based on a repeating sequence of the newly mastered chords. The students sing along as they strum their backing accompaniment. Rusinek (2008) has written persuasively of the power of a classroom ensemble to re-engage disaffected learners in a Spanish school context.

However, it is worth stopping to consider what outcome might be intended from such activity. Is there any goal other than a perfect performance? Does this performing activity merely seek to develop skills at the expense of understanding? At best, students master their part through the process of rehearsal and then maintain it within the ensemble. While it is laudable that they are at least *doing* music, these could be seen as pretty limited examples of promoting musical understanding through a whole-class performance.

Task 9.3 Benefits and limitations of whole-class performing

Irrespective of the wider lesson aims or purpose of the specific activity, many teachers are keener to break down the class into smaller groups for practical work. Expand and complete the following table to weigh up the benefits and limitations of whole-class performing.

Benefits	Limitations
• Every student gets the same experience. • The teacher can monitor what every student is doing.	• Risks being a showcase for confident performers.

In both the whole-class performing scenarios discussed so far, there is very little scope for students to add their own ideas to the performance and the whole enterprise is initiated *and* determined by the teacher. Students are not required to choose what or when to play, and a teacher regarding the session as little more than a rehearsal could well disapprove if students attempt to add their own material or decoration. The best they can expect is perhaps some input into the structure of the performance: which sections are repeated, how many verses they perform, and the like.

Even within the context of whole-class performance, by relaxing the teacher's control and giving the students a real-time stake in the outcome, what would otherwise simply be a performing activity becomes a far richer opportunity to develop creativity and a broader concept of musicianship. As Elliott notes with reference to his praxial view of music education: 'A music class in which the ensemble director finds, solves, and reduces all music problems himself or herself is *not* a reflective practicum. Inducting students into musical practices involves teaching students to think critically, independently, and creatively' (Elliott 1995: 287).

Case study

The following scenario of a performing activity is based on material devised by the teacher, which consists of a number of musical ideas around a basic modal tonality (see Figure 9.1). By using the Aeolian mode on A, they conveniently fit diatonic tuned percussion and the white keys of the keyboard so the majority of students play instruments readily available in the classroom. Those in the group who play other instruments have been encouraged to bring them to the lesson too. The simplest of the ideas are Idea A, a series of long-held descending notes, and Idea D, a repeating syncopated rhythm on a single note. Most of the other ideas are characterised by their basic scalic nature or sequential repetition.

Having assigned students to instruments, the teacher teaches them the short musical ideas quickly, through a process of call and response. After a few preliminary attempts in which the teacher orchestrates the beginnings of a performance from the group (Idea A on bass guitar, joined by Idea B from some keyboards, Idea C on tuned percussion and all held together by a steady beat on the drum kit), control is given over to the students. The teacher counts them in and sits down as a member of the group ready to join in on her clarinet. The performance begins in the way that the class has previously rehearsed, but this time students are encouraged to drop out and re-enter the performance at will. Fragments of melody come and go and the more experienced instrumentalists attempt more ambitious melodic ideas. At one point the drumming stops but the sense of pulse is now well established and the class carries on regardless. Gradually, almost one by one the performers drop out until we are left with a lone bass guitarist playing the slowly descending scale and the performance is finally wrapped up with a decisive tonic note A.

On a further performance, students are encouraged to swap between a couple of the patterns as the music progresses or, if they wish, introduce their own pentatonic riffs on the notes A, C, D, E and G. The performance gradually evolves as individuals experiment and then settle down into their new pattern.

Note how these performances have evolved organically as a result of the students' decisions 'in the moment'. As a result, no two performances of this material would be the

Figure 9.1 Musical ideas in the Aeolian mode

same, other than having the same repetitive and hypnotic momentum. The activity here is *determined* by the students. It is not simply a performing activity in which the young people are used to realise the teacher's intentions. Pedagogically, the key point here is that it is an open-ended task in which, albeit within the framework established by the teacher, students have the opportunity to make creative decisions, to improvise, and to participate in real-time composing. This is a performing activity going much further than mastery of technical skills. It is a genuine opportunity for getting to know music by 'homing in . . . from different angles in order to become aware of its richness of possibilities' (Swanwick 1979: 42).

Such an approach is a move closer to the collaborative large-group music-making experience of creative workshop practice, which is more typical of the non-formal sector. The teacher acts more as a facilitator than leader of the performance and there is an assumption that the outcome will evolve over time through experimentation, interaction and gradual refinement. While the students are actively making music they are drawing on the interrelated skills of performing, listening and composing.

There has been strong advocacy for bringing non-formal teaching practices into the formal school context over the past decade, and this has been an important strand of the

Musical Futures approach to teaching and learning. There is a significant section in the Teachers' Resource Pack (D'Amore 2009) showing how spontaneous creative experiences modelled on workshop practice can be shaped into satisfying large-group performances in the classroom, and this is a very effective way of integrating the musical skills of performing, composing and listening.

To the novice teacher such a way of working may seem daunting, since control, if not completely handed over to the students, is certainly being shared with them. On the other hand, being able to start off and see where things lead might also appear quite attractive, certainly in the context of the outcomes-obsessed climate of most school practice. But the way in which music here is created, shaped and performed is actually far from a 'free for all'. It is both organised and goal directed. The difference lies with the teacher, who has to be more open and prepared to go with the flow of the material generated by the group (Renshaw 2005). Nevertheless, even in what appears a more democratic process, the musical material is still largely generated by the teacher, even if the students have a significant role in determining the outcome, as can be seen in Figure 9.2. Task 9.4 helps you to think about what it would take to give the students autonomy and total ownership of their large-group music making.

Task 9.4 Creative workshop practice

Here are some comments from beginner teachers who have been experimenting with creative workshop practice:

> 'You're there to enable them to do something rather than to teach them something.'

> 'With this very live, very reactive model, if you're attentive to what's going on in the room, you should always get some sort of result.'

> 'There's no possibility of them getting it wrong because they're always working at their own level. You (the teacher) are always looking for what's good about it and you're really measuring success in terms of participation rather than in terms of outcome.'

> 'It's about getting everyone involved, no matter what their ability is.'

> 'It's making music accessible to everyone . . . Every single individual can get something out of that way of working, and it's not exclusive.'

What are the main themes coming out here?

These comments are all positive about this way of working. You might be more circumspect. What would be your concerns?

What do you see as the musical and organisational challenges *you* would face in exploring creative work in a large-group context?

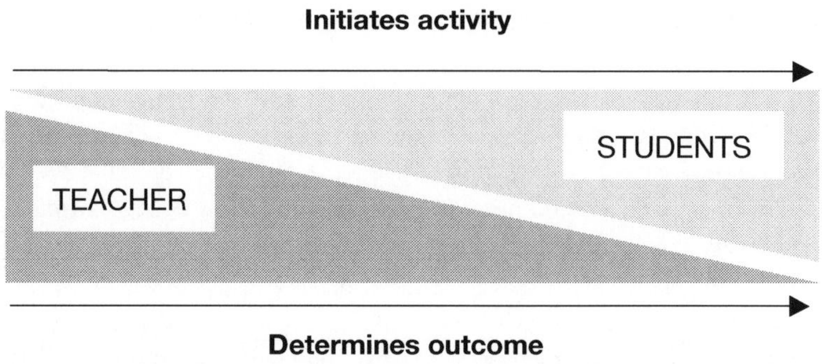

Initiates activity

Figure 9.2 Determining outcomes versus initiating activity

The ideal ensemble for large-group music making does not have all musicians playing the same instrument. This is not to say that large groups of young people playing instruments such as the violin, recorder or ukulele are not common in the education context (consider the first access to whole-class instrumental learning in English primary schools), but even here a group that includes different sizes of the core instrument (treble and tenor recorders, cellos as well as violins) provides a more varied and interesting ensemble. In order to exploit timbre, dynamics, short sounds, sustained sounds, different playing techniques (striking, plucking, blowing), students need access to a range of instruments and ideally the facility to generate and manipulate sounds through technology too. This is also why it is important to encourage students who learn an instrument to bring it along to curriculum lessons, although it is equally important not to overlook other more immediate sound sources such as the voice. The mixed ensemble where students are listening and responding to different timbres and textures has far more potential and mirrors the line-up of most 'real-world' musical groups.

Singing as a whole-class activity

Before moving on from large-group performing it is worth looking briefly at singing as a whole-class activity. This can be some of the most inclusive music making in the classroom and yet, for some teachers, the most daunting. Teachers who lack confidence in singing tend to avoid it altogether, and therefore their students miss out on what is undoubtedly an important way to internalise sound and make music with others. Singing is possibly the most inclusive form of music making, because the musical resources are the young people themselves.

Developing a singing culture in the curriculum is not easy, and merely including random songs in music lessons on a fairly regular basis does not guarantee success any more than having keyboards in classrooms has ensured that every student becomes a competent pianist. But successful teachers recognise students' interest in song and are aware of the culture of singing to which they aspire. Rather than passing judgement on the success of popular vocalists and television programmes such as *X Factor*, they capitalise on their popularity to 'normalise' the act of singing into both a social and educative activity. It is hard to sustain a view that boys 'won't sing' or 'don't sing' when boy bands regularly feature in the TV finals on Saturday night.

The scarcity of good singing in secondary schools is a constant theme in official reports, and Ofsted (2012) noted that singing was a major weakness in nearly half of the secondary schools visited for subject inspections in the previous three years. It would seem that many teachers are not promoting singing in the curriculum, either on the basis that they do not feel confident about it or perhaps because they tried it a few times and quickly became frustrated when the results were half-hearted and disappointing and therefore gave up. These are the teachers who address the problem by introducing a songwriting unit into their scheme of work and then express surprise when no one wants to sing! There is little doubt that a singing culture is established once students are as confident using their voices as other sound sources, when singing becomes simply something that we do in music lessons. But even consciously choosing music with which you know the class has some affinity is no guarantee of success. Other considerations, such as standing or sitting, in groups or rows, with or without music/lyrics, will all impact on engagement as well as the quality of the outcome. Spruce (2009: 41) exemplifies this in an excellent little scenario in which a beginner teacher transforms singing in his class from one lesson to the next simply by replacing his initial round-the-piano community-singalong approach with a genuine performance occasion using backing track, microphones and amplifier. By teaching some basic riffs that fit with the backing and getting small groups taking the lead, he gets an enthusiastic performance going and the class productively discussing phrasing, texture and subtleties of performance practice.

Performing and creating music in small groups

Organising young people to work in small groups has been a common strategy for creative work in music lessons since the 1970s. The reasons for this are both educational and pragmatic: socio-constructivist theories suggest that students learn more effectively working collaboratively with others, and distributing three or four small groups in venues around the department in addition to having a couple of groups working in the main classroom is about the best most schools can arrange to divide up a class of 25–30 young people. Of course, a group of four or five musicians is a common performing ensemble in many musical traditions too. This size of group allows for a diversity of opinion, although we have to be careful that students on the fringes do not become mere 'passengers'.

The emphasis on integration of skills means that the majority of group work in music lessons involves both performing and composing. The members of the group are collaborating to develop new music (or at least to put a new spin on existing material) *through* performing. The make-up of the group therefore can have quite an impact on the outcome. As the teacher, you can determine the composition of the groups how you like and this might well vary for different units and different tasks. For example, informal learning pedagogy in the past ten years has promoted working in friendship groups. There is a sound reason for this in that it accords with self-directed music practices outside of school on which such an approach is based, but this does not mean that students working with their friends has to be the default arrangement in all classroom situations and contexts. There are pros and cons of different groupings which are worth considering, as Task 9.5 asks you to reflect on.

Task 9.5 Organising group work

The first column in the chart below lists a number of ways in which you could organise group work in music lessons. Complete the chart to summarise what you see as the benefits and limitations of each one.

Before you start, think carefully about the nature of 'ability' in the first two rows. Are you interpreting this as *musical* ability or *performing* ability?

Grouping	Benefits	Limitations
Ability groups		
Mixed ability groups		
Deliberately arbitrary groups		
Single-sex groups		
Friendship groups		

The matter of instrumental/vocal fluency and the teacher recognising and building on young people's existing performing skills is important in group work. As a teacher you are required to 'set goals that stretch and challenge young people of all backgrounds, abilities and dispositions' and 'know when and how to differentiate appropriately' (DfE 2012). It is hardly stretching and challenging, then, if you allow a talented instrumentalist to leave his/her instrument at home. Conversely, you may be knowingly setting up some students to fail if you conceive the brief in such a way that they all require quite high levels of proficiency on, say, a keyboard in order to participate. This comes back to the basic premise of music education. If we see its function as developing musical *understanding* through performing, composing and listening activity, it is not necessary for everyone to *do* the same thing. In the example below, five students further their *understanding* of the blues by taking quite different roles in a group performance. But, as a result of this performing they become acquainted with and 'get to know' the blues.

Blues example

Player A has been taught the twelve-bar blues chord pattern in G on the keyboard and plays G///| G///| . . . etc.) throughout the performance.

Player B has been shown by the teacher how to play chords G, C and D on the guitar and is tentatively shadowing Player A on an acoustic guitar.

Player C is not a confident performer but, with the chord pattern written in G in front of him, is able to add the root note of each chord at the beginning of each bar on a bass guitar, largely on open strings.

Player D, a self-taught drummer, adds a bluesy rhythm on the drum kit.

Player E, who has had individual lessons on the alto saxophone for some time, has been given the notes EGABD written on a stave (i.e. a transposed G pentatonic blues scale for an E flat instrument) and is using them as the basis for a solo improvisation supported by the rest of the group.

Performing on keyboards

In spite of everything above promoting performing as a large- or small-group instrumental or vocal experience, for many students performing in curriculum music lessons is still largely restricted to keyboards. It is not hard to understand why the availability of relatively cheap electronic keyboards in the late 1980s led to their adoption by most secondary schools. The potential for having students working in pairs at keyboards with headphones in the same room and not disturbing each other seemed the answer to teachers' prayers. The fact that keyboards also had a range of voices, funky rhythmic accompaniments and the possibility of auto-chord backings made them seem really modern in comparison to existing classroom instruments such as recorders and tuned percussion. But thirty years later it has to be questioned what kind of experience we are really giving our students if the majority of their performing is on a couple of octaves of a shared keyboard. Table 9.1 lists some of the issues of less-than-ideal practices seen on a regular basis.

Of course, with some thought in terms of both room layout and lesson planning, it is possible to address some of these issues and it is certainly not being suggested that there is no longer a role for keyboards in the classroom context. It is perhaps better that we think of the keyboard as just another instrument available for use (ideally, not fixed to a particular place in the classroom but more like any other instrument in that it is able to be taken to a location where the students wish to make music), and then it can truly fulfil its part as one of the most versatile instruments at their disposal.

Progression in performing

This chapter began with discussion about what we are aiming to achieve through performing in the classroom context and noted different opinions between focusing on technical mastery and regarding performing as just one of a number of interrelated activities through which young people are led to understand the richness and possibilities of music. If we are focusing on technique, it may seem fairly easy to define progression in performing in terms of improving accuracy, fluency, expression and the like, but when the emphasis is on developing more holistically in terms of musical understanding, progression in performance becomes subsumed within broader concepts of musicianship.

Table 9.1 Issues and difficulties using keyboards

Issue	Difficulties
Inappropriate performing space, e.g. keyboards around perimeter of room facing the wall	• Makes it very difficult to relate to other performers through eye contact/physical gesture. • If required to perform to class, with backs to audience performers unable to engage with audience. • Any scaling up into larger-group/whole-class performance impossible for reasons above.
Two students at one relatively small keyboard	• Poor hand positions. Student on RH side has to play with contorted wrist position (and often resorts to playing with left hand). • Students rarely use both hands (which is authentic practice on a keyboard instrument). • Negotiation of musical learning made more difficult if both wearing headphones, as not able to easily discuss about what they are trying to achieve.
A distinct role for both performers	• Both performers are working on the same part, which would ideally be in the middle of the instrument. Attempting to play in unison, they rehearse at wrong pitch. • Alternatively, they do have distinct roles, which they would ideally benefit from being able to rehearse at separate instruments, at least in the early stages.
Lack of differentiation	• This is not unique to using keyboards, but commonly there are up to thirty students working in pairs at keyboards around the classroom, all of them trying to perform the same thing. Would this be the case in a small-group performance?
Perception as to whether the task would be seen as 'real' music	• Working on joint keyboards like this only happens in classrooms – perception that it doesn't in any way relate to students' own musical experiences beyond the classroom – issue of validity.
Appropriateness of using keyboards for the musical learning at hand	• Lack of sustain, dynamics etc. • Use for units of work that would not use keyboards.

We therefore need to be cautious that we don't simply assume that getting better at performing is indicated by a student's capacity to do ever more difficult and complex things. This is a quantitative rather than a qualitative assessment.

It is similar to the popular perception in the world of classical music that assumes that a keyboard virtuoso performing a fast and furious work by Liszt is automatically a better performer than another pianist giving a poetic interpretation of a relatively simple Schumann miniature.

When there was an attainment target expressed as a series of levels in the English National Curriculum for Music (i.e. up to 2013), technical skills, skills of interpretation, ensemble, rehearsal, memory and performing from notation were all reflected in the performing element of the level descriptors. The quantitative at the expense of the qualitative was perfectly illustrated in the phrase in the level 3 statement: '. . . perform rhythmically simple parts with a limited range of notes'.

Summary

In this chapter we have:

*   asked you to explore your own beliefs about the value and purpose of performing in the classroom;
*   examined how a young person's performance contributes to their wider musical understanding and understood how to develop different pedagogies and strategies for performing as part of an integrated music curriculum;
*   explored the importance of students having the opportunity to play a musical instrument and sing as part of a rounded musical education.
*   suggested that, although these are valuable skills to acquire, they should certainly not be the sum total of musical experience in school and that a curriculum seeking to develop instrumental technique alone falls a long way short of developing true musical understanding.

Certainly, we want our students operating as practising musicians but, in doing so, we must help them develop a closer relationship with music itself. In that way, there is a good chance that they will develop their musical understanding *and* develop confidence as a performer.

Further reading

Anderson, A. (2012) Developing performing opportunities, in J. Price and J. Savage (eds) *Teaching Secondary Music*, London: Sage.

Savage, J. (2007) Is musical performance worth saving? The importance of musical performance in teaching and learning, in C. Philpott and G. Spruce (eds) *Learning to Teach Music in the Secondary School*, 2nd edn, London: RoutledgeFalmer, pp. 135–148.

Although discussion in both of these chapters is in the context of previous versions of the English National Curriculum, they contain key messages about good performing practice in schools,

D'Amore, A. (ed.) (2009) Section 2: Non-formal teaching, in *Musical Futures – An Approach to Teaching and Learning – Resource Pack*, 2nd edn, London: Paul Hamlyn Foundation.

This resource and the Musical Futures website (www.musicalfutures.org) contain a wealth of ideas and advice on classroom workshopping.

10 Listening and responding and the ideology of aesthetic listening

Gary Spruce

Introduction

There is a paradox at the heart of music education, which is that listening, the musical activity that many young people involve themselves in most frequently outside school, is often the aspect of the music curriculum they find least attractive and, in the way in which it is typically taught, the one in which they achieve less well. In the course of this chapter we try to identify some of the reasons for, and strategies to address, young people's negative attitudes towards listening, and their consequent underachievement in this area of the music curriculum.

Significantly less research has taken place into how young people's musical understanding can be developed through listening than through composing and performing, and fewer resources have been developed to support its teaching. This relative neglect is perhaps symptomatic of a belief that the way in which listening is best taught is essentially straightforward: students listen to music and through analysing the way in which the 'musical elements' fit together, and informed by historical and stylistic information, they gain an understanding of its meaning. Their understanding is then most effectively articulated through verbal and written responses.

This unproblematic perception of the pedagogy of listening is rooted in assumptions about the nature of music and the relationship between 'the music' and 'the listener' that, although seemingly universal and self-evident, have developed in tandem with, and in order to reflect and support, the traditions and protocols of western art music – constituting what we refer to in this chapter as the ideology of 'aesthetic listening'. This ideology has then influenced the way in which listening is taught.

In this chapter we explore the assumptions and beliefs that underpin aesthetic listening. We then go on to explore the impact of aesthetic listening on music teaching and learning through analysing three hypothetical examples of the way in which listening is taught in the music classroom. Following this, issues associated with the personal construction of musical meaning and responses other than verbal and written ones are considered. Finally, we suggest ways in which listening can be taught through integration with composing and performing activities.

The main argument of this chapter is that a much richer relationship exists (or can exist) between music and the listener than that which is often promoted in formal music education, and that this richer relationship can lead to young people engaging more positively and more successfully with listening and responding activities. Such a relationship acknowledges and values:

- responses that go beyond than just verbal and written ones;
- the role of the listener in constructing musical meaning;
- the diversity and plurality of musical practices in the world;
- integrating listening with performing and composing.

Objectives

By the end of this chapter you should be able to:

- understand the strengths and limitations of 'aesthetic listening';
- describe the assumptions underpinning the way in which listening has tradition-ally been taught;
- identify ways in which listening activities can be 'opened up' to reflect and develop a wider range of musical learning, understanding and experience and thus become more inclusive.

What is meant by the 'ideology of aesthetic listening'?

Task 10.1 Your own experience of listening and responding in school

Note down the kinds of listening activities you were asked to do at school. Structure your notes under the following headings:

- the kinds of music you listened to;
- how you were asked to respond to the music;
- the musical skills and knowledge that were intended to be taught through listening and responding activities;
- what you actually learnt.

It is likely that the listening activities you have identified in Task 10.1 are one of two types (or perhaps a combination of both):

1   'Music appreciation': you might have been asked to suggest what it is that the composer is trying to express through the music – say, in terms of a particular emotion, place or narrative – referring perhaps to the use of the 'musical elements' to support your

answer. In other words, what message or meaning is being communicated by the composer through the music.

2   'Aural analysis': you might have analysed the music in terms of its structure and elements – its pitch, rhythm, harmony, timbre and texture and how these fit together.

Both these kinds of listening activities and the responses to them that are expected reflect the ideology of aesthetic listening, which is predicated upon a number of beliefs about the nature of 'good' music and the way in which it makes and communicates its meaning. These beliefs are that:

- the meaning of a piece of music is what the composer intends it to be (or what we are told by 'experts' it is intended to be);
- musical meaning is articulated through the interplay of the musical materials. Consequently . . .
- musical meaning is fixed and independent of social context or function. In other words, good music is *autonomous* music.

It therefore follows from these beliefs that:

- musical meaning flows in one direction: *from* the music *to* the listener;
- the role of the listener is to listen 'knowledgeably' and thereby gain understanding of the 'true' meaning contained within the music;
- the role of the teacher is to teach this knowledge.

The role of the listener in aesthetic listening

It is not our intention in this chapter to suggest that 'aesthetic listening' is an inappropriate way of engaging with music *per se*, but rather, as Dibben puts it, to recognise that '"contemplative" listening, the act of listening afforded to audience members by Western classical concert music is just one of a number of ways of listening' (Dibben in Clayton 2003: 201) and consequently just one way in which young people can respond to music.

The argument here is that aesthetic listening assumes that only one relationship can exist between the music and listener, that of listener-as-audience. Listener-as-audience is predicated upon the belief that listening is an essentially discrete activity, distinct and separate from composing and performing. The sonic materials of music are cognitively processed 'in the head' and musical meaning construed. The degree of success with which the listener construes the 'correct' musical meaning is taken as an indicator of that person's musical understanding. The 'correct' meaning is what the composer intends it to be, and such meaning is uncovered through detailed analysis of the musical materials.

The ideology of aesthetic listening is located in the wider concept of 'objective knowledge'. In *The Courage to Teach*, Parker Palmer (1998) argues that there is a myth that: sees truth as a set of propositions about objects; education as a system for delivering those propositions to students; and an educated person as one who can remember and repeat the experts' propositions.

Palmer identifies four elements of this 'objectivist myth of knowing':

> *Objects* of knowledge . . . reside 'out there' somewhere, pristine in physical or conceptual space, as described by the 'facts' in a given field.
>
> *Experts* [teachers] are people trained to know these objects in their pristine form without allowing their own subjectivity to slop over onto the purity of the objects themselves.
>
> *Amateurs* [students] are those who do not presently possess these objects. They must depend on experts for objective or pure knowledge of the pristine objects.
>
> *Baffles* allow objective knowledge to flow downstream while preventing the subjectivity of the amateurs to flow back up – possibly contaminating the intellectual purity of the *objects*.
>
> (Palmer 1998: 100–101)

The common characteristic of objective knowledge and aesthetic listening is that neither recognises the role of the learner/listener in *constructing* meaning and understanding.

The impact of aesthetic listening on the music curriculum

In this section we are going to consider the strengths and limitations of aesthetic listening in terms of developing young people's musical understanding and the extent to which it provides them with a valuable and rich musical experience. To this end, three hypothetical approaches to the teaching of listening are critically analysed, each of which exemplifies a particular aspect of aesthetic listening as identified in the previous section.

Musical meaning is what the composer intends it to be

Task 10.2 Musical meaning and 'high status' musical knowledge

Read Scenario 1 and note down what you think it tells you about:

* the kind of musical knowledge and understanding the teacher values and rewards;
* the musical understanding and perception of each of the three students involved;
* what the teacher understands as the relationship between the musical work, the composer and the listener.

Scenario 1

A Year 7 class (11 year olds) enters the classroom as a recording of 'Mars' from Holst's 'Planets Suite' is being played. The students sit behind desks, and the teacher plays the music once more. She then asks them what they think the music is 'about'. They

(continued)

(continued)

respond enthusiastically. Marcus says that it reminds him of a storm and refers to the loud dynamics and the use of brass and percussion instruments. Phyllis remarks how the 'rhythmic ostinato' (she uses this term) makes her think of machinery in a factory. The teacher makes encouraging noises of the 'good but not quite right' kind. At the back of the class Samuel has his hand is raised and is giving every indication that he will burst if not given an opportunity to answer. To avoid this catastrophe, the teacher asks him for his response, which is: 'It's "Mars, the Bringer of War", Miss.' 'Excellent,' says the teacher, 'how do you know that?' 'My father told me. He plays it in the car all the time,' says Samuel. 'Well, *well* done,' says the teacher and gives him three merit points. She then moves on to the next part of the lesson.

There are many positive things in what the teacher is doing here, particularly the way in which the lesson *begins* with musical activity and how students' responses are actively sought. However, the teacher is deeply committed to the idea that although students' personal responses to the music are to be encouraged, they are to be more greatly valued (and rewarded) the closer these responses accord with the perceived intentions of the composer. So, however much musical understanding and perception a person might bring to bear on the music, it will be never be more valued than simply possessing the knowledge of what the composer intended (or what we think s/he intended) the meaning of the music to be. In this scenario the teacher is happy to move on once she has the 'correct' answer. She does not explore the extent to which Samuel's answer is indicative of his musical understanding. She is content that he has got the 'correct' answer. It is a pedagogical approach rooted in the assumption that the meaning of a piece of music is what the composer desires it to be, that this is not open to negotiation and that the role of the listener is, as Small says, 'simply to contemplate the work, to try to understand it and to respond to it, but that she or he has nothing to contribute to its meaning. That is the composer's business' (1998: 6). Musical meaning is seen as flowing in one direction: from the composer via the musical object to the passive listener.

Musical meaning is articulated exclusively through the relationship and interplay of the musical materials

Task 10.3 Musical meaning and musical materials

Read Scenario 2 and make notes on:

*   the knowledge that is considered to be important in developing musical understanding;
*   the extent to which what students are being asked to do reflects the way in which they (or you) listen to music outside the music classroom.

Scenario 2

A Year 9 class is studying the 'Gavotte' from Prokofiev's 'Classical Symphony'. The students are given a work sheet divided into five sections, each one headed by a different musical element: pitch, rhythm, harmony, texture and timbre. They are asked to respond to the music under each of these headings, and their responses form the basis of a class discussion into how the composer achieves particular musical effects. The students are then asked to listen to the music again, this time identifying its structure.

In this scenario, teaching is predicated upon an understanding that as meaning is what the composer intends it to be, it follows that such meaning must be encoded within the musical materials and therefore is got at through the atomistic and 'distanced' analysis of the elements and structure. Musical knowledge and understanding are understood here as the ability to aurally deconstruct the music into its discrete 'elements', explore the character of these elements separate from the musical whole and finally 'reconstruct' the work to see how the musical elements 'fit together'. This is the understanding of the relationship between the music and listener upon which [my italics] 'Prolific twentieth-century "listeners' guides" offer intellectual expositions of the expressiveness in the musical work (*not in the listeners*) focusing on the musical text and teaching listeners "how the music fits together"' (Finnegan in Clayton 2003: 182).

Clearly there are benefits to be gained from being able to analyse the component elements of a musical work in order to understand how they fit together. It enables students to consider the ways in which musical elements are organised to create the sonic 'lingua franca' of, in this case, classical music. There are then opportunities to transfer learning to students' own composing activities. However, as a musical experience *in its own right*, such an approach has significant limitations.

One problem with this approach is that the music is being thought of as akin to a painting in a gallery – as an object. Consequently, the relationship between the music and the listener is seen as the same as that between the viewer and the painting. Both the listener and the viewer study the art object in a distanced objective way, contemplating how its formal properties contribute to an aesthetically complete whole. However, is the *experience* of looking at a painting in any way similar to the experience of listening and responding to music? Perhaps not. A painting in a gallery is by its very nature an object. Its often framed presentation is fixed in time and space and distanced from the viewer – it is 'out there'. Consequently, thinking of music as an object leads to the idea that music is, or can be, experienced in a similar 'distanced' way. However, both Handel and Bowman (in Elliott 1995: 126) argue that there is a qualitative difference between listening and looking/ observing. Handel argues that 'Listening is centripetal; it pulls you into the world. Looking is centrifugal; it separates you from the world . . . looking makes each of us a focused observer, listening makes each of us a surrounded participant'. Bowman makes the critical point that experiencing music is not static (like observing a painting) 'but temporal and, therefore, full of ambiguity . . . a moment-by-moment renewal . . . We see the world as a noun and hear it as a verb' (in Elliott 1995: 127).

The metaphor of noun and verb is a potent one in that it challenges the deeply rooted idea of music as object. Thinking of art objects (paintings, sculpture etc.) as nouns means that they are fixed and unchanging. One can contemplate them both holistically and atomistically, moving at will from the object as a whole to contemplating the way in which its elements contribute to that whole. The totality can be observed in a single moment. The idea of talking about these objects in a distanced way – analysing the relationship between the whole and its parts – is arguably legitimate. However, the reality of musical experience as a 'verb' – as an active, fluctuating, temporal, moment-by-moment experience – throws into question the distanced, analytical approach, at least as an exclusive way of understanding the way in which one constructs and construes musical meaning. Indeed, research by Smith (1973) and Cook (1990) suggests that whereas people *can* listen to music atomistically in terms of the musical elements or musical structure if *required* to do so, few (even 'trained' musicians) do so as a matter of course.

Task 10.4 Adopting an holistic approach to traditional listening and responding tasks

Devise a series a questions based around a listening activity that is predicated upon an holistic approach to music response and upon the idea of music as an 'active, fluctuating, temporal, moment-by-moment experience'. Examples of questions might be:

- What is the music like?
- What happens in the music?
- Where do you feel the climax of the piece occurs?
- What point in the music do you find most exciting/moving/effective?
- What is it about the music that you find least effective?
- Where did you feel that there was a really interesting use of rhythm/ instrumentation/harmony?

Now develop a sequence of more atomistic-type questions (those typically used in listening tests) to help students analyse how these effects were achieved. Think about how you can make strong links between these two sets of questions.

Good music is autonomous music

If the meaning of a piece of music must be what the composer intends it to be, and if musical meaning is articulated exclusively through the musical materials, it follows that musical meaning is fixed and remains the same in whatever context the music is heard. Such music can then be said to enjoy an autonomous existence. The notion of musical autonomy is a key aspect of the ideology of aesthetic listening, and is reinforced through the way in which people typically engage with western art music: in the concert hall or through recordings. This model of musical engagement is then mapped onto the classroom, where students sit in neat rows behind desks (a kind of surrogate concert hall) listening to recordings of music respectfully, in a detached manner and informed by knowledge.

Kivy makes the point that recordings, which play an important part in listening activities, reinforce the ideology of aesthetic listening by creating '. . . the false allusion that listening is private and passive' and' . . . that music is a collection of autonomous sounds alone' (Kivy in Elliott 1995: 102). In fact, as Elliott points out, for most people in the world (and consequently most musical practices), listening is far from private and passive but an activity where' . . . people join together in the communal and ritual actions of listening, watching and participating empathetically as music makers bring forth unique musical events and experiences' (Elliott 1995: 102).

Students' negative reactions to listening in the classroom can occur as a consequence of a requirement upon them to engage with music which they have experienced as part of these 'communal and ritual actions' in a way that to them seems (and indeed *is*) alien: through the ideology of aesthetic listening. Now read Scenario 3.

Scenario 3

Simon is a beginner teacher. On Friday afternoon he takes 9A for their 'listening lesson'. They are a class with a 'reputation'. Simon decides that the best way of surviving his encounter with 9A is to base the lesson on some music that they know and like. He chats with some of the students and identifies a song that is particularly popular with many of them. He downloads the track and creates a 'listening worksheet', which asks the students to listen to the music in terms of the musical 'bits': harmony, melody, rhythm etc. and to write down their responses. He adopts the school's policy for behaviour management, requiring the young people to sit in rows behind desks in boy-girl-boy formation. At first the lesson goes well. The students are pleased that they are being asked to work with music they know and like. However, they show little enthusiasm for 'analysing' the music and even less for writing down their responses. Instead, they begin to react to the music in the way they would in the youth club – they being to move to it (albeit within the confines of the physical limitations of the classroom) and to talk over the music. The teacher tries to quell what he perceives as this indiscipline. The students comply, but the lesson is characterised by a sullen acquiescence.

As in all the scenarios, there are positive things in what the teacher is doing, particularly the way he is trying to break down barriers between curriculum music and music outside school. However, the lesson is less than successful because Simon assumes that young people's alienation from listening activities in the music classroom can be addressed simply through changing the musical focus to something to which they can more easily relate. In fact, the issue is the *way* in which they are being asked to respond to the music. Such is the assumed universality of aesthetic listening that he can conceive of only one way of musical meaning being construed: through distanced, objective analysis, with the students in the role of listener-as-audience. He doesn't recognise that responses to music need not be exclusively distanced and cognitive but can also be physical and emotional. Moreover, whatever the mode of response, the opportunity to construct personal meaning is critical to an authentic and meaningful engagement with music.

Task 10.5 Thinking about different ways in which people respond to music

Choose a piece of music from a tradition other than western art music. Make notes about the music in terms of the following:

- the way in which the music is created;
- how the music is communicated to 'the listeners' and the way in which they respond and relate to it.

Note down some ideas of how this music might be used in the classroom in a way that is similar to how it is experienced in its original context.

Personal construction of meaning

The ideology of aesthetic listening is located within the concept of 'objective knowledge' – an understanding of knowledge as being somehow 'out there' waiting to be engaged with and understood. However, as Small has written: 'Knowledge . . . is the relationship between the knower and the thing known. . . . There can be no such thing as completely objective knowledge, knowledge of the external world exactly as it is, since everything we can possibly know about it is mediated by the way we, the knowers, work on the stimuli to convert them to usable knowledge . . .' (Small 1999: 14). It follows from this that, as Carey says, '. . . emotions and ideas do not reside in artworks but in the people responding to them [and] their responses display infinite variation' (Carey 2005: 78). Consequently, 'Musical meanings are negotiated not absorbed; constructed not given; appropriated not bestowed. The processes and experiences we call musical, then, never reside in a hermetically-insular "aesthetic" realm, but are part of our lived, social reality' (Elliott 1995: 125). This lived social reality includes responses to music that go far beyond the purely distanced verbal and written ones.

Emotional and physical responses to music

Young people attending a Bruce Springsteen concert described their experience of the music in the following way [my italics]: 'It gets you physically, because you're dancing, you're moving around, you're waving your arms, you're clapping your hands ... It's just an energizing experience and it's a spiritual experience. So, it gets your *mind, body and soul'* (Daniel Cavicchi quoted by Finnegan in Clayton 2003: 185).

Clearly the holistic (mind, body, soul) response to music is very important to these young people. It is not difficult, then, to imagine how responses to music that are restricted to the written and verbal may seem irredeemably impoverished. Indeed, Philpott suggests that, 'Part of the reason for the alienation of some older pupils is that the needs of the body are severed from the mind' and that 'connections need to be constantly reinforced between cognition and our bodily sense' (Philpott and Plummeridge 2001: 89).

What Philpott and the pupils are doing is rejecting the mind–body split explicit within Cartesian dualism. In a telling passage, Small argues that:

> Properly understood, all art is *action* – performance art, if you like, and its meaning lies not in creating objects but in acts of creating, displaying and *perceiving*. It is an activity in which humans take part in order that they may come to understand their relationships – with one another and with the great pattern which connects. In all these activities we call the arts, *we think with our bodies*. They negate with every gesture the Cartesian split between mind and body.
>
> (Small 1998: 40) (emphases not in original)

Small's notion that 'we think with our bodies' is supported by Elliott, who argues that a young person's musical understanding, and what he describes as their 'listenership', are best developed and assessed through 'thinking' and 'knowing' 'in action' (Elliott 1995: 97). In other words, musical understanding is demonstrated through the 'physical doing' of music. It follows, therefore, that young people's responses to music are likely to be most authentic and illuminating if such responses take place through musical activity. So, one listens to music and responds to it, demonstrating one's knowledge, understanding and perception through composing, improvising and performing; that is, through the integration of musical activities.

Implications for the teaching of listening

Where students are enabled to respond to and appraise music in a range of ways, where personal construction of meaning is valued, and where listening is integrated with composing and performing, there is created a context in which they have ownership of their musical learning and where rich musical learning can take place.

Scenario 4

Lara, Jennifer, David and Gerry are 15-year-old GCSE music students who have formed a rock group to meet part of the requirements for the performing aspect of the GCSE music exam. Most of their repertoire is cover versions. Having selected the music they want to perform, they learn their parts individually through repeated listening to recordings. When listening to the recordings, they focus not just on the building

(continued)

(continued)

bricks of rhythm, pitch and harmony but also on the nuances of the recording. They then rehearse collectively, and once the piece is 'hanging together' they work on the 'interpretation', collectively informed by their personal reflections on the music gained during their individual study of the recording. They decide which aspects of the recorded performance to keep and which of their own ideas to include in order to make the performance 'their own'.

One of the key aspects of this scenario is that the musical decision making emerges from immersion in the music. However, neither the recording nor any notated form of the music is treated as fixed (as encapsulating definitive musical meaning). The construction of meaning occurs not just through verbal discussion but as 'thinking-in-action' – as an ongoing, individual and collective process; musical meaning is constructed as the interpretation develops. Different ways of shaping a phrase, bending a note, swinging a rhythm, and different guitar and drum effects are all tried out, *listened to*, *responded to* and then accepted or rejected. The students are engaged in making informed, artistic and intelligent decisions about their music making. This thinking-in-action is also much more holistic, being physical as much as cognitive – what feels right is what feels right bodily, emotionally and intellectually.

Task 10.6 **Finding out how students use listening to support performing and composing**
Talk to some students who play in a rock band about the ways in which they learn the music. Focus your questions particularly on the listening and responding skills they deploy in creating the performance they want.

Planning an integrated approach to listening and responding

In the final section of this chapter we look at a skeletal plan of a sequence of three music lessons based upon the song 'Strange Fruit', which refers to the lynching of Black Americans during the first part of the last century (see Table 10.1).

These lessons show how:

*   performing and composing might be used as the means by which students respond to their listening;
*   the English National Curriculum requirements for music might be met through an integrated approach to listening;
*   students can demonstrate their listening and responding skills and musical understanding through responses other than written ones;
*   opportunities might be created for students to be involved in the construction of musical meaning.

Task 10.7 Applying the principles of this chapter

Read carefully through the lesson plans in Table 10.1. Then, using a template of your own devising, plan a lesson or sequence of lessons that meets the four criteria above (preceding this task) and focuses on developing students' understanding of music through listening and responding. Make the lesson:

- specific to a class that you know and are likely to teach;
- build on the students' prior learning;
- link into your partner school's Scheme of Work and any National Curriculum requirements within which you are working.

Table 10.1 Applying the principles: an example

Learning and teaching activities	English National Curriculum Programme of study for music	Commentary
Lesson 1		
A recording of Billie Holiday singing 'Strange Fruit' is playing as young people enter the room. The young people are asked to identify the style of the music and most are able to identify it as jazz. The teacher asks them about their reactions to it. Where they might expect to hear such music? Why it sounds like jazz? The young people have clear ideas about where such music is likely to be heard but only a few can really describe *verbally* what it is about the music that makes it sound like jazz	understand and explore how music is created, produced and communicated	The lesson begins with musical activity Clear links are made between the music and the contexts in which it is likely to be heard. Their 'knowledge of the external world' (Small op. cit) is used to enable them to create appropriate meaning The teacher identifies those able to appraise music verbally
The teacher asks them to identify one short phrase that, for them, really sounds jazz-like. They do this and listen to it a few times. They divide into groups, some working on keyboards, others vocally and others using ICT. The teacher asks them to compose a *short* phrase, which sounds like jazz and is similar to the one to which they have been listening. They explore musical ideas and motifs for 10 minutes. Some young people are able to produce musical ideas that are typically jazzy and reflect the phrase they have heard, other young people struggle. The class discuss why some ideas are more successful than others in reflecting a	understand musical structures, styles, genres and traditions, identifying the expressive use of musical dimensions to listen with discrimination to the best in the musical canon	Activities are set up to enable young people to demonstrate their understanding of jazz through composing, improvising and performing The exploration of musical ideas means that musical meaning emerges from the young people rather than begin imposed upon them From this (*rather than from verbal descriptions*) the teacher is able to assess those

Task 10.7   *(continued)*

jazz style. Some of the keyboard players refer to their use of 'black notes', the singers to 'bending the notes' they exemplify what they are saying with musical examples The teacher talks briefly about the idea of 'blues' notes (referring back to a previous topic on the blues), swung rhythm and 'bent' notes. The young people spend five more minutes working on their phrases in the light of their learning, and perform them to each other		young people whose listening has enabled them to understand the characteristics of jazz Musical understanding developed in previous lessons is used to inform their understanding of jazz and their ability to construct their own meaning
Lesson 2		
Young people now compare the Billie Holliday version of 'SF' with one sung by Sting. They discuss differences in the performance, listening particularly to the extent to which the performances conform to their expectations of what jazz should be like		Responding and responding skills are now used to compare different performances of the same music drawing on learning from the previous lesson
Young people listen to a jazz number performed/recorded 'straight' by the teacher. They are given the lyrics to a verse and chord symbols but no musical notation. They are asked to work on a 'jazz performance' of this verse, drawing on their understanding of jazz style to create a convincing interpretation. Young people then perform their versions to each other, discussing the perceived strengths and weaknesses of each informed by their learning	Improvise and compose, extend and develop musical ideas by drawing on a range of musical structures, styles, genres and traditions	Responding skills are now strongly linked to young people performing skills and interpretative understanding
Lesson 3		
Young people discuss with the teacher the meaning that lies behind the words of 'Strange Fruit' and from this they explore the role of jazz and blues in Black American Culture They are given the lyrics of a Black American protest song and compose music for it- not notated but created and learnt aurally, drawing on their learning through responding during the previous lessons	develop a deep understanding of the music that they perform and to which they listen	

Summary

In this chapter we have considered how we can create a context for listening and responding in the curriculum that

- embraces and acknowledges a much wider range of musical responses;
- acknowledges the different ways in which people 'learn musically';
- integrates listening and responding more fully with performing and composing.

In other words, we have developed and discussed an approach to listening and responding that is characterised by its musical inclusivity.

Further reading

Dibben, N. (2003) Musical materials, perception and listening, in M. Clayton, T. Herbert and R. Middleton (eds) *The Cultural Study of Music*, London: Routledge, pp. 181–193.
Fautley, M. (2014) *Listen, Imagine Compose*, Birmingham: Birmingham City University, www.soundand music.org/projects/listen-imagine-compose (accessed 4 August 2015).
Hargreaves, D. North, N. and Wallas, M. (2000) 'English and American adolescents' reasons for listening to music', *Psychology of Music*, 28, 2: 166–173.

These publications deal with the cultural issues surrounding listening and appraising exposed in this chapter, and also some practical implications for the music classroom that arise as a result. The research report 'Listen, Imagine, Compose' provides a rich resource for understanding, first, how listening, composing and performing can be addressed in an integrated way, and second, effective ways of working in partnership with composers and other professional musicians.

11 Framing conceptions of technology for learning in music – implications for pedagogy

Duncan Mackrill with Alison Daubney

Introduction

From social networking to computer games, instant access of information and communication anywhere, technology permeates young people's lives, particularly out of school. This accessibility, portability and natural engagement with different technologies opens up opportunities for its innovative use in the curriculum, particularly to capitalise upon young people's motivation for music. Within school, too, technology has become an increasingly important tool and a necessary element of a rounded music education experience. Its importance and potential are recognised within the National Curriculum for Music (DfE 2013b) and the National Plan for Music Education (DfE and DCMS 2011). Many teachers training today will be very familiar with technology such as computers and mobile technologies and use them every day, and in this chapter you will have the opportunity to consider how you might use these technologies in your teaching to develop your pupils' musical learning and engagement.

While technology in school opens up exciting possibilities, maximising technology's potential for facilitating musical learning in the school requires careful consideration and planning in order to capitalise upon young people's motivation in ways that are meaningful, relevant and pedagogically sound. The following is an important principle we adopt for this entire chapter:

> it is not whether technology is used (or not) which makes the difference, but how well the technology is used to support teaching and learning. There is no doubt that technology engages and motivates young people. However this benefit is only an advantage for learning if the activity is effectively aligned with what is to be learned. It is therefore the pedagogy of the application of technology in the classroom which is important: the *how* rather than the *what*.
>
> (Higgins *et al.* 2012: 3)

Over the past thirty years, the use of music technology in education has moved from the introduction of hardware such as synthesisers, portable keyboards and four-track cassette recorders to computer suites running industry-standard music software and full multi-track studios. Programs such as Cubase, Sibelius, Logic and Garage Band are well established, particularly at Key Stage 4, and there is already literature on all these important aspects of using technology in music – for example Crow (2007: 180–186). Therefore, readers are encouraged to refer to this and other literature on these areas and to develop their expertise in using a sequencer, score writer and multi-track recorder.

The focus of this chapter is on more recent and mobile learning technologies and how these might be used to develop musical learning and teaching. However, to give the bigger picture, Table 11.1, building on Crow's (2007: 184) categories of music software, is included in order to present a broad overview of the range of technologies available and indications of their potential uses in relation to musical learning.

Further examples are to be found throughout the chapter. There are, of course, many generic technology tools, including Interactive Whiteboards (IWB) – for example to model using a virtual keyboard so that students can see (and hear) what is being played; and websites such as YouTube, with a huge selection of music across many genres that is a fantastic resource for music teachers to use across all key stages. If YouTube is blocked by the school's firewall, you should contact the network manager to allow at least teacher access.

In recent years, many school music departments have made capital investments in PC or Apple Mac computer suites. This is to be welcomed, and has certainly helped to equip departments to deliver GCSE, A level and BTEC courses with significant technology components. While access to computers set up specifically for music is clearly very beneficial, a significant problem is frequently the amount of time spent trouble-shooting and ensuring that students are able to log on, retrieve and save their work quickly and easily. A number of music departments employ music technicians who can offer valuable support across the department to teachers and students, not just with technology, and they are a most valuable asset!

Task 11.1 School perspectives

Ask the curriculum leader for music in your placement school about their view of technology and its use in the music classroom:

- What do they think are the most useful technologies to use?
- What technology would they buy for the department if they were given a budget of £5,000 or £20,000, and why?
- What would this enable them to do that they cannot do now?
- How would it develop their students' musical learning?
- What changes would they need to make to the curriculum as a result, and to their delivery?

Some may argue that the more music computers in a department the better. However, it is our view that a more balanced approach to introducing technology is required, which includes both music computers and mobile technologies, and that this is beneficial both pedagogically and to make the most of limited funds.

Table 11.1 Technologies available and potential uses

Technology	Examples	Uses include
Sequencer	Cubase, Logic, Sonar, Pro Tools, Reason, Studio One, Mixcraft	Making multi-track recordings via MIDI or audio to build up a piece track by track; editing and mixing; using virtual instruments and effects to play back sounds; ability (in some programs) to produce scores and parts
Loop-based sequencer	GarageBand, FL Studio, Acid, Music Maker	Auditioning and selecting ready-made loops from a pool (drag and drop) to build up a composition; ability (in some programs) to edit loops/instrumentation and record new tracks
Score and notation software	Sibelius, Finale, MuseScore, Notion	Producing scores and parts with the ability to play these back
Theory and aural skills	Musition, Auralia, Musictheory.net	Understanding theory and aural skills; drill and testing
DJ decks (hardware) and live performance software	Numark, Pioneer, VirtualDJ, Tractor DJ, Abelton Live	Controlling and interacting with audio files/CDs etc. and loops in a live environment
Rehearsal group mixer	Jam Hub	Enabling up to seven instrumentalists/singers to work together on headphones, each with their own individual mix. Results can also be easily recorded
Loop stations	Boss RC	Playing live and building up loops (repeating phrases) layer by layer – these are often used by guitarists and operated by foot pedals
Audio recording	Audacity (free), Wavelab	Recording sounds, editing (including pitch) and adding effects
Sampler software	HALion, Propellerhead NN-XT	Recording sounds, editing (including pitch) and triggering them from other hardware or software programs
Electronic keyboards	Portable keyboards	Selecting from a wide range of instrumental sounds; using a chord and/or rhythmic backing; listening via headphones or out loud
Synthesizers	Various by Korg, Roland, Yamaha etc.	Enabling sounds to be created or edited – frequently used in performance
Portable audio recording	Tascam DR or Roland R portable recorders	Making live stereo recordings in the classroom or on location
Multi-track audio recording	Boss BR, Tascam DP, Zoom R multi-track studios	Building up a multi-track recording – often one track at a time – to produce a professional-quality recording, including effects
Video recording	Tablet, Zoom, Flip camera (mobile phone)	Videoing work in progress or final performances to build up a portfolio of pupil work; projecting on the board; sharing with pupils/parents via school network; creating a series of short video 'how to' tutorials to build up skills related to specific units of work that can be accessed as required when uploaded to the school's learning platform
ePortfolio	School or web-hosted learning platform	Pupils creating and accessing their own portfolio, including audio and/or video of their work in music over time. Sharing these with parents/carers.

Objectives

By the end of this chapter you should be able to:

- demonstrate an awareness of a range of technologies available for both teacher and pupil use in the music classroom, particularly mobile and emerging technologies;
- begin to know when and how to integrate technology effectively into units of work to develop students' musical learning;
- explore how technology can be used in music to enhance assessment in ways that are beneficial to both teachers and pupils;
- understand the potential benefits and problems in using technology in the classroom, including classroom management, health and safety and ethical issues.

Motivation and engagement: learning anywhere

There is plentiful evidence that young people are motivated by technology. A systematic literature review by Smith *et al.* (2005) found that learners aged 11–16 were more motivated to learn if the lessons were perceived to be relevant, interesting and fun – using technology effectively has the potential to contribute all of the these criteria. Additionally, they report that 'authentic learning tasks are more likely to cognitively engage pupils' (2005: 4), defining authenticity as 'how situated and related to the real world school learning situations appeared to pupils' (p. 46). It is also important to ensure pupil engagement in the assessment process.

Many teachers have considered that the use of technology in music may motivate boys more than girls. Interestingly, from our own research (Daubney and Mackrill 2012) with students in Years 6 and 7, while more boys reported using technology for music in school, more girls had a personal music collection and were actively involved in using technology (including karaoke) for music at home than boys. Thus, focusing upon gender differences may not always be useful or relevant. The headline figures from our sample of 150 Year 6 state school students from seven different areas of England show that over 85 per cent own their own mobile phones and have access to laptops, tablets and other forms of technology. They are clearly adept at using it informally and without formal instruction, including for music, as this example from Simon, aged 11, demonstrates.

> Sometimes when I listen, I think, 'oh I like that'. I might think I want to learn it, so I would go onto a website that would give you the lyrics, guitar, like, tabs. I go on this one called Ultimate Guitar and it gives you the tabs for the song, so listening to it, really, really that's it.

In the past, there was a view that young people go to school to learn. However, there has been a significant change over the past few years in the access to music out of school and in the way young people engage with it through the development of technology. We need to recognise the considerable learning and music experiences young people have involving technology outside school, which they bring to the classroom.

The following are some of the important changes:

- the significant improvement in the roll-out of Wi-Fi, enabling a fast internet connection at home, school and on the move;
- the move away from CDs and purchasing music in the high street to the MP3 download and accessing music online via YouTube, Spotify and other streaming music sites;
- the increase in the number of children with their own laptop and a lowering of the age at which children own their own computer (or tablet);
- the development of the smartphone, which is effectively a computer in your hand with internet access and a range of music apps that are relatively inexpensive to purchase;
- the popularity of tablets – again with internet access and access to a wide range of music and generic apps.

Our job as teachers is to work out creative ways that capitalise upon motivation and skills developed outside the classroom and use these to contribute to meaningful and musical learning experiences in school, which both build on young people's experiences and help to develop their musical and/or technological learning.

Whenever you consider using technology, ask yourself the following questions:

1   Can I identify the benefits for me as teacher and/or the students in my class by using this technology?
2   Does using the technology enable students to do something that they couldn't otherwise do without it, where it would be less effective or would take them much longer to complete?
3   Does the use of the proposed technology have the potential to improve the quality, or capacity, of work and learning?
4   Is the task I am asking the young people to complete musical?

If the answer to any of these questions is 'No', or you are unsure, you should seriously question why you are choosing to use technology, or perhaps that particular technology tool.

A few caveats:

- Technology should not be a bolt-on but instead be the 'norm'. However, just because we may have different technologies available to use, we don't have to use them all the time. For example, in the case of dedicated computer suites, though there may be challenges around the availability of classrooms, it is important to avoid teaching the practical aspects of a topic such as African drumming using computers instead of drums!
- Beware of interpreting excitement or amusement necessarily as engagement.
- Ensure that introducing the technology does not reduce opportunities for developing musical understanding and promoting creativity. For example, drag and drop software where anything 'fits' may be little more than an activity to keep young people amused

without careful planning and implementation, and no 'auditioning' skill required by students.

Task 11.2 asks you to consider these issues in relation to planning a lesson, to ensure the use of technology is appropriate to the learning.

Task 11.2 Selecting appropriate technology tools

Choose a lesson from a unit of work in your placement school that you are going to teach and list the technology resources available to you. Referring to the four questions above, consider which ones might be appropriate to include and how you can use them to develop students' learning and creativity.

We now have portable, instant 24/7 access to the internet and each other, and this 'learning anywhere' approach has significant implications. The opportunity to access resources and obtain instant information on how to do something – play a chord, use alternative fingering, find music that is similar to something else they know etc. – makes learning without formal tuition much more feasible. While there is no alternative to the experience of playing real instruments and developing skills on instruments, this changing relationship with technology should challenge our ideas about teaching, pedagogy and young people's learning both in and out of the classroom.

Task 11.3 Students' uses of technology for music outside school

- Spend a little time in one of your lessons (or ask to do this in tutor time), asking students in one of your Year 7 or 8 classes how many of them use technology for music in their lives outside school, and in what ways.
- Discuss your approach with the class teacher beforehand. You will need to be sensitive when introducing this, as some students will not have the latest smartphone or access to technology. Therefore, it is suggested that you avoid asking students to put their hand up to indicate whether they have a particular device or use technology in a particular manner, and instead simply invite them to share how they use different technologies for music.

Questions you might ask are, for example, do they have an MP3 player (or do they use their phone) and a music collection? Are there any musical games, such as the PlayStation, that are popular? Do they teach themselves to play an instrument and, if so, do they use any particular websites?

- Once you have carried this out, reflect on their answers and make notes on the key responses, noting any answers or examples that surprised you.
- As a result of this knowledge, what implications might be there for your own planning and teaching?

More recent technologies

Developments in technology are rapid, and frequently new or emerging technologies become the 'norm' in just a few years. At present, it seems that the majority of 'new' technologies for use in education can be broadly categorised into one of two groups, either mobile or web-based technologies (as summarised in Table 11.2) – although a number of devices can, of course, be both mobile and web-based, e.g. a smartphone.

In addition to these mobile or web-based technologies, two other hardware developments that can be used to support live performance work are worthy of note.

First, the JamHub, which allows up to seven instrumentalists and singers to rehearse together using headphones, each with control of their own individual mix of the group. This works well for multiple bands or groups in a classroom to work together and is particularly well suited to an informal learning approach. The results can also be easily recorded.

Second, loop stations. These are live performance tools that enable the user to build up layers of loops, and many also include built-in effects. These hardware tools are designed particularly for guitarists, singers and beatboxers, but can be used by other instrumentalists, and educationally they provide a good modelling tool as an introduction to loop-based software.

Table 11.2 Mobile and web-based technologies

Mobile			Web-based	
Device	Function	Examples	Category	Examples
Mobile phone, portable digital recorder, tablets	Recording and playback of audio/ video	MP3 player, video and/or audio recorder	Cloud-based software programs	Soundation, Musition, Auralia, Noteflight, O-Generator
			Cloud music players	iCloud, Google Music
Tablets (e.g. iPad, Galaxy, Nexus, Xperia), iTouch, smartphones	Music-specific apps	GarageBand, PocketBand, Music Studio, Traktor DJ, ReLoop, Spotify, FL Studio	Music sharing (ePortfolio) or collaboration softwares	Edmodo, Makewaves, Ohmstudio
	Music instruments /tools	Metronome, Guitar tuner, virtual instruments, e.g. Alchemy, Drum Set	Teach-yourself, and access-anywhere music videos and online music	YouTube, Ultimate Guitar, Spotify, Grooveshark

Task 11.4 Making your own technology shopping list

While being realistic, consider what you would use if you could have any technology you wished. Now begin a list of what would be on your own technology shopping list for your music classroom in the future. Is it the same as that identified by the teacher in Task 11.1? If not, why might this be?

Mobile technologies

Mobile phones and smartphones

Over the past few years we have seen a significant change in the types of technology being developed commercially, and this has also impacted on its use in schools – for example, the explosion of smartphones, delivering what is effectively a portable computer in your pocket. Though this was led by Apple with their iPhone, Android now has some 85 per cent of the market share worldwide (International Data Corporation 2014). While Apple still has strong sales in the UK, it is a premium-priced product and you should ideally look for music apps that are available on both platforms.

There is an ongoing debate regarding the use of mobile phones in the classroom, but more schools are cautiously moving towards regulated use. Mobile phones fall into the category of 'bring your own device' (BYOD), and clearly there are implications for education in terms of teaching, equity and pupil learning; these issues need to be carefully considered and addressed when weighing up the potential benefits for their use. However, the great educational potential of musical technology is beginning to be recognised. For example, Ofsted advocate their use in their triennial report on music (2012), recognising the value of mobile phones for musical learning – see page 38, section 100 and the associated videos.

In the music classroom there is a range of potential benefits to their use in a controlled, regulated environment:

- Young people may make an audio or video recording on a mobile phone or tablet (subject to permission) of their own work in progress to refer to next lesson.
- Video tutorials or examples of modelling by the teacher can be uploaded to the school learning platform for students to download and view (on a smartphone, iPod Touch or tablet) as required, whether they are working in the main classroom or in rehearsal rooms.
- Photographs of group work undertaken may be taken – for example graphic scores – using a mobile phone or tablet and shared with the rest of the group to enable work to continue out of class.
- A backing track or chord chart etc. may be downloaded to a mobile phone, MP3 player or tablet for use in group work in rehearsal rooms.
- Smartphone apps such as GarageBand or PocketBand or a simple metronome or drum pattern etc. can be used to support practice.

As previously mentioned, there is substantial evidence that students use mobile technology extensively outside the classroom for informal learning and engagement with music; the balance between the extent to which learning in schools should simply replicate/build on this, or offer something different, should be carefully planned, otherwise the value of learning in school is questionable.

Lastly, there is a need to educate young people about the importance of respecting intellectual property rights and to develop a sense of what is acceptable behaviour when using technology.

Cloud applications

'Cloud' is a general term usually used in connection with virtual storage and potentially sharing facilities, or software applications that are accessed via the web allowing you to save data to be stored online. It can effectively be used as an audio/video-based portfolio of musical learning and progression over time, which also has the capacity to store scanned scores, notes, teacher observations etc. In addition, using cloud storage is one way a portfolio of evidence can be created, taking into consideration pupil ownership and portability, although there is little evidence of this happening other than in the Early Years Foundation Stage (EYFS).

Some software programs are now being distributed as cloud-based applications, so instead of purchasing the software from a supplier and installing it on each computer, licences are purchased (usually on an annual basis) and the software is delivered from the cloud to any computer on the system. It has only recently become viable to deliver large programs, where high-quality audio recording and processing in real time are required, via cloud applications, but these can be cost-effective and are often popular with IT managers in schools.

Apple, Google and Amazon have all produced their own cloud music players to enable you to store and stream your own music collection on any mobile device from virtually any location. Using a cloud player enables you to select music from your own collection as listening examples to play in the classroom from your mobile or a computer. However, you may need to arrange access to the site or Wi-Fi by contacting the school network manager.

The challenge now is how to change our pedagogies to address these new technologies, as Task 11.5 asks you to consider.

Task 11.5 Students' use of mobile technologies

Take a unit of work you are to teach at Key Stage 3 and identify opportunities where allowing students to use mobile phones, MP3 players or portable audio/video recorders (or a combination of these) would benefit their learning or your teaching. Please refer to the list of potential benefits above.

Things you will need to consider include:

- the school and/or department's position on the use of mobile phones or personal MP3 players;
- issues of equity to ensure that those students without a mobile or who do not have the latest smartphone do not feel 'second best' (for example, emphasise that using personal phones is optional and organise a rota for using any departmental digital recorders, tablets etc. – those using their own mobile can then release their allocated 'slot' for others to use the department equipment);
- checking to see who may not be photographed or videoed (the school should have a register for this);

(continued)

Task 11.5 *(continued)*

- who will have the responsibility for making any recordings and how this will be managed;
- what will happen to any recordings/photographs/backing tracks at the end of the lesson, i.e. will they be stored in the department, on the virtual learning environment (VLE) or will youngsters have the responsibility for bringing them into the following lesson? In the latter case, what back up plan do you have in case they forget to do so?

Now do the same for a Key Stage 4 music class. Discuss these ideas carefully with your mentor and senior staff as appropriate, finding out their perspective and whether your proposal fits with the school's policy on the acceptable use of mobile phones. If it is agreed by your mentor, introduce your ideas in your teaching and evaluate their success.

Specific examples of cloud applications include:

- *Soundation* - an online music studio with over 700 loops and sounds, virtual instruments and effects where students can share the results of their work online http://soundation.com and www.musicfirst.co.uk/store/all/soundation-4-education
- *Noteflight* – this notation program enables students to work on their scores at school or at home and their teacher to view, edit and comment at home – see http://music first.co.uk/store/brands/noteflight/noteflight
- *OhmStudio* – a real-time online digital audio workstation allowing users to collaborate with each other to create music – see www.ohmstudio.com/
- *Bandlab* – a new collaborative songwriting and recording system app for a tablet. The app itself is free, with users paying for cloud storage instead – see www.bandlab.com/

Tablets

In the past few years, tablets have become the latest technology 'must-haves' for personal use and now, increasingly, in education. There is no doubt that they bring some exciting opportunities for both learning and teaching. Tablets can engage and motivate students, the apps are inexpensive (enabling students to purchase them to use at home etc. where the tablet is not provided by the school) and they already come with some intuitive, well-designed productivity and organisation tools. There is evidence that where tablets are used as one-to-one devices (where each pupil has their own tablet to use in all lessons as well as at home), and where the necessary pedagogic changes are implemented, there are significant benefits across the curriculum. Table 11.3 outlines the benefits of using tablets for musical learning and assessment.

Table 11.3 Possible uses of tablets

Concept/use	Possible uses
Provides a computer in our hand – sound, screen, mic etc. are all in one portable unit	Teachers or pupils can easily make video or audio recordings of completed work or their work in progress. This can then be replayed via a projector for the whole class, or on the tablet itself in a future lesson to remind pupils of their previous work (useful for ongoing composition or performance activities).
	Videos demonstrating how to play a particular rhythm or chord sequence can be prepared and made available for pupils to access as required.
	Key evidence of pupil work can be saved and collated and notes made on pupils 'on the hoof' as teachers go around the class.
Portability	Allows easy internet access anywhere with a Wi-Fi connection so tablets can be used to support musicians as they work – for example in finding lyrics, chord progressions, guitar tab, accompaniment backings etc.
	Pupils with a one-to-one tablet can continue to work at home, using the same software as at school, providing opportunities to set 'musical' homework.
Support tool for teachers	Enables teachers to play MP3 files, set quizzes etc. and create simple backings to support singing or instrumental work – for example using GarageBand (iOS) or PocketBand (Android).
Presentation and collaboration tool	The teacher or pupils can present their ideas to each other using an app such as Explain Everything or Nearpod.
	Pupils may work in a group to compose using the tablet as a recording device or to play a backing track.
Sequencing	Pupils work individually or in pairs to compose and build up their own piece a layer at a time. For example, using GarageBand or PocketBand, or a more complex app such as Cubasis (iOS).
Ability to plug in a range of other devices via an inexpensive hardware interface	Using a hardware guitar/instrument interface that includes amp simulation and effects allows guitarists to work on headphones without the need for a bulky, expensive amp.
	Tablets can also be used as mixers and controllers for more advanced sequencing and audio recording programs.
ePortfolio	Pupils create and access their own portfolio, including audio and potentially video of their work in music. For those with one-to-one devices, this portfolio can also easily be shared with parents/carers.

Using tablets in music offers some real benefits, but there are some important caveats of which you should be aware. For example as with introducing any technology for the first time we need to be aware of the inevitable element of 'novelty value'. In addition, it is all too easy to believe that students are learning just because they appear engaged with the technology or are quiet, but tablets can offer new opportunities for young people to be distracted, with them easily able to message their peers or use apps other than those intended. Consequently, as always, establishing ground rules for their use right from the start will be important here. Adopting tablets in any classroom requires a significant pedagogic shift, from the traditional view of the teacher at the front of a class to that of learning using one-to-one tablets. You should therefore take every opportunity to talk to and observe how other teachers use tablets in their classrooms.

The four principles for using technology in the section on 'Motivation and engagement: learning anywhere' should continue to be adopted, but in addition it is worth considering the following when using tablets:

- Apps are generally designed to be intuitive and to do one specific thing easily and well. While this can be good, it challenges our pedagogy, developed over the past ten or fifteen years, of working with industry-standard music (or generic) software that is intended to be comprehensive and have everything you need in one package. However, some app developers are beginning to create apps that can link and communicate with others – so, for example, one might compose a track in one app but the playback could use sounds from another app, e.g. Sampletank.
- Tablets are also primarily designed for personal use rather than having many users successively on the one device, so where multiple classes share the same set of tablets, it is more difficult to save and retrieve students' work from one lesson to the next as the device is not their own. Consequently, their work will need to be saved, or at least backed up to the school's network to ensure it is available for the next lesson. This will require the support of the school IT manager. It is hoped that the industry will work to address this issue.
- When selecting apps to use, evaluate how productive its use will be for the students in your classes. Avoid 'instant' music apps that don't encourage musical learning, and consider whether it would be better to use a computer or a different technology instead, or even no technology at all. For example, entering music notes on a stave, or editing audio or MIDI tracks in a sequencer, will be much easier and productive for most students with a conventional computer and a mouse.

It is not possible within the confines of this chapter to address other important issues about the use of tablets in the music classroom, such as bandwidth, network administration, insurance, protective cases, breakages and how to manage the use of sets of tablets, but there is more information on many of these issues to be found elsewhere, and a good place to start is on the Tablets for Schools website.

Tablets are powerful and valuable technology tools, but it will be important for students to also have access to conventional computers, which still offer more functionality, in order to deliver some aspects of the curriculum, particularly at Key Stage 4 and above. Both technologies are important and support students' learning in different ways.

Lastly, we have concentrated on the whole-class use of tablets, but there is much to be gained from using a single tablet in the classroom as a teacher (see Table 11.3), and you are encouraged to do so – it could well transform your teaching! Task 11.6 asks you to consider available apps and the implications of using them within a whole-class setting.

Task 11.6 Selecting and using apps

Find out what apps your peers, other teachers and students use and find most useful in their teaching or learning. These can be music-specific apps or those designed for teaching generally.

- Try these out and decide which ones might really help to develop the musical learning of the students in your classes.
- If possible, observe other teachers using these apps.
- How would you change your pedagogy to use the app(s) effectively, and what changes in learning outcomes do you anticipate?

Issues

While the potential for technology is great, inevitably there are a number of other emergent issues that the use of technology throws up. The most pressing of these involves assessment, transition from primary school and continuing professional development for music teachers. Unfortunately, within just a chapter there is insufficient space to deal with these in any detail, but instead we urge teachers to refer to other relevant chapters in this book on these topics and think about the impact of technology on their own learning and the learning experiences they plan and provide for their pupils.

We must also mention opportunities that technology provides for pupils with special educational needs (SEN), including touch-screen computers and tablets, Soundbeam and other controllers to enable pupils to access and make music, control sounds and express themselves. Drake Music champion a great deal of work in this area and it is suggested that you investigate some of the ideas on their website.

Assessment

As with other art forms, we consider that assessment is integral to the teaching and learning process, rather than being treated as a separate entity. When used well, technology opens up tremendous possibilities for different types of assessment.

It is clear that Ofsted (2012: 38) advocate the value of technology as a formative part of the learning process, as well as ways for teachers to meaningfully evidence musical progression:

A well-ordered catalogue of recordings over time, supported by commentaries and scores, provides a very effective and compelling way to demonstrate students' musical progress. Where there was good practice, teachers capitalised on students' interest in and facility with internet and mobile technology.

We support this approach. Portable digital recorders, or tablets, are particularly useful and you are encouraged to record, store and assess recordings of pupils' work, both completed and as work in progress. Importantly, by carefully selecting examples of the latter to share with the class and regularly giving clear, formative feedback, pupil learning and progress can be significantly improved.

While this is only the tip of the iceberg on this important aspect, we have included examples of how technology might be used to support assessment and students' learning at many points throughout this chapter. Task 11.7 provides you with the opportunity to bring these ideas together in considering one unit of work.

Task 11.7   Technology in assessment

Drawing together ideas from this chapter, choose a unit of work that you are preparing to teach and identify opportunities to integrate the use of mobile technologies as part of the assessment and learning process.

Transitions in education

Much has been written about transition from primary school to secondary school and the inherent dangers of secondary school teachers ignoring their pupils' prior musical experiences. Technology is not only found in secondary schools – there is also considerable use in primary schools, but research (Daubney and Mackrill 2013) indicates that this is not frequently used for music! Additionally, through the Wider Opportunities programme, many pupils arriving in Year 7 will have experienced at least a term of instrumental lessons at some point during their time at primary school.

There are many ways in which technology can help to support learning across transition, but perhaps the most significant of these could be the development and use of a sound-based musical profiling system. Pupils can then create their own portfolio of musical learning throughout their school years, documenting their musical development through audio and, where possible, video examples across time, both in and out of school. Their portfolio would then transfer with them when changing schools. Such a system is currently in place in parts of Scotland and is also advocated in the National Plan for Music Education (DfE and DCMS 2011).

Continuing professional development (CPD)

When any new technology or pedagogic approach is introduced, one of the key components of its success and effective impact is the quality – and often the quantity – of the CPD that is delivered, and we agree with Higgins, Xiao and Katsipataki's (2012) view:

> Training for teachers (and for learners), when it is offered, usually focuses on technology skills in using the equipment. This is not usually sufficient to support teachers and pupils

in getting the best from technology in terms of their learning. On-going professional development and support to evaluate the impact on learning is likely to be required.

(Higgins, Xiao and Katsipataki 2012: 5)

Learning to use a new piece of kit is different from understanding its use pedagogically, and this will inevitably take time, but there are advantages of the explosion in new mobile technologies: many are intuitive, as they are designed for the mass market, not specialists. You are also more likely to have good generic skills with mobile technologies already if you have a smartphone or portable digital recorder. Therefore, teachers at all levels should consider the pedagogic implications of using different technologies rather than just mastering basic skills.

However, you do not have to master every technology yourself. For example, there is considerable scope for using technologies such as DJ turntables, loop stations etc. in both the composing and performing components of Key Stage 4 exam specifications, but it appears that they are seldom used. We suggest that this is often linked to a lack of teacher confidence and experience in relation to using such technologies. This is understandable, but providing you as the teacher understand how to use the technology pedagogically, you do not have to master every technology and you can leave it to your pupils. This approach may be applied to a broader range of technologies, and with a current focus upon 'partnership working', particularly through the formation of music hubs, there may be others working in your local area who have experience in using technology in a range of settings. It would be useful to find out about other local organisations and any teachers/practitioners who offer technology-based opportunities to your pupils in different settings, and think about how these contacts may be useful for your own professional development and also to enhance your pupils' learning opportunities.

Summary

In this whistle-stop tour of technology we have:

- demonstrated the breadth of the word 'technology' and some of the potential uses in music education, especially with mobile and emerging technologies;
- emphasised that the world outside the music classroom is certainly changing faster than the world inside; technology is at the heart of much of this change, and the students you are educating today learn informally in ways that are often entirely different from those you may have grown up with and so may challenge your traditional view of teaching and teachers;
- shown how technology can support and nurture musical learning both directly and indirectly;
- shown the need for you always to be mindful that the learning you promote and the ways in which you encourage the use of technology are worthwhile and relevant.

When planning to use technology, we always need to think about pedagogy and how the use of the technology will assist or develop students' learning and promote creativity, progress and musical understanding. We should also accept that technology in school music education has a role to play in providing stimuli and solutions that learners have not already found for themselves, which they are motivated to take back to their own 'authentic' environments outside the music classroom. Otherwise, one might ask, why bother?

Further reading

Mackrill, D. (2009) The integration of ICT into the music classroom, in C. Philpott and J. Evans (eds) A *Practical Guide to Teaching Music in the Secondary School*, Abingdon: Routledge.

Daubney, A. and Mackrill, D. (2013) *Music Technologies – Playing the Home Advantage*, Music Education UK. Online, available at: http://issuu.com/musiceducationasia/docs/musiceducationuk_issue_04 (accessed 15 August 2015).

DfE (Department for Education) and DCMS (Department for Culture, Media and Sport) (2011) The Importance of Music – A National Plan for Music Education. Online, available at: www.gov.uk/government/uploads/system/uploads/attachment_data/file/180973/DFE-00086-2011.pdf (accessed 15 August 2015).

Of particular interest will be Annex 2: 'Music technology', pp. 36–41.

These readings and online sources further explore the potential of technology in music teaching and emphasise the importance of teachers being able to reflect critically on new developments in a digital world.

Websites

Drake Music: www.drakemusic.org (accessed 3 March 2016)

Technology support for teaching music with young people who have special educational needs.

Jamhub: www.jamhub.com (accessed 3 March 2016)

Music hardware for use in classrooms.

Musical Futures: www.musicalfutures.org/resources/c/mfpilot2013 (accessed 3 March 2016)

Musical Futures resource exploring ways to incorporate mobile technologies and singing in Year 7.

Ohm Studio www.ohmstudio.com (accessed 3 March 2016)

A collaborative digital audio workstation that can facilitate the sharing of young people's performances and compositions.

Ofsted: www.youtube.com/watch?v=EFcwPkGOWCO; www.youtube.com/watch?v=EFcwPkGOWCO (accessed 3 March 2016)

Videos on using technology in assessment.

Techknowledge for Schools: http://techknowledge.org.uk (accessed 3 March 2016)

Research reports and advice for using tablets with whole classes.

12 Addressing individual needs and equality of opportunity in music education

Chris Philpott and Ruth Wright with Keith Evans and Sally Zimmermann

Introduction

> Inclusive education has grown from the belief that education is a basic human right and that it provides the foundation for a more just society. All learners have a right to education, regardless of their individual characteristics or difficulties. (UNESCO 2003)

Inclusive education is about addressing individual needs and providing equality of opportunity. At the heart of inclusive education is the recognition that each child is an individual and has different learning needs. The challenge for music teachers is to identify these individual needs and plan to meet them through teaching and learning.

The chapter begins by examining those issues around individual needs and equality of opportunity that have the potential to impact on all young people in terms of their access to music education. Here we identify what we mean by individual needs and some of the principles that underpin an inclusive approach to music education. We examine some of the factors that can work against children's access to a music education and how these might be addressed through differentiated approaches to music teaching and learning. Using 'gender' as a case study, we then explore one example of how social and cultural factors can affect young people's experiences of music education.

In the final part of the chapter we turn to those young people who may have exceptional and special education needs. We look at the English legislative and policy frameworks, which set out the support that these young people should receive, followed by three exemplars of what this support might look like when enacted within music education. Then, as an appendix to the chapter, there is an interview with Sally Zimmermann, a leading practitioner and expert in music education with young people with special educational needs. This appendix, and its associated activity, explore the particular challenges faced by young people with special educational needs in accessing music education and how these challenges might be addressed by music teachers.

Objectives

By the end of this chapter and its appendix you should be able to:

- define the concept of inclusion in the music classroom;
- define the concept of differentiation and its application in the music classroom;
- know how to use a variety of teaching and learning strategies to address individual needs;
- understand how common, unique and exceptional needs can be met through differentiation;
- understand some of the challenges to accessing music education experienced by children with special educational needs and how these might be addressed.

What are individual needs?

The individual needs of students in the music classroom can be understood in terms of:

- the *common* needs of all students, for example an entitlement to music education;
- the individual and *unique* needs of *all* students regardless of, for example, gender, social class or culture;
- the *exceptional* shared needs of students who experience, for example, hearing impairment, autism and learning difficulties. (Adapted from O'Brien 1998)

Addressing individual needs is about *inclusion*, and this is achieved by ensuring that all young people receive their entitlement to music education. Inclusion is also achieved thorough effective *differentiation*, and effective differentiation is about ensuring that the learning we plan is appropriate for the needs, interests and aspirations of all students in our classes and thus facilitating their musical development. Effective differentiation results in *accessibility* both within the curriculum *and* the extended curriculum, i.e. those activities outside of timetabled music lessons. An *accessible* music curriculum recognises the right of every young person to teaching and learning that inspires and motivates them to be the best musician they can be in a way that is *relevant* to them. Task 12.1 asks you to consider how your needs have been met as a learner in music education.

Task 12.1 Exploring how your personal needs have been met

Identify the individual needs you have had as a developing musician. Think about individual needs, not only in terms of 'difficulties' you may have experienced but also in terms of your aspirations and interests. Discuss with other beginner teachers both your own and their individual needs, and the extent to which these have been met through formal and informal music education.

Some principles of inclusion

The National Curriculum for England (DfE 2013a) is underpinned by some fundamental principles of inclusion which can be aligned to those identified by O'Brien (see Box 12.1). As you plan your teaching, you can evaluate the extent to which your lessons address these principles. Task 12.2 provides you with an opportunity to explore your understanding of these principles.

Box 12.1 Some principles of inclusion

1   Setting suitable challenges for all students (addressing common needs).
2   Responding to students' diverse needs (their individual and unique needs).
3   Overcoming potential barriers for individuals and groups of students (their exceptional shared needs).

Adapted from National Curriculum for England (DfE 2013a) and O'Brien (1998).

Task 12.2 Exploring your understanding of the principles of inclusion

Using each of these principles of inclusion as a heading, make lists of your thoughts on them as indicated in italics:

1   Setting suitable challenges (common needs) – *list some of the possible learning challenges in music. How might the challenges you set differ throughout the age and attainment range?*
2   Responding to students' diverse needs (individual and unique needs) – *list as many individual needs as you can. What might be the effect of the need on the young person's learning if not addressed by the teacher?*
3   Overcoming potential barriers for individuals and groups of students (exceptional shared needs) – *What kinds of barriers to learning do you think exist and have come across in your own school context? How might you adapt your material or design your tasks to remove the barriers?*

You may wish to return to this task from time to time, adapting your suggestions in the light of further reflection or additional information.

It can be argued that the *common* needs of students are addressed by the National Curriculum, which represents an entitlement to music education, although it is the role of the music teacher to set *suitable learning challenges* within the context of this curriculum. The *unique* needs of all students can be addressed by *responding to their diverse learning needs* through well-differentiated planning and strategies for learning. The *exceptional shared needs* of students (embracing what is referred to as special educational needs) can be addressed through *overcoming barriers* to their learning. Later in this chapter we shall consider each of these principles in turn and exemplify them through case study examples.

Identifying students' individual needs, interests and aspirations

In order to cater for individual needs, you need to know your students and understand them as musicians. One of the best ways (indeed, perhaps the only way) of doing this is to observe them participating *in music*, paying attention to the ways in which they make and respond to music. As we have stressed elsewhere, a good music lesson is one in which youngsters are actively engaged in performing, composing and responding to music for the majority of the time. For example, when students enter secondary school for this first time, it may be a good idea to conduct a series of diagnostic activities over the first term as they settle into their new school environment. These might include call and response, singing or rhythm work that enables you to observe simple musical skills such as the ability to recall and imitate pitch and rhythm. Simple whole-class songs or instrumental performances will allow you to observe students as they engage with music making: furthermore, their response to a composing or improvising stimulus can provide important information on creativity. By being aware of where students are at in terms of their musical development, we can ensure that we plan appropriate learning for their individual needs, and this helps to secure motivation for future learning.

It is important in all lessons to allow yourself some time to stand to one side and observe students working, and then use this information in planning future lessons. This will involve you in assessment for learning, which includes:

· gathering and interpreting evidence about students' learning; and
· using that evidence to decide where students are in their learning, where they are going and how to take the next steps.

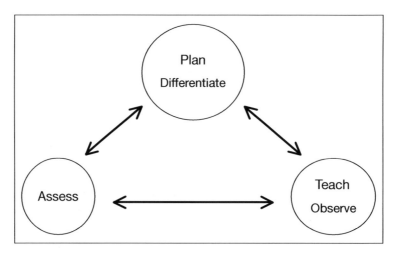

Figure 12.1 The teaching continuum

It is clear, therefore, that we should be monitoring the effects of our differentiation on young people's achievement and using these observations to inform our teaching and future planning. Thus, the processes of planning for differentiation, teaching, observing and assessment for learning creates a continuum (see Figure 12.1).

Task 12.3 Applying one's own understanding of individual needs

Choose a class that you know and have taught or observed extensively, and ask yourself the following questions:

- What could I tell a visitor about the musical attainment of each student in this class? In other words, do you know what the young people in your class know, understand and can do?
- Am I offering all students in this class an opportunity to succeed by showing what *they* know, understand and can do?
- Are they all engaged in musical learning?
- Can everyone access the work? For example, have I planned for students with physical disabilities?

We return now to the three principles of inclusion identified earlier in this chapter, to discuss the implications of each for planning and teaching.

Setting suitable challenges (common needs)

It is important that all young people are given opportunities to experience success, and also progress in their musical learning. In order that this can occur, they need to be presented with content and tasks that are appropriate to their developmental levels and individual needs. This process is called differentiation. Differentiation can mean a variety of things, from structural differentiation through streaming and banding to individualised learning packages. For the purposes of this chapter, however, we assume that differentiation is the process through which you identify the most effective learning and teaching strategies for each learner and/or groups of learners. The aim of differentiation is that by understanding differences between students you can bring about achievement, develop self-esteem and sustain motivation for *all*. As Green says, 'In addressing differentiation we are recognising and celebrating the range of different strategies that pupils use in order to learn, as well as the different rates at which they might learn' (Green 1997: 9).

Indeed, it can be argued that differentiation is synonymous with good teaching. Differentiation is a broad concept, and in planning for differentiation Dickinson and Wright (1993) have established a model which is set out in Figure 12.2.

We now briefly explore the implications of each aspect of the model for teaching and learning music.

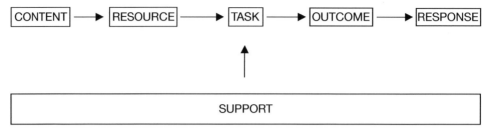

Figure 12.2 A model for differentiation

Differentiation by content

It could be argued that it is not appropriate for all students to study the same content at the same time in the same classroom, and the National Curriculum does not demand this. Providing a range of lesson content to suit different groups of students could be a more effective way of addressing their needs. For example, there is no reason why one group should not be working on creating a cover version of a current popular song while others are composing in response to a painting, if this best enables individual needs to be met. The organisational aspects of such a strategy might seem daunting, but it could be argued that music is particularly well placed to achieve this through composition and performance activities. Such an approach could certainly flourish with GCSE or AS/A level classes, which often involve smaller groups and opportunities for more individualised work.

Differentiation by resource

The possible variety implied by the differentiation of content, and when youngsters are composing, performing and responding to music, requires a rich range of resources that can be carefully matched to their needs. For example, it is important that our collection of recordings enable, as far as is possible, students to experience music 'authentically' when we use recorded music to stimulate and support their work. Resources are also important when addressing any barriers to learning. For example, technology can often be used to enable all (including those with special educational needs) to demonstrate and develop their creativity.

Differentiation by task

Differentiation by task involves providing a range of activities matched to students' levels of development, interests and aspirations. This can be particularly appropriate for performing activities, where roles in a classroom ensemble, for example, can be differentiated according to their individual skills and attainment. What is of critical importance is that, however simple or difficult the task, it should be perceived by the students as being of musical value and worth performing.

It is also possible to differentiate composing tasks by, for example, adapting the brief, the stimulus or structure to meet the needs of all students in the class. It is often the case in composing activities that group work is adopted as a method of organisation at Key Stage 3 and where young people can provide mutually beneficial (and differentiated) support to each other. Differentiated composing tasks are perhaps less problematic when there is the possibility of individualised work at GCSE or A level or when using music technology.

Differentiated tasks that require students of all levels to respond to music can be planned through types of questions (both verbal and written) which allow them to show what they understand and know. The use of probing questions can also extend lines of thought or help them to think in greater depth about their work.

Differentiation by outcome

Differentiation by outcome involves the setting of a task that allows each youngster to accomplish it according to their developmental level. Indeed, there is a sense in which music differentiates itself by engagement (see Swanwick 1988). This is especially so in areas of problem solving involving composing and responding to music, where students can engage with the music at their own particular level of musical development. This means that they can work in the same groups on the same projects even if their engagement is qualitatively different. Nevertheless, care needs to be taken to ensure that higher-attaining youngsters are challenged and lower-attaining youngsters are given sufficient and appropriate support.

Differentiation by support and response

Differentiation by support and response is often an intuitive part of the teaching process; we tailor our support, including our verbal feedback, according to the individual needs of our students (assessment for learning). It can, however, go beyond this to providing support from learning support/teaching assistants, visiting instrumental staff and by liaising with outside agencies such as the local music hub to provide specialist support for higher-attaining youngsters. It is also possible to use students at different levels of attainment to work with one another to extend the learning of all.

Understanding and being able to draw on these forms of differentiation is a critical skill for effective inclusive learning. Task 12.4 asks you to consider the forms in relation to your own experiences, while Task 12.5 involves planning lessons using appropriate forms of differentiation.

Task 12.4 The forms of differentiation

Evaluate the forms of differentiation you have witnessed or used so far. Map your observations against the headings in the model above (Figure 12.2). In what ways have the forms of differentiation manifested themselves in your experience thus far? For each mode of differentiation, imagine and note further examples of music that could be used.

Discuss the results of this exercise with your mentor and/or other beginner teachers.

Task 12.5 Planning for differentiation

Imagine you have a Year 7 class of twenty-five youngsters. Six students in the class have instrumental lessons either in or out of school and you are aware that some have had a year of 'First Access' whole-class instrumental learning in their primary school (mainly clarinets, ukuleles and djembes). Many of the class seem quite 'intuitive' musicians, although few are 'readers' of music. One or two students have coordination problems but enjoy the subject. There is a wide range of ability in terms of reading and writing the English language.

Plan one or two lessons that involve performing, composing and responding to music for this class on a topic of your choice. What planned differentiation is appropriate?

Points to consider:

- the core knowledge and understanding you want for all as a result of the lesson(s);
- identifying and allocating parts and roles in performance;
- extending the most able;
- supporting the learning of the less able (N.B. the notion of 'more' and 'less' able is not solely about the ability to perform on an instrument);
- resources: How can any worksheets you use be differentiated? Are instructions and questions suitable for all students? What types of questions can you use: open, closed?

Differentiation is a complex and challenging process for the beginner teacher to implement, but as with most dimensions to pedagogy, these skills can be learnt, and the much of the best practice lies with teaching music musically.

Responding to young students' diverse needs (individual and unique needs)

We have a duty to plan for all of our students to have equal access to the music curriculum, including girls and boys, those from diverse cultural and social backgrounds, those with special learning needs, those with English as a second language and youngsters with mental or physical disabilities. We discuss special learning needs later in the chapter, but we also need to be aware that their social and cultural experiences have a profound effect on how students might respond to the materials and activities presented to them in school. As Green suggests:

> ... children from different large-scale social groups tend, by varying degrees, to be involved in different musical practices, to attach different meanings to music, to prefer different kinds of music, and to relate differently to music as individuals within their

groups. These differences occur not only in their lives outside the school, but also their engagement with music in school.

(Green 2001: 51)

The ways in which music is created, disseminated and received vary considerably between different musical styles and genres. For example, the role of notation in rock music is much different to the role it plays in western art music. Furthermore, the division of the roles of composer, performer and audience articulated in western art music have little relevance in some genres of African music. Children come into school with sets of musical values, priorities and aspirations derived from the musical practices that they have engaged with as part of the various social or cultural groups to which they belong. Some awareness of these differences can help us greatly in our planning and teaching.

It is impossible in a chapter of this length to discuss addressing the complete range of individual and unique needs in the classroom, and so we will explore this principle through a case study example based on gender. Equality of access to the music curriculum for boys and girls is, of course, an issue of individual need. We discuss this particular individual need by way of illustrating the range of issues that arise when responding to wider diverse needs, and possible approaches adopted to address them.

Case study example: gender and music education

For some time there has been concern expressed over the underachievement of boys in our education system (Younger and Warrington 1996; Francis 2000). In addition, a growing body of research in music education (Green 1996; Hallam 1998; Wright 2001) has high-lighted the importance of understanding gender differences and the broader social influences that affect the relationship between gender and achievement in music. It is important that teachers embrace these issues and devise appropriate learning strategies to address them.

The following issues appear to arise from research into gender and society, gender and music, gender and music education:

* the general underachievement of boys in music at school;
* the apparent paradox that boys are disproportionately over-represented in the music profession;
* the stereotypical patterns of achievement and attitude among boys and girls at school;
* the gendered meanings placed on music, which are determined by the structure and nature of society;
* the 'loss' of a female history of music.

These issues are further amplified by quotations from the literature in Box 12.2.

Box 12.2 Gender and music education

Boys have traditionally been under represented among those learning to play an instrument. Approximately twice as many girls play instruments as boys. Girls also do better in school music examinations. Despite this there appear to be no gender differences in measures of musical ability on music tests.

(Hallam, 1998: 55)

It is now known that women have been involved as performers and composers in all periods of history from antiquity to the present day – one consistent factor is that women have tended to work in specialised areas of music rather than across the whole musical field as represented by men of their area.

(Green 1996: 41)

Historically, men have dominated the music profession as composers, conductors and performers in jazz and pop groups. It is therefore perhaps surprising that, given the predominance of successful male role models, the explanation for the greater numbers of girls learning to play instruments, singing in choirs and being involved in other musical activities is seen as reflecting the stereotyped views of music as being a 'feminine' activity.

(Hallam 1998: 55)

Green's research (1996b) into music teachers found that they said the following things about *girls*: they sing, prefer keyboard or orchestral instruments, are better at playing classical music, are committed, are conservative composers, are less imaginative than boys, are in the main mediocre.

Green's research into music teachers found that they said the following things about *boys*: they don't sing, prefer electric guitars and drums and attendant pop music, are aesthetically adventurous in composition, are a rare breed yet often gifted and creative.

A great deal of music by women composers has been denigrated for its effeminacy; other music has been more favourably received as displaying positive feminine attributes such as delicacy or sensitivity; a tiny amount of music by women has been incredulously hailed as equal to music by men.

(Green 1996: 127)

Task 12.6 Gender and music education

Think about your own experiences as a musician and music teacher. Consider the following questions in the light of personal experience:

- Are there any gender patterns to those who adopt various roles in the music industry: teachers/composers/conductors/instrumentalists e.g. drummers, flautists, guitarists?
- In what ways are girls' and boys' behaviours similar or different in music lessons?
- Are there differences in achievement between girls and boys across the different areas of the music curriculum: performing, composing and responding?
- Which instruments do boys and girls choose?
- Is there a gender difference in the uptake of GCSE music?
- Have you used or experienced the use of the work of female musicians and/or composers as examples in music lessons?
- Can you explain the differences between girls' and boys' achievement and involvement in music (both in and out of school)?

This case study aims to exemplify how we might understand individual and unique needs, and the following strategies are suggested as ways in which gender issues might be addressed in the music classroom:

- making sure that you value a wide range of style, genre and tradition, and where possible providing opportunities for all to pursue their interests;
- being sensitive to the possible perception by boys that making music and especially classical music is a 'feminine' activity;
- promoting singing among boys, e.g. boys-only vocal groups;
- providing access to a wide range of instruments, technology and vocal work for all;
- being sensitive to the 'lost' history of the female in music and to curriculum materials that explore women's role in music, e.g. by playing music by women composers from all traditions;
- being open to the possibility that the history of music is an opportunity to explore the gender issue as part of the music lesson;
- avoiding making assumptions based on gender by offering both sexes the same opportunities.

As can be seen, these strategies are a judicious mix of positive discrimination and equality of access. The social and cultural forces that promote gender differences in the classroom are powerful, and given that the classroom is only a microcosm of wider society, gender is a tough issue to address, but one where teachers *can* have an impact.

Overcoming potential barriers for individuals and groups of students (exceptional shared needs)

In addition to the common and individual needs of all students, there are also those who have exceptional shared learning needs for whom we need to provide relevant learning experiences. These exceptional needs fall into the following categories:

- those who are exceptionally able;
- those with specific physical and/or learning difficulties;
- those with emotional and behavioural difficulties.

There is a legal imperative for young people's exceptional needs to be catered for; for example, see Box 12.3 in relation to disability. While such legislation can present many challenges for schools, such needs can *largely* be met by planned support and the differentiation of materials and tasks. We have a responsibility to plan for adequate time, classroom organisation and access to equipment such that *all* can participate effectively in music education. Part of this will involve you in identifying areas of the curriculum that may present particular problems for specific individuals such that you are able to plan for their participation.

Box 12.3 Students with disabilities

All schools have duties under the Equality Act 2010 towards individual disabled children and young people. They **must** make reasonable adjustments, including the provision of auxiliary aids and services for disabled children, to prevent them being put at a substantial disadvantage. These duties are anticipatory – they require thought to be given in advance to what disabled children and young people might require and what adjustments might need to be made to prevent that disadvantage.

(DfE/DfH 2015, Special Educational Needs and
Disability Code of Practice: 0 to 25 years [Para 6.9])

The first point of reference is usually the young person's Statement of Special Educational Needs or Learning Disability Assessment. These are gradually being transferred to a more integrated system of Education, Health and Care (EHC) plans as a result of the Children and Families Act (2014). Such documents detail the exact nature of the physical or learning difficulties faced by the youngster. While the needs of these students can be met to a large extent by differentiation, you may also need recourse to specially adapted equipment. Those with physical and other learning needs may well have access to a learning support assistant, and it is important that you involve these professionals in your planning and preparation. They are likely to know an individual very well and can make a valuable contribution to you differentiating for their needs. Together you can form a powerful team to maximise an individual's and/or groups of students' musical learning.

Case study example 1: exceptionally able students

The concept of inclusion covers the full spectrum of attainment. In providing for the most able, it is important that there is an early identification of their learning potential. Once this has been established, you can plan for them to be challenged through enriching and extending activities.

Pratt and Stephens (1995) suggest a number of ways in which the exceptionally able student might be identified. These include the ability to memorise music quickly and accurately, demonstrating a strong creative impulse and sensitivity to musical expression, possessing a particular affinity with a musical instrument or being able sing accurately in tune with natural expression.

Differentiation for these youngsters can include the following strategies:

- providing tasks of well-defined challenge;
- setting high expectations in terms of outcomes;
- challenging them through the use of a wide range of ICT software and hardware;
- directing them to opportunities for guided independent study and research;
- allowing them access to work from a later key stage or to work with others from older age groups (i.e. considering stage rather than age);
- developing a rich range of supporting resources;
- open-ended problem solving, e.g. self-directed learning;
- allowing them a role in the teaching of their peers, i.e. when we teach, we learn.

Case study example 2: using technology to support students with learning difficulties and/or physical difficulties

Technology offers one of the most important means of access to music for young people with exceptional needs. Some examples include:

- Using a touch-screen tablet with an 'app' connected to suitable amplification.
- Touch-panels that 'sound', connected to MIDI software. These panels can be sensitive to pressure, speed and touch, and represent a good way of accessing musical improvisation and composition for all students.
- Light beams that stimulate electronic sounds when interrupted in different ways by any part of the body. Similarly, these can be sensitive to the speed and type of movement.
- Software that utilises 'blocks' of sounds or samples and takes away many of the technical and physical barriers to composition and performance, but still allows young people to structure the 'blocks' and samples into real compositions and arrangements.

Interactive whiteboard technology also offers great benefits to those with exceptional learning needs. For example, a tablet can be used to allow students with limited mobility to control the board from their seat, while large fonts and bright colours may help visually impaired youngsters to see the display more clearly.

Case study example 3: students with emotional and behavioural difficulties

Young people with emotional and behavioural difficulties (EBD) can find composing, performing and responding to music a challenge. Furthermore, those with EBD can find the idea of self-expression and creativity somewhat daunting in a whole-class situation. However, Packer (1987, 1996) offers the following positive advice when differentiating for EBD in the music classroom:

1   Conform to a primary 'project'-based model; for example, try to tie the work in with other extra-musical ideas and areas of the curriculum.
2   Make the work active and fun.
3   Try to build in some familiarity. Students with EBD can identify with the familiar and can be resistant to change.
4   Build in early success. Allowing these students to succeed can be the most valuable thing you can do for them.
5   Dare to be imaginative and unconventional. Explore new ways of working that allow them to succeed, and focus on what they can do and not what they can't.

As can be seen, much of what constitutes effective music teaching applies to *all* students whether or not they have EBD. For example, music lessons should always be *musical*, with plenty of opportunities for composing, improvising, performing and responding. Where appropriate, various levels of structure can be included (the discipline of music itself is very good at providing this if we allow it), and yet more open-ended approaches are also possible once good relationships have been established. As ever, it is important to celebrate and record success.

Most of these strategies have the potential for being fully integrated into the music classroom alongside all other individual needs. As with all exceptional shared needs, however, there is a danger that differentiation for such young people is seen as being something special and apart from the rest of the class. One of the most powerful features of music as discipline is that it is capable of embracing participants of all types and with a wide range of needs. If the music classroom is to be truly inclusive, in line with the UNESCO statement at the head of this chapter, then such equality of opportunity is an imperative.

Inclusion and the extended curriculum

So far this chapter has explored inclusion from the perspective of the classroom. Also important is how we ensure that musical activity in schools beyond the curriculum is accessible to all youngsters and meets their interests and needs. A school that prides itself on excellence in public performance might actually be less successful than it seems if you consider it from a perspective of inclusion and equality of opportunity. Is the *number* of young people involved in the extended curriculum actually a good indicator in this respect? What other measures could you use to assess inclusion in the extra-curricular offer? One possibility here is to make sure that there are opportunities for the work of the classroom to be both fully represented and developed in the extended curriculum.

Task 12.7 Inclusion and the extended curriculum

How can the extended curriculum be adapted to meet the needs of all youngsters? Make notes, using the principles and issues of inclusion explored in this chapter.

Summary

Providing access to the music curriculum for all students is not an easy task, but it is at the heart of the music teacher's work. Ensuring equality of opportunity involves a good deal of thought and hard work, but can be achieved with creative teaching and music making. If we are committed to a truly liberal education – one that develops the whole person – then music as a way of knowing and means of expression is a fundamental entitlement of our young people. In this chapter we have noted that:

- the National Curriculum has a strong statement on inclusion and we have a duty to ensure that all have access to a broad and balanced music curriculum irrespective of race, gender, social background or ability;
- we achieve inclusion by setting suitable learning challenges, responding to diverse learning needs and overcoming potential barriers to learning and assessment;
- differentiation allows us to provide suitable learning opportunities for individual needs, although we may also need to make special provision for those with specific learning requirements;
- whatever their needs, young people need to be motivated to learn, and this can be achieved by providing a music curriculum that is relevant to their musical interests and aspirations.

Go now to the Appendix to this chapter where we will explore greater depth issues around music education and special educational needs with Sally Zimmermann.

Further reading

Green, L. (1997) *Music, Gender, Education*, Cambridge: Cambridge University Press.
Ockelford, A. (2008) *Music for Children and Young People with Complex Needs*, Oxford: Oxford University Press.
Packer, Y. (1987) *Musical Activities for Children with Behavioural Problems*, London: Disabled Living Foundation.
Patterson, A. and Zimmerman, S. (2006) *No Need for Words: Special Needs and Music Education*. Online, available from The UK Association for Music Education – Music Mark: Musicmark.org.uk (accessed 3 March 2016)
Wright, R. (2001) 'Gender and achievement: the view from the classroom', *British Journal of Music Education*, 18, 3: 275–291.

These publications offer an analysis of gender and EBD issues and also suggest possible strategies for addressing these individual learning needs in the classroom.

Appendix: music education and 'special educational needs' – definitions, challenges, opportunities

An interview with Sally Zimmermann, conducted by Gary Spruce.

Introduction

Sally Zimmermann has been music adviser at the Royal National Institute of Blind People (RNIB) since 1994, before which she worked in mainstream and special schools in London as a music teacher and music and communication tutor. She has written and presented widely on music education with children who have learning difficulties and recently has been involved in the 'Sounds of Intent' project with the Institute of Education, at the University of London, which has been looking at the musical behaviour and development in children with complex needs.

Could you begin by saying what would be your starting point for thinking about special education needs?

I think we need to step back and start from the premise that as a teacher in a school we have a responsibility for musically educating, engaging, encouraging and sustaining all young people. There is then a need to give particular attention to two particular groups: first, those formally labelled as having special educational needs (SEN) and, second, those whom you find hard to show are making progress in your lessons. You need to find time to identify each cohort and you have a particular responsibility towards those young people who fall into both groups.

How are these young people identified?

It's a relative definition of pupils who are basically not coping with the local offer. So you could have a school with a very high proportion of pupils who, for want of a much better description, are low-level learners and therefore SEN doesn't come into the equation because that's the level that you're pitching your work at. Conversely, you could be working in a grammar school setting, where your definition of SEN is completely different.

So it's context bound then? A child can be SEN in one context and not in another?

It's meant to be context bound, and it's meant to relate to young people who can't do what is the norm in that context.

This goes right back to the Warnock Report (1978) and the whole concept of special educational needs. Warnock was very keen that young people didn't get labelled, but unfortunately this is still what happens. Currently, about 1.6 million children in England form the SEN cohort – that is one in every five pupils – and 2.8 per cent of pupils have Statements. The original Code of Practice (2001) divided the types of need into four groupings which are still in use, if a little tired. These groups are

- Communication and interaction
- Cognition and learning
- Behaviour, emotional and social development
- Sensory and/or physical.

How can we ensure that children with formally identified SEN are included in music lessons?

I think that there are two linked issues here: social inclusion and educational inclusion.

In terms of the former, one key issue is how children with SEN – and particularly those with communication issues – are 'included' in peer group working, and this needs thinking hard about.

For example, you ask your class to go into groups, to choose a well-known song and make their own arrangement of this. How are the groups chosen? Have the class sorted themselves into friendship groups, and you have people left over? Do they arrange themselves into groups of their perceived music standards, letting the keen top groups do most the work? If you select the groups, do you go for consistency and building up working relationships, or for variety, including in the number in a group? Somehow in peer-led work you have to engineer the situation for groups to want to have pupils who work in different ways, or who struggle to keep up or who do not want to do what is decided by the majority.

Then there's the timid student who just does not want to sing or play. He may take a simple part given to him in rehearsal, but dare not play in the performance to the whole class. Perhaps this hesitation could be explored musically by using a drone in the piece, which moves from one player to another, perhaps overlapping. The shy person plays or sings this drone in turn without drawing attention to himself. This music merging into an established texture may produce emotionally valuable, and educationally assessable, results.

At the end of the practical task, rather than asking for a live performance to the class, recording in practice rooms and then playing back just the sound track, or even playing back other class's work for the mood analysis, defuses the social elements from the musical content and can sometimes be a more effective investment of time.

Children who are identified as having some form of special educational needs are sometimes accompanied in classes by support teachers or classroom assistants. Are there any particular issues here for music teachers?

Liaising with support staff can be particularly tricky for music teachers. As music teachers work with many pupils, the sheer number of relationships to maintain is challenging. These classroom assistants can be immensely helpful in that they are often working with the same young person or groups of students across the most subjects and thus know them and provide continuity for them. However, they also come with their own memories and expectations of music lessons, which may not accord with what you are trying to achieve in your classroom (or they may not understand what you are trying to achieve), and this 'dissonance', if communicated to the young people, has the potential for making the world more baffling for pupils and stressful for teachers. Making music involves risk taking. At Key Stage 3, music teachers trust pupils to work independently. Support staff might be better researching and preparing accessible resources rather than sitting in on rehearsals, restricting peer social dynamics.

Could you describe some of the particular barriers and issues around communication and interaction, sensory, the cognition and learning and ways of addressing these?

OK. So let's take examples of children who have different kinds of special needs. Let's say in relation to communication, behaviour, cognition and hearing and visual impairment.

Communication

For those young people who experience difficulties with communication, I think music has great power and is possibly unique in terms of how it can engage those young people who find it hard to express themselves and/or listen to someone else and to take on board what they're saying. The effectiveness of a music lesson with these young people is often related to the amount of music going on in a lesson vs the amount of teacher talk. My advice would always be that the more music and the less talk there is, the more chance there is that you're going to 'catch' those for whom talk is a problem area, potential conflict or 'wind-up' situation or whatever. I think music has a huge amount to offer for these young people.

Autism

The chances are that the young person with autism is not going to appear to be listening to any of your opening exposition at the beginning of a class where you are recapping on what you did last week. Not likely to put his or her hand up when you're asking the class to say what happens next or what they did last week. Not going to volunteer to go off in a group etc. but more likely to be fiddling with the wires on a keyboard that aren't straight. What are you going to do? OK, one strategy is that you can just let him drift, and providing he's not going to come to any harm then he's getting something from just hearing the music that's going on around. That's the baseline.

But how can we build on this? One way is to see if you can find the opportunity to observe what he does and if there is something that you can pick up on and use as a musical feature. If the young person is pacing up and down at the back of the room, it may be that that pace is actually related to something you're doing musically. In fact it's quite likely it is, because we're talking about fairly base human responses here – of engagement with a beat or pulse. You then might be able to work with his pulse. Then, as soon as you've got a musical gesture, you've got something you can work with.

Then, when everybody else goes off in groups to do something, you can go and spend some time not necessarily talking to this young person, but replicating the gesture or making up a sound that goes with it and see if you can get some sort of musical engagement going. There may well be other students in the class (particularly by the time you get to Year 9) who might be very good at helping with this, because they've been with this young person day in, day out. You might be seeing hundreds of children in a week, but the child with autism is in that class all the time and all the other young people have had the time and opportunity to work out far more sophisticated strategies for working with him or her than you have.

Cognition

There's often a lot of counting involved in performing music. Working in music with a child who has no concept of number presents particular challenges. So, in this example, the group were composing answering phrases, we had done quite a lot of clapping work and we'd realised that even if you clap a different answer to an opening phrase given by somebody in the class, the chances were it was the same length. Anyway, this girl was fine doing this sort of activity, but when they were sent away to go and pair up and clap question and answer phrases, she'd lost this idea of filling a measured space. So we looked at movement again and we did some work with her. We looked at the fact that she walked steadily from one side of the room to the other side, one side and then the other side, and while we were doing this, could we fill the time from one side to the other? We avoided counting, but had a physical measure. It also happened that in the corridor we had tiles, black and white tiles, and we could begin to pattern with what she was doing out there. So we avoided counting, but she was following a sequence that was visual.

Visual impairment

One of the important things to remember when working with children who have special educational needs is that it is possible to provide for their particular needs through an activity that all students can engage with and benefit from.

A class are exploring the fact that you can represent sounds with symbols. And they've been working for some time on how music has different textures – basically melody, harmony and a bass line – but you can put these textures together. They've been working in fours, and in one group there is a student who is blind, but intellectually she's probably in the top quarter of the class and she's having violin lessons. She's leading her group because it's actually easier for her to lead what's going on than to follow subtle gestures.

Her group, which includes three other girls, are working well. She's playing a melody on her violin and there's the keyboard and bass guitar and drums. They begin to think how they are going to represent their music. The other girls are all very happy to raid their pencil boxes and make representations of the music on paper. But the blind girl is struggling to know what to do.

What the classroom assistant comes up with is a huge floor tile covered in Blu-Tack and the blind girl starts putting plaster and string and shapes on it, but delineating the four lines and checking the verticality of it to check that she's got the drum part in alignment with the signs. The other girls, of course, are far more interested in this than in their own little two-dimensional pictures, and they chip in. The child does Braille labels and the other girls want to know what the Braille labels mean, so they do little translation labels. Eventually, at the end of the topic, after they've performed it and after the rest of the class have looked at each other's scores, they actually like the blind student's score quite a lot, because more of them can look at it because it's bigger. There is a slight problem about mounting the results up on the board, and so a digital photograph of the tile is taken.

So not only was the blind student absolutely involved in doing exactly what the rest of the class were doing, not only was she learning about the symbolic representation of music, which is actually quite hard for a blind person to realise because music is just out there as an aural phenomenon, but she's been teaching her peers about how she can manipulate in two dimensions, how she can label things up and understand what the labels are etc. There's been a lot of additional awareness built up in this class, not about disability but about *difference*.

Hearing impairment

In the world of hearing impairment, the musical connection is made through the vibrations that things produce and feed back, so one important thing to note is that if you are using digital technologies, these might not produce these acoustic vibrations on which the hearing-impaired pupil depends. So this might mean getting the huge bass xylophone out, as a change from keyboards with headphones. Somewhere lurking in the classroom there are still things, pieces of wood, that will amplify sound for you, and again it's a journey that you can take as a group, at least a group in your class, if not the whole class. It's part of the culture in your class that this is how a particular person is learning, and we are all going to share in that learning and find out a bit more about vibro-acoustics.

What support is available for young people who have identified special needs and those who teach them?

Just as SENCOs draw on outside assistance for particular types of disability and special need, so music teachers can draw on music organisations for help. Every school in England falls within a 'music hub', and schools are encouraged to ask their hub for support. Many hubs themselves have partners who regularly work with young people with SEN, those from disadvantaged backgrounds and those deemed at risk of harm. Several high-profile groups, including Youth Music and Sing Up, have had remits to reach all young people.

There are also extensive special arrangements in place for students with SEN and/or disabilities with all the grade music examination boards as well as through the Joint Council for Qualifications for GCSE and A level examinations. (The current JCQ guidance runs to 114 pages.) Modified papers for candidates with sensory impairments and permission for the use of word processing, readers and amanuenses can all be requested. All special arrangements are based on the candidate's normal way of working.

A whole industry of special music technology has arisen and is widely used in special schools, but is yet to make a significant impact in mainstream schools. Soundbeam (www.soundbeam.co.uk), Skoog (www.skoogmusic.com), Apollo Creative (www.apollo creative.co.uk) and Optimusic (www.optimusic.co.uk) can give whole classes a chance to return to basic musical elements, with those with and those without the dexterity or physical control to play conventional instruments on an equal footing.

Finally, we hide ourselves in music and we use music to find ourselves. We use music to get us going and we use music to calm us. Music is the subject we learn before we are born and stays with us to our dying moments. For many of those for whom the rest of school can be a struggle, music lessons can be the key to success.

Task 12.8 Supporting children with SEN in music lessons

Take the plan for a lesson that you have previously taught and, drawing on your learning from this chapter and the previous one, annotate or rework it in order to include and accommodate a young person identified as having special needs. You may be drawing on the young person's learning plan or statement. However, it is more likely that you will be drawing on your own observations and experiences of this youngster within a music-specific learning environment.

Write a short commentary that outlines how you will:

- enable the communication, behavioural, cognitive, hearing or visual needs of the young person to be met;
- ensure that the young person is fully included in the musical activities that take place;
- draw on the musical and social skills of the other young people in supporting and including the young person.

In addition, describe how in teaching the lesson and meeting the needs of the young person, the class come to understand the needs of the young person as an issue of 'difference' rather than 'disability'.

13 Assessment in music education

Chris Philpott with Keith Evans

Introduction

Derek Rowntree (1977) poses the following questions about assessment: Why assess? What is there to assess? How do we assess? How do we interpret? How do we respond?

Our answers to these questions are, to a certain extent, governed by our views on the very nature of music itself. In this sense assessment is never neutral but, along with most other aspects of education, contested. The 'what' and the 'how' of assessment in music have always been a source of controversy, and different ideologies have placed a different emphasis on the relative importance of certain types of musical knowledge.

In this chapter we promote the following values in relation to assessment in music education:

- Assessment is about coming to know the musical understandings of the students we teach and thus coming to know the effectiveness of our own teaching. It also involves students knowing themselves and knowing each other (see Rowntree 1977).
- After Swanwick we argue that 'to teach is to assess' (1988: 149). In coming to know the musical understandings of our students, assessment is not a 'bolt-on' to the process of learning and teaching but woven intricately into it.
- We need to devise methods of assessment that are 'fit for purpose', i.e. that are able to help us come to know our students in relation to all types of musical knowledge and understandings.
- We need to make that which is most important to us assessable, rather than that which is easily assessable important. Assessment should be about that which is intrinsically musical in music, no matter how tough this task is.

Objectives

By the end of this chapter you should be able to:

- understand the nature of assessment *for* learning in music education;
- know how questioning can be used formatively;

(continued)

(continued)

- know how to use feedback formatively;
- understand how self- and peer-assessment can be used to enhance musical learning;
- understand assessment *of* learning in music;
- understand the issues that arise when making any assessment judgements about music;
- understand these issues in the context of self-directed musical learning.

Before reading on, we suggest that you address Task 13.1 to explore your own experiences of assessment.

Task 13.1 Looking back at assessment

In what ways have you been aware of being assessed in music? What was assessed and how were you assessed? Draw up a table of your memories and share with other beginner teachers and your mentor.

Ways of coming to know students as musicians

In one way, music is the most assessed of disciplines both in the school context and beyond; for example, graded examinations, competitions, tests of musical ability and the 'pop charts'. We are used to placing values on musical products of all types, although this experience has sometimes caused a rather skewed view of what counts as assessment in music.

There are two broad ways of categorising assessment, listed in Box 13.1.

Box 13.1 Two categories of assessment

Assessment for learning	Assessment of learning
Formative assessment – questioning, feedback, target setting, discussing criteria, 'closing the gap' activities, self-assessment e.g. in relation to performance or composition	Summative assessment – performance examination, composition portfolio, written tests, aural tests, tests of musical ability
Divergent assessment – open style, facilitating approach, pupil focused: 'any assessment for which the first priority is to serve the purpose of promoting students' learning . . . it is usually informal, embedded in all aspects of teaching and learning . . . (and this) becomes formative assessment when the evidence is used to adapt the teaching work to meet learning needs' (Black *et al.* 2003: 2)	Convergent assessment – closed style, 'can do' approach, teacher focused: 'for the league tables or the GCSEs, the main assessment methods are formal tests: these usually . . . involve tests that are infrequent, isolated from normal teaching and learning, carried out on special occasions with formal rituals . . .' (Black *et al.* 2003: 2)
What students know and can do	*Whether* students know and can do

Each of these broad categories contains different ways in which *we* can come to 'know' the understandings of young people and ways in which they come to know themselves. However, there is a sense in which they represent a false distinction, for in the process of assessment *for* learning we constantly gain summative snapshots of our students, and summative 'results' from assessment *of* learning can and should be used formatively.

Task 13.2 Categorising assessment

Revisit Task 13.1 and Box 13.1.

* How do your own experiences of assessment fit into these categories?
* Which assessment styles have you used yourself as a teacher?
* Which styles have you observed in schools or other settings?
* Share your findings with another beginner teacher.

Assessment for learning in music

We will explore four ways in which teachers can develop formative assessment for learning in music education, i.e. questioning, feedback, self- and peer-assessment and the formative use of summative tests (Black *et al.* 2003).

Questioning

Questioning, as a strategy for coming to know our students, is an important tool for all teachers. Brown and Edmondson have suggested the following reasons for asking questions:

* to encourage thought and understanding of ideas and procedures;
* to check understanding, knowledge and skills;
* to gain attention and aid management;
* to review, revise, recall and reinforce;
* to teach the whole class through young people's answers;
* to give everyone a chance to answer;
* to use able students to encourage others;
* to draw in shyer students ;
* to probe after critical answers;
* to allow expression of feelings, views and empathy. (Brown and Edmonson 1984, quoted in Kyriacou 1991)

In relation to formative assessment for learning, the knowledge gained about young people by asking these questions enables the teacher to adapt their responses in order to maximise further learning. The assessment evidence derived from questioning can feed into planning and is also fully integrated with teaching itself.

Most questions can be categorised as *open* or *closed* and *high order* or *low order*. An open question might be: 'Is this a successful passage and if so, why?' A closed question could be: 'What style of music have we just listened to?' A lower-order question might simply ask the young person to identify the instrument that plays the opening fanfare, while a higher-order question might ask a young person to describe the way in which the music achieves a particular expressive effect.

Closed and lower-order questions are almost always capable of leading onto open and higher-order questions. So, a question concerning the identification of musical style can then lead on to the student being asked to justify their answer through reference to the music's character and using appropriate terminology. It follows that effective questioning can be used as a tool for differentiation and progression when teachers respond as a result of 'coming to know' the students in their classes.

Task 13.3 Questions in music education

Make a list of questions that you might ask students while they are working on a composition. If you have a particular situation in mind from your practice (observed or taught), use this. Box 13.2 will help you here.

Box 13.2 Questions in music education

In the music classroom, questioning can be used to:

1 focus attention on the music holistically: for example, the style of the music, or the general atmosphere created by it (What happens in this music? What is the music like?);
2 discriminate between the various strands of the music (How does the accompaniment contrast with and support the melody?);
3 identify how the interrelated dimensions of music contribute to the whole (How does the composer combine dynamics and speed in this piece and what effect is created?);
4 describe and specify (What musical device is used in the 'middle eight'?);
5 interpret and explain (What 'feel' is created by this music and how does the composer achieve this?);
6 analyse and synthesise (How does the composer achieve contrast?);
7 speculate and hypothesise (What would happen if we . . .?);
8 evaluate (Does this idea work, and if so why?).

Good practice in the use of questions as part of formative assessment for learning includes spending effort framing questions that are worth asking, i.e. questions that explore issues and develop students' understanding. It also involves allowing them the time to think, with an expectation that all contribute to the discussion, and then planning follow-up activities to check that the question has had an impact upon learning and teaching (see also Black *et al.* 2003). Such an approach to questioning places particular emphasis on the need to make students think, for thinking promotes the development of a rich understanding. Furthermore, open-ended questions have the greatest chance of making this happen.

The implications for music education are that questioning needs to be conducted in the spirit of musical criticism, and in this sense assessment for learning *is* musical criticism – not necessarily focused on the 'value' of the music but speculating on, hypothesising on and analysing what we hear or what we might hear. Assessment for learning as musical criticism also encourages students to ask their own questions as part of the critical process, when engaging in dialogue with teachers and peers alike.

One drawback of questioning is that it can lead to an over-reliance on verbal or written responses. One of the principles of assessment for learning is that students are given opportunities to show and develop their understanding through a variety of different media. To this end, musical criticism can be witnessed when, for example, they make music, move to music or create a sculpture in response to music.

Task 13.4 Observing questioning

In what ways do the teachers you have observed and/or been taught by use questions as a device for formative assessment for learning? Use Box 13.2 as a guide. Have you ever felt part of a dialogue with a teacher in the spirit of musical criticism? Compare your notes with another beginner teacher.

Feedback

An important part of formative assessment for learning is feedback. Vygotsky (1986) noted a psychological underpinning for the importance of feedback through what he called the zone of proximal development (ZPD). The ZPD is the gap between that which a young person can understand on their own and their potential understanding in collaboration with teachers or peers. The support offered to 'close the gap' between these points is known as 'scaffolding', and feedback is an important device for scaffolding to 'close the gap'. Good practice in feedback identifies what has been done well, identifies areas for development and suggests ways in which the improvements can take place.

In the music classroom we can interpret this as a three-part process, which is exemplified in Box 13.3. You are asked to reflect on this process in Task 13.5.

Task 13.5 Closing the gap in music

Reflect on some situations from your own learning, or learning you are now observing in school, and write down some scenarios for 'closing the gap' as seen in Box 13.3.

Box 13.3 Scaffolding in music to 'close the gap'

A blues improvisation (Key Stage 3)

1   Aleya, you have produced a lively improvisation over the riff.
2   Do you think you might try to 'swing' the music a little more, in keeping with the blues style?
3   We can try this together/Listen to Jono's group and join in with them/Listen to this CD.

A composition based on 'variation' (Key Stage 4)

1   Jack, I like the way in which your variations add 'ornaments' to the original tune.
2   What other ways are there for you to change this tune? Have you considered changing the timbres or accompaniment or key or harmony (with suitable models)?
3   Listen to John Iveson's *Frere Jacques* variations, make notes on what he does to the original tune and think about some further ideas for your piece.

Improvisation (Key Stage 5)

1   Dika, that was a really fluent improvised solo.
2   In this 'area of study' there is a wide range of approaches to improvisation, e.g. a more 'minimal' approach than you are currently engaging with.
3   Listen to some of the trumpet solos on Miles Davies' 'Kind of Blue'. Can you emulate some of the approaches he takes to improvisation?

Another important part of feedback in music is modelling. Indeed, part of the task to 'close the gap' might be for the young person to listen to musical models scaffolded by the teacher or indeed to 'jam' with them. This is the case with Aleya in Box 13.3. In some musical communities, where social learning is prevalent, this type of feedback happens all the time and is often unconsciously intuitive on the part of teachers and students alike.

It is entirely appropriate for teachers to make active interventions when feeding back on students' work, although this needs to be carefully judged. You need to become skilled at sensing when they need, and are open to, guidance. Unless you are sensitive to this, feedback and interventions in what is already a successful creative process can breed resentment and alienation. Feedback from a teacher is always on a spectrum from 'leave well alone' to more active interventions.

The effectiveness of feedback can also be enhanced if the criteria for success are shared and mutually understood between students and their teachers. Such criteria can include:

*   criteria from syllabi and curricula;
*   criteria devised by the teacher for what counts as success;
*   criteria devised by the students themselves for what counts as success;
*   criteria devised in a collaboration between the students and their teacher.

While we take a deeper look at criteria for success later in this chapter, it is clear that if both teacher and young person understand the criteria for success, feedback not only makes sense, but acts as a reference point for target setting and thus closing the gap.

Self-assessment

Sharing criteria is also vital to the process of self-assessment. If young people understand and are aware of criteria, they can assess themselves, but why would we want them to do this? Self-assessment has the following advantages:

*   It engages us actively in our own learning.
*   It breeds ownership and autonomy in learning.
*   It can promote thinking skills and metacognition (the conscious awareness of one's own thinking process).
*   It promotes an understanding of what we have learnt.
*   It promotes an understanding of how we have learnt.

However, there are also some dangers in self-assessment, for it can breed cynicism in a culture where there is an expectation for an external figure of authority to make judgements. The solutions to such issues lie in the careful modelling of self-assessment. If we are asking the right questions, i.e. questions that cause young people to think, and are also sharing criteria for success, then the process has the potential to deliver significant gains in motivation and ownership of learning. Self-assessment can breed an understanding of what has been learnt and also how the learning has taken place.

In self-assessment we can use the questioning skills developed earlier in the chapter. For example, as part of a composing task, the student's self-assessment could involve them reflecting on:

1   the musical content of their work (e.g. an analysis of the structure);
2   the creative process (how did the piece come about?);
3   what they have learnt by composing the piece;
4   how the piece relates to the brief and/or criteria for success;
5   the skills they have developed;
6   how their approach to composing might have developed as result of these reflections (Under what conditions am I at my best as a composer? What other conditions might facilitate me as a composer?).

Task 13.6 Writing a prompt for self-assessment

Using a recently completed project from one of your placement schools, write a series of self-assessment prompts for young people, using the ideas explored above.

Peer-assessment

Peer-assessment has all the benefits and issues associated with self-assessment for both the peer assessor and the person whose work is being assessed. For example, in the case of composition, the former gains a window into someone else's solution to a musical 'problem', and the latter gains a new perspective on their own work. However, letting another young person 'mark' your work can be problematic if not handled well, and such collaborative assessment needs a good deal of modelling and practice to make it work.

Peers can be asked to comment on the positive points they hear and to make polite suggestions for consideration in a spirit of musical criticism. While peer feedback *can* be based on criteria for success, there is no necessity for peers to give an overall grade, and we should remember to focus the formative process on learning. Indeed, Black *et al.* experimented with a 'comments only' approach to assessment and concluded that grades and marks offered by *anyone* are of relatively limited value to learning.

Formative use of summative tests

As a link to the section on the assessment of learning, it is worth looking at the formative potential of summative tests. If a teacher sets a test or examination and gives a mark or a grade in music, youngsters should always be encouraged to reflect on these 'results' and review what they tell them about their learning. This type of reflection can be used, for example, to set targets for learning and when preparing for further summative tests, e.g. as part of revision. There are also other ways in which they can be formatively engaged with the summative process:

- Students can be encouraged to set questions for themselves to help them understand the assessment process and to plan for their future development.
- Students can be given the opportunity, through self-assessment, to apply examination criteria to their compositions and performances and to rework them in light of this process.

The point is that summative tests can be seen as part of formative assessment *for* learning.

The formative styles of assessment noted above are of particular importance in the music classroom. At the outset we suggested that assessment methods need to be fit for purpose in order to 'get at' what is musical about music. The formative process allows students to behave musically and is flexible and open enough to be able to capture the nuances and subtleties of the discipline. If we believe that musical understanding is at the heart of musical learning, formative assessment for learning has a huge role to play when teachers facilitate and recognise this in the classroom. Assessment for learning is about allowing young people to become musicians and for teachers to come to know them as musicians.

Assessment of learning

While there is often a false distinction between assessment for learning and assessment of learning, there are times when we need to make summative judgements about our students.

Indeed, there is a long tradition of placing value on musical products, e.g. where a composition or performance is judged to be 'better' than another in a competition. The most fraught issue within summative assessment of learning is the writing and use of criteria for making these judgements. How do we write criteria when judging the creative process? How can we write criteria that capture what is musical about music? How can criteria be written that allow us to make judgements about compositions or performances from different styles and traditions? Such questions are at the heart of music education and our answers to them reveal the things we consider to be important in music. Having said this, the writing of criteria is notoriously difficult, and while this section of the chapter allows you to engage with these issues, it will not solve them!

Writing criteria for summative assessment of learning

The issues surrounding writing criteria are explored at first in relation to composition and performance at GCSE level. The assessment of creativity, imagination and craft in composition presents music educators with some of their biggest challenges, encompassing many of the problems inherent in making judgements about good and bad art. When writing and using criteria, we are always confronted by issues surrounding taste, values and subjectivity. GCSE awarding bodies have been bold in laying down criteria for judging composition, and Box 13.4 summarises some approaches to setting criteria for composition at GCSE level, taken from draft specifications submitted to Ofqual for approval in summer 2015.

Box 13.4   Approaches to assessing GCSE composition and example criteria

Pearson Edexcel

Each composition is marked out of 10 against three assessment grids: 1 Developing musical ideas, 2 Demonstrating technical control, 3 Composing with musical coherence.

From 2. Demonstrating technical control

    1-2 marks: Textures are narrow in scope and unvaried
    5-6 marks: There are no serious misjudgements in the handling of textures but they may lack variety
    9-10 marks: Textures are varied, complex, and/or clear as appropriate to the style.

Pearson Edexcel (2015)

AQA

Each composition is marked out of 6 against six assessment grids: 1 Rhythm and metre, 2 Texture and melody, 3 Harmony and tonality, 4 Timbre and dynamics, 5 Structure and form, 6 Composing log.

(continued)

Box 13.4 *(continued)*

From 1: Rhythm and metre

6 marks: It is expected that a minimum of **four** of the following techniques/devices will be in evidence: change of metre/compound time/augmentation/diminution/cross rhythm/syncopation/dotted rhythm/triplets/rubato/tempo change.

4 marks: It is expected that a minimum of **two** of the following techniques/devices will be in evidence: change of metre/compound time/augmentation/diminution/cross rhythm/syncopation/dotted rhythms/triplets/rubato/tempo change.

From 2: Texture and melody

6 marks: It is expected that a minimum of **four** of the following techniques/devices will be in evidence: homophonic and polyphonic texture/scalic, triadic conjunct and disjunct movement/three different types of ornamentation/ostinato or riff/improvisation/imitation/canon/antiphonal texture/blue notes/passing notes

4 marks: It is expected that a minimum of **two** of the following techniques/devices will be in evidence: homophonic and polyphonic texture/scalic, triadic conjunct and disjunct movement/three different types of ornamentation/ostinato or riff/improvisation/imitation/canon/antiphonal texture/blue notes/passing notes.

AQA (2015)

On the basis of the examples in Box 13.4, there are some critical questions that arise for the writing and use of criteria in the summative assessment of composition:

- Is consistency or variety a measure of musical worth? Does this differ according to the style or tradition in question?
- Are certain styles and traditions prejudiced by the criteria, such as those that do not value 'varied and complex' textures?
- Are we as teachers likely to be biased towards compositions that exhibit complexity or those that we 'understand'?
- Is it possible to break down a composition into its 'parts' to make a judgement about the whole?
- Does a scheme of assessment that values the number of techniques/devices that are included in the composition reflect its creative worth?

Swanwick finds such criteria problematic:

Adding up marks awarded under checklist seems an odd way to engage in musical criticism. To be useful criteria statements should indicate qualitative differences rather than qualitative shifts. It is not so difficult to devise these descriptions provided that there is serviceable model of musical criticism, *an adequate theory.*

(Swanwick 1988: 151)

There are similar issues surrounding the marking of performance at GCSE where judging the performance is based upon (a) a set of criteria which are then (b) differentiated by the difficulty of the piece being played. Once again, Swanwick is concerned about an over-reliance on quantitative differences between levels of difficulty and technical virtuosity.

Task 13.7 Assessment of performance at GCSE level

Collect the criteria for assessing performance for the GCSE board in use by your placement school and answer the following questions:

- Do you feel that the criteria are valid descriptions of performance?
- What are the issues surrounding criteria differentiated by the difficulty of the piece being played?
- Are those who have instrumental lessons at an unfair advantage here?

Swanwick's concern with the problems surrounding quantitative criteria arise from his own work on producing qualitative descriptions for shifts in levels of musical development and engagement. For Swanwick, assessing the holistic engagement with music is the only worthwhile measure. His model for development moves from a youngster's initial concern with the sensory materials of music through to their engagement with the expressive and structural use of materials to a philosophical commitment to music. This is not the place for a detailed analysis of his work; however, a flavour of his qualitative approach to an holistic assessment can be found in Box 13.5.

Box 13.5 Swanwick's levels of engagement with music

- Awareness and control of *sound materials*: shown in distinguishing between timbres, levels of loudness, duration or pitches, technical management of instruments or voices.
- Awareness and control of *expressive character*: shown in atmosphere, musical gesture, the sense of movement implied in the shape of musical phrases.
- Awareness and control of *musical form*: shown in relationships between expressive shapes, the ways in which musical gestures are repeated, transformed, contrasted or connected.
- Awareness of personal and cultural *value* of music: shown in autonomy, independent critical evaluation and sustained commitment to specific musical styles. (Swanwick 1999: 81)

Swanwick's levels were never intended to be used as examination criteria, and in many ways are not suitable. However, their strength lies in their grounding in research and the emergent theory of musical development and engagement.

However, one of the issues surrounding an overarching theory such as this is that it cannot capture the 'local' needs of teachers and their students. Summative criteria are most useful when they arise out of the actual work being carried out by teachers and students themselves.

We have seen that writing criteria for making judgements about musical composition and performance is notoriously tough, and yet you should not be discouraged by this. The most useful and effective criteria can be those written by you as teacher in relation to what you (and your students) believe to be a successful outcome for a lesson or unit of work. In this sense it is good to have local, learning-specific criteria which have meaning for individual classrooms. Such local criteria could have the following features:

- be clear and easily understood by all involved in making judgements (teacher and students);
- be explicitly related to the objectives for learning themselves;
- focus on the musical outcomes, although others can be included, e.g. effort, social cooperation etc.

Task 13.8 Writing 'local' criteria

1   Collect a unit of work from school and make notes on the assessment strategies used and how the outcomes are judged (if indeed they are).
2   For the same unit, write your own criteria for success at three positive levels and discuss these with your tutor and/or mentor.
3   For a unit of work that you have taught or are about to teach, devise some success criteria and share these with colleagues for comment.

Write an initial set of guidelines for yourself when writing criteria.

Assessment and the National Curriculum for Music

Some of the issues surrounding the writing and use of criteria for formative and summative assessment can be illustrated by the recent history of the National Curriculum for Music in England.

In 1999, The National Curriculum in England (DfEE 1999) brought music into line with other subjects by setting out criteria for making judgements about young people's musicianship in the form of attainment-target-level descriptors to be used when making an holistic, and 'best-fit' judgement at the end of Key Stage 3. In the fifteen years of its existence, until the system of levels was scrapped across all subjects in 2014, this attainment target with its nine incremental steps of outcomes offered teachers an important model of musical progression, which they found useful when getting to grips with the ephemeral world of assessment in music. However, in line with the criticisms noted above, the model assumed that musical progression can be marked by the acquisition of a breadth and complexity of musical knowledge. On this account, what level would a composer of blues achieve if she refused to move out of her preferred genre? Would this make her a less well-developed musician?

Furthermore, the attainment target levels in music became problematic, as they were appropriated by the day-to-day assessment and tracking practices of schools. Attainment levels that had been devised to make an holistic statement about musical understanding at the end of Key Stage 3 were distorted to the extent that many schools used them to assess individual 'local' pieces of work. Latterly, many music teachers found themselves inventing sub-levels (which did not officially exist) in order to satisfy the demands of data-driven accountability in schools. Teachers were often trying to reconcile what their students were doing musically with an atomised version of the attainment target levels, a practice heavily criticised by school inspectors (Ofsted 2009, 2012). Their conclusion was that the use of the National Curriculum levels was getting in the way of musical achievement in the classroom.

The removal of levels from 2014 as a means of recording and reporting young people's attainment has presented an opportunity for music teachers to devise and promote assessment practices that are fit for the purpose of assessing music in the context of their own schools. This is both a real challenge, as we have seen, and yet an exciting one, where, potentially, teachers and students will have more control over what counts as success, achievement and progression both during and at the end of Key Stage 3. As a beginner and then qualified teacher, you will need to consider where you believe students need to be by the end of Key Stage 3 and how they get there. Task 13.9 will help you to begin this work.

Task 13.9 Designing and assessing outcomes for Key Stage 3

1   Choose one specific area or theme of musical learning and define what you might expect young people to know, understand or be able to do as a result of your teaching by the end of Key Stage 3. These outcomes need to be realistic in the context of curriculum music yet at the same time aspirational.

2   How will you recognise your anticipated outcomes when young people compose, perform and respond to music?

3   Taking each of these anticipated outcomes, try to create two statements that can serve as intermediate and incremental stepping stones on the journey to the end of the key stage. Consider carefully the quality of musical knowledge and understanding and *not just quantity* (i.e. do more of).

4   Share your work with other beginner teachers or music teachers in your placement schools.

Through the process of Task 13.9 you will have established an outline trajectory for your young people for the end of Key Stage 3. However, while such overarching 'levels' can inform holistic, best-fit summative judgements, they are not useful criteria for assessing the day-to-day work of young people in the classroom. As we have seen, this is more readily addressed by 'local' criteria developed by teachers or even the students themselves, perhaps as part of their own self-directed learning.

The assessment of self-directed learning

The issues surrounding assessment in music are brought sharply into focus by the emergence of self-directed learning through initiatives such as Musical Futures. What is the role of assessment in self-directed learning? All of the strategies noted above, associated with assessment for learning and assessment of learning, are legitimate practices here when they arise out of the young people's self-directed objectives and criteria for success. Consider the example in Box 13.6.

Box 13.6 An example of self-directed learning

A group of youngsters decide that they will learn and perform a song during their music lesson. After doodling on instruments individually, they haphazardly perform an approximate version of the introduction to the song. Jo has worked out the main riff and teaches this to the others in the group. Jack begins to sing the vocal line above the riff. They cannot quite work out all of the chords they need, and ask the class teacher to support them in learning these. They continue to play the song with the 'bits' they have worked out for themselves and been taught by the class teacher.

In the example in Box 13.6, summative assessment *of* learning *could* take place based on the criteria for success set by the youngsters themselves, and the teacher can share their perceptions of progress on the basis of such criteria. In relation to assessment *for* learning, the teacher can make interventions based on a diagnosis of the youngsters' self-driven needs and can give feedback to achieve their self-declared learning outcomes. However, the strategies of self- and peer-assessment hold a certain primacy in self-directed learning, and these are most commonly integrated into the very act of making and playing music itself. Without sensitivities to such use of assessment in self-directed learning, teachers risk compromising the ownership of the music and thus alienating young people (see Philpott 2012).

Successful assessment for self-directed learning has the following features, which arise out of our previous analysis in this chapter:

- the use of 'local' criteria that arise out of the self-directed objectives of young people;
- promoting the primacy of self- and peer-assessments using these criteria;
- teacher interventions using criteria that are based on the needs of the young people themselves;
- an acceptance by teachers that there are times when no assessment interventions are appropriate and trusting that learning will take place.

Task 13.10 The assessment of self-directed learning

Using Box 13.6, write a summary of the what, how and where of assessment that is faithful to young people's self-directed learning.

For teachers of music, self-directed learning involves a subtle and nuanced pedagogy and is challenging work. There will be concerns that leaving young people to set their own objectives and to establish their own criteria for summative and formative assessment is a tall order. However, there is enough evidence of the rich engagement of young people arising out of the *Musicals Futures* research (see Green 2008) to suggest that we can trust them to make the most of taking genuine ownership of their learning when presented with opportunities to do so.

Collecting assessment evidence

Whatever work is undertaken in the classroom, the music teacher has a responsibility to collect evidence for the musical achievement as a result of learning and teaching. It is important for you to collect a wide range of evidence such that the subtle nuances of musical learning can be 'captured'. Here are some practical suggestions:

- digital audio and video evidence of composing and performing (both interim work and final outcome);
- written work, e.g. worksheets, scores etc.;
- verbal and written, self- and peer-assessments;
- 'jottings' made by you on significant features of the students' work, e.g. verbal responses during appraisal, their role during group work, significant contributions made to compositions etc.;
- a record of attendance, achievement grades, comments, homework set and completed.

Can you think of other types of evidence?

Collecting assessment evidence using a wide range of media should be seen as part of the daily routine of teaching, such that it can constantly inform the learning process as you come to know your students.

Such evidence is easiest to collect when students and teachers have created assessment criteria specific to the musical work in hand (i.e. the 'local' learning), as a basis for formative and summative assessment. Such evidence can underpin learning and teaching and be used to build an ongoing musical profile of a student where assessment is embedded in practice. To reiterate Swanwick: to teach is to assess.

Summary

In this chapter we have seen that:

- there are two broad categories of assessment that can be applied to the music classroom, the formative and the summative;
- what we assess and how we assess are related to what we value most highly about music;
- assessment for learning (formative) strategies allow us to come to know the subtle nuances of our students' musical learning;

- summative assessments of learning can also be used formatively;
- writing criteria for assessing success is a problematic process;
- criteria based on 'local' learning can be the most significant for teachers and young people alike;
- the assessment for self-directed learning can employ all strategies outlined in this chapter;
- there is a the need to collect a wide variety of assessment evidence when coming to know your students as part of the teaching and learning process.

Further reading

Fautley, M. (2010) *Assessment in Music Education*, Oxford: Oxford University Press.

Fautley, M. (2012) 'Assessment in classroom music', *Music Teacher*, March: 40–41.

Philpott, C. (2012) The assessment of self-directed learning in music education, in C. Philpott and G. Spruce (eds) *Debates in Music Teaching*, London: Routledge, pp. 153–168.

Swanwick, K. (1999) *Teaching Music Musically*, London: Routledge.

These readings explore ways in which assessment practice can and should be tailored to the uniqueness of music. They highlight how some common assessment practices might be detrimental in our subject and emphasise that our focus should be on assessing that which is inherently musical.

14 Collaboration

Julie Evans

Introduction

Collaboration is an important aspect of many human interactions, but just because different parties work together does not necessarily mean that they collaborate *effectively*. Collaboration is a complex process and involves establishing good communication and trust, and respecting and using the different skills and knowledge of individuals. Effective collaborations can be very powerful: 'When we collaborate, creativity unfolds across people; the sparks fly faster, and the whole is greater than the sum of its parts' (Sawyer 2007: 7).

Of course, all secondary school teachers have to collaborate with others, within and beyond the school. This chapter will consider a range of collaborations that all secondary school teachers have to develop and some that are specific to the role of a secondary class music teacher. Collaborations may involve the challenging of existing hierarchies and developing new ways of working, and some models of collaboration and conditions for effective collaborations will be proposed in this chapter.

Objectives

By the end of this chapter you should be able to:

- understand a range of collaborations that all secondary school teachers have to develop;
- understand some collaborations that are specific to the role of a secondary class music teacher;
- understand some models of collaboration;
- establish some conditions that are essential for effective collaborations to flourish.

Collaborations that all secondary teachers need to develop

All secondary school teachers have to develop:

* collaborations with other colleagues, within and beyond a department/faculty;
* cross-curricular collaborations within the school;
* extra-curricular collaborations within and beyond the school;
* collaborations with feeder primary schools;
* collaborations with students.

In some departments, such as science departments, collaborations between a whole team of teachers will be essential in order to ensure equality of learning experiences for students at all key stages and, hopefully, to share and develop good teaching practice. These collaborative partnerships may not be comparable to those of all music teachers, some of whom are *solely* responsible for all of the musical learning in a school.

Teachers in all subject areas have to collaborate regularly with non-teaching colleagues and with colleagues who have responsibilities that are not subject specific. This includes colleagues from within the school, such as teaching/learning support assistants, specialist technicians, colleagues with particular responsibility for and expertise in supporting students' special educational needs and disabilities, as well as teachers with management responsibilities at all levels. Task 14.1 asks you to identify those people with whom you may need to collaborate within your setting.

Task 14.1 Key personnel, collaboration and effective learning

Make a list of names and roles of the key personnel within your school who have specific responsibilities and with whom you will have to collaborate to ensure effective learning, e.g. those who have management responsibilities, from the head teacher to your immediate line manager; those who have responsibilities for supporting students with special educational needs and disabilities (SEND); teaching/learning support assistants who work with any students you teach etc. Suggest why you need to collaborate with each colleague and how you can develop collaborations.

Name of colleague	Role	Why do you need to collaborate with this colleague and how can you develop collaborations?

Additionally, all teachers have to know how to, and be able to, collaborate to varying degrees with a wide range of colleagues from other agencies beyond the school, for instance social workers, the police and health professionals.

Cross-curricular collaborations within the school

Music is often included in cross-curricular collaborations within secondary schools. A common model used in many secondary schools is project-based learning. This may be used for a variety of reasons. In some secondary schools, project-based learning is used across the whole of Year 7 to facilitate the transition of students from Year 6 in a primary school to Year 7 in a secondary school. Project-based learning is one strategy used even more extensively in some schools, often across the Key Stage 3 curriculum, to develop students' thinking skills and problem solving, as opposed to them simply 'receiving' knowledge from teachers. Well-planned cross-curricular learning that includes a musical element can enhance students' learning in combination with other subjects, although its value as a discrete subject should never be forgotten.

Case study

India is the project topic for Year 7 in a rural secondary school for a whole term. One key teacher is responsible for coordinating the students' learning in English, history, geography, art, PE and music throughout the whole of Year 7. They have another key teacher who coordinates their learning in maths, science, design and technology and computing. Having a small team of key teachers creates stability for the Year 7 students, who have been used to having one key teacher in Year 6 in their primary school. The music teacher collaborates with art and dance teachers to create a performance, which is shown to parents and carers at the end of term. The school does not own any authentic Indian instruments, beside four pairs of tabla, but students are encouraged to bring in and use any of their own instruments on which they can 'bend' notes, and others use the school's tabla and electronic keyboards set to create quite realistic sitar sounds. A key learning objective is established for all three subjects, which is that by the end of the project students will *have explored repeated patterns in Indian art, dance and music.*

This case study exemplifies some important principles of cross-curricular collaboration. The first is that only three subjects are combined. Jonathan Barnes suggests that:

> The cross-curriculum models of the 1970s and 1980s often foundered on the contrived inclusion of *all* subjects on every Topic Web. In today's best cross-curricular practice, only two or three subjects are necessary to bring a balanced understanding to a theme. A serious danger of interdisciplinary work is that the boundaries between the subject disciplines become less distinct and progression within subjects is weakened.
>
> (Barnes 2011: 206)

He also suggests that 'in delivering cross-curricular themes, teachers should identify and focus on clear, appropriate, subject-based learning objectives' (Barnes 2011: 207). In the case study, the sole learning objective is further strengthened by being equally relevant to the three subject areas, thus consolidating the students' understanding by linking together different aspects of their learning across subjects. Devising learning objectives that are equally relevant to different subject areas can take time, but this will add cohesion to the learning opportunity and ensures that students can make links across subjects, as opposed to exploring the same or similar ideas in isolated subject silos.

Of course, all cross-curricular collaborations may not be as extensive as in schools that are committed to project-based or competence-based learning. It is often left to individual teachers to establish effective cross-curricular collaborations. Such collaborations involve more time-consuming planning than solo planning, and it can be demanding to try to establish truly 'appropriate' learning objectives that fit different subjects. It is only through having appropriate shared learning objectives that cross-curricular learning can effectively enhance students' understanding, as learning is transferred, links are made and themes are established. A clear example would be where a year group are learning about Black civil rights in history lessons. With some quite simple collaborations between teachers, the students could concurrently learn how to write their own protest songs in their music lessons, underpinned by learning some protest songs from past and present times. Their knowledge and understanding in both history and music would be enhanced, as evidenced in the discipline-specific output from each.

Task 14.2 Planning for cross-curricular learning

Plan and collaborate on leading a cross-curricular learning opportunity for a class/group of students that you already teach. This could be anything from a single lesson to a sequence of learning opportunities. Ensure that you underpin the cross-curricular learning with some of the key principles that have been established:

- Only combine two or three subjects.
- Devise learning objectives that are appropriate to all subjects.
- Ensure that students' learning takes place across all subjects.

Extra-curricular collaborations within and beyond the school

Secondary class music teachers will be expected to develop extra-curricular activities involving music for young people of all ages. Some of these activities, and particularly those within the school, will involve collaborations with other teachers. For instance, the production of a musical will involve collaborations with teachers of drama, dance and even design and technology. An evening focused on the arts will involve collaboration with staff from all the arts disciplines within the school. Other collaborations resulting from extra-curricular activities within the school will be with other colleagues, such as administrative staff who advertise and sell tickets, with parents and carers who may need to provide transport for the students or may attend resulting performances/events and, most importantly, new collaborations with young people.

Music teachers will also have opportunities to develop extra-curricular collaborations beyond the school. Students should be encouraged to perform at a whole range of venues, from concert halls and arts centres to more informal venues such as old people's homes and early learning settings. Collaborations can be forged to allow students to work and learn in a variety of contexts beyond the school, such as in a professional recording studio or in a specific context where they can play particular instruments such as taiko drums or a gamelan.

Music teachers are privileged to have opportunities to form very impactful relationships with students who take part in extra-curricular activities, and these undoubtedly enhance the relationships already forged in curriculum lessons.

Collaborations with feeder primary schools

The transition from primary to secondary school is an exciting moment in young people's lives but also creates the need for specific collaborations. From a secondary class music teacher's point of view, a crucial factor is to learn as much as possible about students' prior musical experiences at the start of Year 7 in order to ensure progression in their musical learning. Of course, young people can talk about or, better still, demonstrate their musical understanding. However, they may not reveal everything that they have previously experienced. For instance, it is an aspiration that every student leaving a state-maintained primary school in England will have had the opportunity to learn to play an instrument through Wider Opportunities/First Access initiatives, and this was stated in *'Wow, it's music next': Impact Evaluation of Wider Opportunities Programme in Music at Key Stage Two*: 'By 2011, programmes will be in place that will result in every child having this opportunity during their time in primary school' (Bamford and Glinkowski 2010).

However, students are often reluctant to admit that they 'play an instrument', perhaps because their whole-class/large-group instrumental learning took place in Year 4, as is very common, which may seem a long way off to them, or perhaps because they have already gained the perception that playing an instrument in their secondary school is not for them. For many reasons, it is essential for an effective secondary class music teacher to develop collaborations with key colleagues from feeder primary schools.

All schools will have generic transition links with feeder primary schools, which will involve collaboration with Year 6 class teachers. From a secondary class music teacher's point of view, it may be even more useful to develop collaborations with the feeder schools' music coordinators/music specialist teachers. These collaborations may be quite pragmatic and involve the passing on of information about the feeder school's curriculum music provision at Key Stages 1 and 2, the students' instrumental learning experiences, their involvement in other musical activities such as shows, choirs and ensembles and their perceived aptitude in music. This can be a mammoth task in itself, for instance in a school that serves a wide catchment area and where there are a huge number of feeder primary schools. However, a secondary class music teacher will not receive the kind of indications of student attainment that a teacher of English, mathematics or science will receive, and a manageable system of gaining information will need to be developed.

The strongest collaborations between secondary and primary schools in relation to music are founded on developing young people's *musical* experiences to facilitate a smooth transition. Musical experiences that may facilitate students' transition from Key Stage 2 to 3 have been promoted by Musical Bridges (www.musicalbridges.org.uk) and Musical Futures (www.musicalfutures.org). One example involves students being involved in a composition project in Year 6, supported by music teachers from the secondary school to which they are moving, as well as their class teachers. When the young people start at their secondary school, the composition project is continued and developed. Such experiences involve a great deal of communication and liaison between colleagues in different schools, but the impact on students can be enormous.

Task 14.3 Planning a transition project

Plan and, if possible, deliver a musical activity for the Year 6 classes in one of your feeder primary schools, which can be built upon in their Year 7 curriculum lessons. If possible, make contact with the music coordinator/specialist in the feeder primary school and plan this activity collaboratively.

Collaborations with young people

Teaching is clearly underpinned by teachers collaborating effectively with their students. However, it can be suggested that secondary class music teachers have *particular* opportunities for developing strong collaborations with young people. All secondary-aged students have strong musical interests and these will be bound up with their personal identities. These are generally quite different from interests that students might bring to school in relation to geography or mathematics, since the majority of young people are not regularly immersed in these subjects. Young people are regularly immersed in music and are likely to have highly developed aural acuity, perhaps in relation to very specific areas of music from their experiences outside school. They also often have knowledge, skills and understanding about areas of music that their teachers do not. This may be as listeners, performers or music technologists. Some teachers may be equally knowledgeable, but there is a danger in teachers *pretending* to know as much about their students' music as the students themselves. The expertise of young people should be recognised and used (as elaborated in the section entitled 'Pyramidical model of collaboration' later in this chapter). Task 14.4 provides an opportunity for you to consider the types of expertise the young people you work with have.

Task 14.4 Sharing music skills and understanding

Select one class that you teach. Within the class, students will have a diverse range of musical knowledge, skills and understanding. For five students, list a particular area of musical knowledge, skills and understanding that they could share with you and their peers.

Stronger collaborations between teachers and young people go much further, even allowing the students choice and voice to impact on curriculum design. Abigail D'Amore outlines a simple process for co-constructing a curriculum, as shown in Figure 14.1.

Provide taster sessions	Consult with students based on their experiences	Design a curriculum	Refine with students	Implement

Figure 14.1 Co-constructing a curriculum
Source: D'Amore (2009: 30)

She suggests that the potential benefits of co-constructing a curriculum with students are that it:

- Enables students to take ownership over their music learning, as the curriculum becomes influenced by the result of asking students what they want from their music lessons
- Makes tangible connections with students' musical lives outside school and moves students' musical experiences beyond the classroom
- Achieves a balance between what students already know they want to do and new experiences
- Makes active music making something that all students are involved in
- Gives opportunities to make sustained progress in key areas, to develop new musical skills and reinforce existing skills

(D'Amore 2009: 31)

Specific collaborations that effective music teachers need to develop

Secondary class music teachers have to develop some very specific collaborations beyond the generic partnerships that all secondary teachers have to develop. These include:

- collaborations with visiting instrumental teachers;
- collaborations with music education hubs and music services;
- collaborations with professional musicians.

Collaborations with visiting instrumental teachers

An effective music department develops strong collaborations with a wide range of visiting instrumental teachers. The professional life of an instrumental teacher can be a very lonely one, in which conversations with adults may be rare. Where collaborations with instrumental teachers are truly effective, all lines of communication will be strong. The visiting teachers will be fully aware of what is going on within the school in terms of musical activity within and beyond the curriculum (as elaborated in the section entitled 'Parallel model of collaboration' later in this chapter). This will allow the musical learning of students receiving instrumental lessons to be 'joined up' with their learning within the curriculum. In an effective music department, instrumental teachers will contribute to the musical activities of the school (e.g. running extra-curricular activities or playing alongside them in performances).

Collaborations with music education hubs and music services

Some visiting instrumental teachers may work independently, but it is likely that many visiting instrumental teachers will work for a local music service. In *The Importance of Music: A National Plan for Music Education* (2011), it was stated that:

> Schools cannot be expected to do all that is required of music education alone: a music infrastructure that transcends schools is necessary. Building on the work of local authority music services, this will be provided by music education hubs from September 2012, following recommendations in the Henley review.
>
> (DfE/DCMS 2011: 10)

One-hundred-and-twenty-three music education hubs were established across England in September 2012. After a bidding process, almost all of the hubs were subsequently led by existing music services, although this had not been a foregone conclusion. However, a major misconception was that the hubs were *simply* the music services working in a slightly different guise. It was intended that all music educators in a geographic area would work together in collaborative partnerships to improve children's and young people's musical learning. The document states that:

> Class teachers and specialist instrumental teachers working together will be able to offer well-planned progressive experiences with high expectations. These will enable all pupils to succeed, including those who do not have the encouragement or support from their parents/carers, or who need additional support for other reasons.
>
> (DfE/DCMS 2011: 10)

Secondary class music teachers are therefore *expected* to collaborate with their local music hubs and/or music services. Most importantly, each hub has had the funding for instrumental and vocal teaching for children and young people devolved to them from Arts Council England and each school has had to liaise with the local hub about their own school's provision for instrumental and vocal learning.

In the most effective hubs, really strong partnerships between music services and schools have been developed.

Case study

In one music education hub, secondary schools in one area have worked together in partnership with their local hub leader to develop local provision for out-of-school music activities for young people from all of the schools involved. Each school has taken on responsibility for leading an activity for which they have particular expertise and resources, and these activities include a symphony orchestra, a samba band and a Gospel choir. The local music service could not have developed all of these activities without collaboration with the schools. Equally, the schools have benefited from how communication between schools has been facilitated by the local hub leader.

Task 14.5 Collaborating with music hubs

Find out about one musical activity that is being supported by your local music education hub and in which students from your school are involved. What are the advantages to the students, your school and the music education hub (or music service)? Ask your Head of Music how they collaborate with hubs to benefit the musical learning of their students.

Collaborations with professional musicians

In *The Importance of Music: A National Plan for Music Education* it is also stated that: 'Hubs will augment and support music teaching in schools so that more children experience a combination of classroom teaching, instrumental and vocal tuition and input from professional musicians' (DfE/DCMS 2011: 10).

'Professional musicians' is a very unspecific term. It could encompass anything from orchestral players in a national symphony orchestra to a local rap artist. Secondary class music teachers should develop collaborations with a wide range of professional musicians, and it is important that these partnerships are relevant to students' needs. It can be a life-changing experience for students to attend their first live symphony orchestra concert, but it may be even more impactful for them to work with a professional musician from their own community and with whom they can have face-to-face contact on a regular basis. These professional musicians may include performers, composers, music technologists and cross-arts practitioners.

What is of great importance is that secondary class music teachers understand that they cannot do it all themselves and do not have the whole range of knowledge, skills and under-standing. Reassuringly, this was supported by the National Plan in which it is stated that:

> A unique challenge of music education is the number of different specialisms, instruments, genres and styles, compositions, and technologies. Although many teachers in schools (particularly secondary schools) are music specialists, they may not have the expertise to develop pupils' skills across a range of instruments or experiences.
>
> (DfE/DCMS 2011:10)

Models of collaboration

When individuals collaborate, they do so in a variety of ways, and the following are some common models of collaboration within secondary schools and within music departments.

Hierarchical model of collaboration

This is a very typical model within schools, within which all sorts of hierarchical models are rife. For instance, a beginner music teacher may be answerable to a head of department and/or and head of faculty. In a hierarchical model of collaboration, an individual is regarded as an 'expert' and will disseminate knowledge, skills and understanding to others in a pyramidal fashion.

For instance, a head of department may be very knowledgeable about music technology and may also be cognisant with the requirements of examination boards. In an effective collaborative hierarchical model, this head of department will be willing and able (for instance, overcoming time restraints) to share knowledge, skills and understanding with other members of the department, in order that they, in turn, can develop students' learning (see Figure 14.2).

Figure 14.2 Hierarchical model of collaboration

The strongest music departments are happy to invert the 'normal' inbuilt hierarchical model. In other words, the beginner teacher will have skills and understanding that even an experienced head of department may not have. For instance, this could be knowledge of performing a specific style of music. It is very empowering to work in a music department where the specific knowledge, skills and understanding of each individual are recognised and where each individual is encouraged to share these with others. Of course, this model can be extended to embrace students who can also act as the 'experts'. For example, a young person who is a keen beatboxer can teach his teachers and peers to beatbox. Recognising, celebrating and allowing students to share their expertise is a key feature of collaborating effectively with young people of all ages.

It is not only between the members of music departments that such hierarchical models of collaboration are seen. For instance, when an experienced djembe drummer is asked to lead a workshop in school, or orchestral musicians run an outreach programme with young people, it is very common for a hierarchical model to be adopted, where the classroom teachers play a subservient role, often relying on the expertise of others.

Parallel model of collaboration

This model can be stronger than a hierarchical model. It promotes the idea that different educators working with the same students have equal but different strengths that can be used in a complementary way to develop their learning. An example cited above can be developed to illustrate this.

Case study

Year 8 classes have two curriculum music lessons within their two-week timetable. The visiting djembe drummer, whose expertise is in leading workshops and performing and who does not hold a teaching qualification, works with Year 8s in their curriculum music lessons on alternate weeks over a term developing basic drumming skills, culminating in the classes being able to perform some complex multi-layered pieces. The classroom teacher attends these sessions and learns alongside the students.

The classroom teacher works with the same Year 8s in the alternate weeks, enabling them to use GarageBand to compose their own multi-layered compositions, using a wide range of African percussion instrument sounds and some of the rhythmic ideas, layering techniques and structures that they have explored practically in their djembe drumming.

In this model the students' experience some 'joined-up thinking' about their musical learning.

This case study exemplifies the parallel model of collaboration (Figure 14.3).

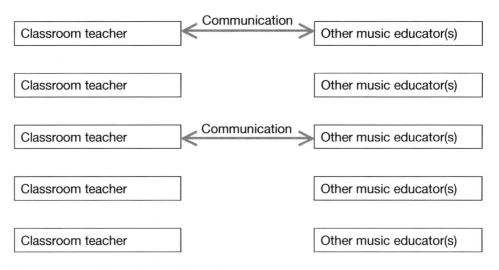

Figure 14.3 Parallel model of collaboration

The parallel model is strengthened by points of communication between the two music educators or sets of educators. Effective collaboration demands extensive and good-quality communication between the two parties involved. Communication need not always be face to face, but regular communication about a student's needs and progress, and practical, organisational issues is essential.

This parallel model of collaboration applies equally to the collaboration between class music teachers and visiting instrumental teachers. A class teacher develops students' musical learning on a regular basis, as do the visiting instrumental teachers. Only too often these two parties work in isolation from each other, with only passing greetings being shared. As Janet Mills suggests,

> Just think how much more progress . . . children could make, musically, if the education system in which they found themselves helped to bring together their music education in class music, in their (instrumental) lessons, when they are playing their (instruments) at home, and so on. No teacher can know everything about the richness of children's individual musical lives. But teachers can give children opportunities to talk about, and to show, the music that they do out of school, and try to build on this. Instrumental teachers can liaise with schoolteachers about the content of their curriculum. And they can give children some composing tasks to carry out during their practice time at home, and listen to the compositions that they have made at home on their own, from time to time.
>
> (Mills 2005: 76)

In order to develop an effective parallel model of collaboration, communication between class and instrumental teachers needs to be developed. This could mean simple strategies such as ensuring that instrumental teachers are given an overview of the units of work that students are engaging with at Key Stage 3, which facilitates the liaison that Mills suggested in relation to the curriculum. So many opportunities are missed when, for instance, students are learning to play a blues piece in saxophone lessons and concurrently learning about the blues in curriculum music lessons. With students at Key Stages 4 and 5 it is essential that instrumental teachers are informed about the requirements of the performance elements of examination specifications in order for them to be able to complement the work of the curriculum teacher and ensure that students are fully prepared.

Episodic model of collaboration

In the episodic model of collaboration, different music educators are responsible for leading students' learning at different points in a linear model.

Case study

The classroom teacher introduces his Year 12s to Steve Reich's New York Counterpoint movement 2, which is a set work for their A level Music course. He facilitates the students in making recordings of tracks, against which they each play a live part, in order that they can learn the work by getting inside the music and gain understanding of some minimalist techniques by actually playing them. Over a period of four weeks the students go on to compose drafts of their own minimalist compositions for a violin, viola, trumpet and bassoon, incorporating some of the minimalist techniques that they have already explored. In the fifth week, four professional orchestral musicians visit the school and play the draft compositions. They demonstrate some instrument-specific techniques and discuss these with the students in order that they might incorporate them into their compositions. The orchestral musicians suggest revisions to the draft compositions, pointing out what works successfully and less successfully on their instruments. The students work on revisions to their compositions over the next four weeks, and the orchestral musicians then return for a second visit to perform the compositions to a small audience of students, their parents and friends. This case study exemplifies the sequential model of collaboration (Figure 14.4).

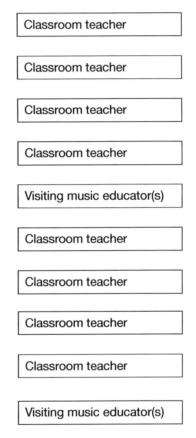

Figure 14.4 Episodic model of collaboration

This model again demands effective and regular communication between the parties involved. As long as this happens, the very different knowledge, skills and understanding of the different music educators can be used to great effect.

Interwoven model

This is a very strong model of collaboration. Different parties work together seamlessly and contribute regularly and equally to developing students' musical learning. The analogy of weaving together threads is useful in that individual threads (the contribution of different music educators and students) are woven together to develop a really strong 'fabric' which represents students' musical learning (Figure 14.5).

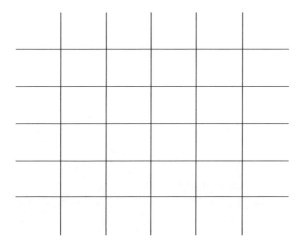

Figure 14.5 Interwoven model of collaboration

As the diagram suggests, each individual 'thread' is of equal value.

Case study

Year 9s in a large academy are composing, performing and recording their own songs over a whole school year. In six curriculum lessons a professional songwriter works with the students, and alongside the class teacher, as they start to compose their songs. She encourages the students to explore melodic lines and conventional structures such as intros, outros and bridge passages, as well as trying out innovative alternatives. The class teacher builds on the initial composition work by encouraging the Year 9 students to use some improvisation within their songs. One of the school's instrumental teachers is a jazz saxophonist, and he works with the Year 9 classes in another six curriculum lessons throughout the year, demonstrating, modelling and supporting the students to experiment with some improvisation. The students suggest their own improvisatory possibilities, using software called Noatikl that one of them has used at home. A local recording studio is booked for three days at the end of the project. The studio manager comes into school to visit each Year 9 class to prepare the students for the recording session. At the end of the school year, performances of all the songs are given in the school's arts centre and they are attended by parents, carers and friends.

Task 14.6 Critiquing the models

What are the benefits and issues for each model in relation to musical learning for the students?

   Draw up a table of your findings.

Conditions necessary for effective collaborations to flourish

When different parties work together, this does not necessarily mean that they *collaborate*. In weak models it is evident that the parties involved are working autonomously, without communication and without regard or respect for each other.

Arts Council England suggest some basic principles that underpin effective collaborative partnership working in music education hubs:

> Partnership working enables organisations to pursue a common vision and work together to achieve more.
>
> Key principles for effective partnership include:
>
> - Trust, goodwill and commitment among members
> - Clear and consensual objectives
> - Good alignment with local context
> - Being inclusive of all those who have the skills and knowledge to usefully contribute
> - Recognition that all partners have something to contribute and willingness to share success
> - Regular assessments of progress made
> - Governance with periodic review to assess whether the partnership is meeting its full potential.
>
> (Arts Council England 2012)

In order to be able to enact these principles for effective collaboration within a school, Southworth *et al.* (in Pollard 2002: 349) suggest that a 'culture of collaboration' must be established. These authors suggest that a school's culture of collaboration is built on four interacting beliefs:

- valuing individuals – as people and for their contribution to others;
- valuing interdependence – belonging to a group and working as a team;
- valuing security;
- valuing openness.

These can be suggested as the conditions for effective collaboration.

It is the valuing of interdependence that is key to establishing and maintaining effective collaboration. In schools with a 'culture of collaboration', Southworth *et al.* observe that:

> Individual staff members . . . valued one another as people, each with his/her identity, personality, interests, skills, experiences and potential. Yet they also appreciated the diversity which this brought to the school. Likewise, interdependence has two aspects. Together the members of staff . . . made a group that was valued because it provided a sense of belonging. At the same time they accepted a collective responsibility for the work of the school so creating a sense of team in which staff helped, encouraged and substituted for one another.
>
> (Pollard 2002: 350)

An effective 'culture of collaboration' may already exist within a school, but collaborations with instrumental teachers, professional musicians and other colleagues will mean that the collaborative community will be extended beyond the existing staff and the students in the school.

It is also essential to remember that all of the collaborations discussed in this chapter are intended to enhance students' musical learning. It is important to reflect on the thoughts of Bruner:

> I have come increasingly to recognise that most learning in most settings is a communal activity, a sharing of culture. It is not just that the child must make his knowledge his own, but he must make it his own in the community of those who share his sense of belonging to a culture.
>
> (Bruner 1986: 127)

An important aim of the sort of collaborations explored in this chapter must surely be to develop 'communal activity' and 'sharing of culture', and this must be an aim for beginner music teachers as well as for educators with a wealth of experience.

Summary

In this chapter we have:

- explored the range of collaborations that all secondary school teachers have to develop and also those that are specific to the role of a secondary class music teacher;
- seen that there are different models of collaboration and that the beginner teacher will need to fully engage with these if they are to maximise the impact on the musical learning and development of the students in their classrooms;
- emphasised the crucially important conditions under which effective collaborations can flourish, central to which is the growth of a culture of collaboration in which all participants feel valued and share mutual understandings in relation to objectives, roles and responsibilities.

Such communal sharing is not only a model for musical learning but for all learning.

Further reading

Hallam, R. (2011) 'Effective partnership working in music education: principles and practice', *International Journal of Music Education*, 29, 2: 155–171.

Ofsted (2012) Music in schools: sound partnerships. Online, available at: www.gov.uk/government/publications/music-in-schools-sound-partnerships (accessed 24 July 2015).

A short survey of music education partnership work in schools highlighting the benefits and pitfalls of partnership working in music education.

Zeserson, K. (2012) Partnerships in music education, in C. Philpott and G. Spruce (eds) *Debates in Music Teaching*, London: Routledge, pp. 209–220.

All three publications here draw on examples from partnerships in music education to demonstrate the nature of successful collaboration and some of the key factors that need to be considered.

15 Music, the arts and education

Chris Philpott

Introduction

This book is about learning how to teach music. However, it is important that we do not see music as an isolated school subject, but its unique contribution to the wider education of our young people. By exploring the relationships and connections between music and other disciplines, we can enhance the teaching of music itself, as well as develop visions for how the whole school curriculum can be organised and taught. This concluding chapter encourages you to look beyond music by focusing on the long-standing debate surrounding the relationship between music, the arts and other subjects in the curriculum. The chapter also challenges you to draw on learning from previous chapters and your current experience as a music teacher.

Objectives

By the end of this chapter you should:

- understand how the arts can be organised in schools;
- understand some of the background history and current trends in arts education;
- understand the argument for the arts being considered a generic family and the consequent implications for educational practice;
- understand the argument for the inherent distinctiveness of the arts and the consequent implications for educational practice;
- understand a possible 'third way' based on the interconnectedness of all knowledge, and how this might manifest itself in the music classroom.

The organisation of the arts in schools

It has been common for schools and policy makers to consider the arts together when organising curricula, timetables and syllabi, and this has been manifest in a variety of ways.

For example, some schools are organised into faculties or departments of creative arts, expressive arts, performing arts. In some cases the curriculum has been taught as combined arts, integrated arts or collaborative arts, where there is an expectation for students to engage with a range of arts in any one lesson, although such approaches are, as we shall see, less common at the time of writing. Some schools timetable the arts together at the same time or as part of a 'carousel' across the year. The types of organisation afford opportunities for common themes and projects across the arts, although arts teachers need the skills and dispositions to make the most of this work.

Task 15.1 The organisation of arts in school

- How were the arts in the curriculum organised in the schools you attended?
- How are the arts organised in your current placement schools?
- Does the organisation afford collaborative possibilities? Are these opportunities exploited?
- Is there any evidence of collaborative arts examination courses in your schools? How are these taught and assessed in comparison to music-only courses?

The arts have also found themselves organised together by policy makers in the form of expressive arts and performing arts examination syllabi at Key Stages 4 and 5 as a possible alternative to specialist and distinct examinations in arts disciplines, e.g. music, drama, dance etc.

Of course, it has been, and still is, very common for the arts to work together as part of extra-curricular productions in schools, although it is increasingly rare for such a model to be replicated in the arts education of the classroom. What is the background to the organisation of the arts in schools past and present?

The arts in education

In the 1980s and 90s, it was fashionable to consider the arts in schools as a family group of disciplines, not just by being related, but for their potential for collaborative work in the curriculum. There was a vibrant debate around such issues, and although at the time of writing the discourses surrounding 'collaborative arts' are still abroad, they have to some extent been overwhelmed by successive policy. For example, the recent trend has been towards the primacy of individual subjects or disciplines as opposed to connections between them, and this has not necessarily worked to the advantage of the arts in education. Two examples of evidence for this are:

1   the finding by the Warwick Commission (2015) that policy most often promotes a 'silo' subject-based curriculum in the sciences and the arts that tends to ignore and obscure discussion around, for example, creativity across the curriculum;

2   the eradication of GCSE, AS or A level expressive and performing arts examination syllabi from 2017 (although they continue to exist as part of the vocationally orientated Business and Technology Education Council examination courses, which are popular with some schools).

Ken Robinson has been an important figure in arts education who has led a variety of projects and authored or edited a number of significant reports (see Calouste Gulbenkian Foundation 1982; NCC 1990; NACCCE 1999). He was one of the architects in the 1980s (and beyond) of a rationale for the arts in education as a generic community; for their connectedness. The question underpinning this work was: What provision should there be for the arts and on what principles should it be based? However, justifying the arts in schools is not the same as saying they are a coherent family, can be grouped together philosophically and practically and that they are fundamentally connected. Robinson and others felt it important for a case to be made for the arts in education as a family as a counterbalance to science, maths and technology (and this is an ongoing challenge for arts educators). The argument typically constructed the arts as a different form of rationality from the sciences, although this logic attracted a critique (and still does) articulating a fear for the 'loss' of the individual arts disciplines where specialist learning is compromised.

In his most recent publication, Robinson (Robinson and Aronica 2015) has extended his views on the fundamental connectedness of the arts into a vision for the whole of education that is also a critique of the 'silo' approach in much recent policy on schooling. Central to his search for connectedness, among other things, is an ongoing concern for creativity as a defining feature of what it means to be human.

However, as we have seen, and in spite of writers such as Robinson, the political and educational pendulum is very much with distinct subjects at the centre of curriculum content, as opposed to the connectedness of educational knowledge and processes.

Task 15.2 The arts in school and society

Why do you think that arts educators feel the ongoing need to advocate for the importance of the arts to school leaders and policy makers alike? Make notes for a 60-second 'elevator pitch' on the importance of the arts in school and society. In order to do this, you should draw on your wider learning from other chapters of this book, from your own reading and from your experience as a musician and teacher.

We now turn to the debate that has underpinned the justification for the arts in education.

Two views of the arts in education

The debate surrounding the nature of the arts and their role in education arose out of a desire to justify the place of the arts in the curriculum. While this is not the place to pursue the issue of justification (more can be found on this in Chapter 1), arts educators have for a long time felt the need to make the case for the arts, both as a group and as individual disciplines, against a backdrop of what is perceived to be a hierarchical dichotomy (see Philpott 1996) between the value of the sciences and arts in society and education. The justification for the arts in school has spawned two sides to the debate: the arts as a generic community versus the arts as distinct disciplines.

The arts as a generic community

One of the most powerful philosophical arguments for the arts as a generic family has come from the work of Peter Abbs (1987, 1989a, 1989b). Abbs' argument revolves around the central concept of the aesthetic, which can be characterised by our sensuous understanding, i.e. being of the senses and understanding through the senses. The arts, he maintains, operate in the aesthetic mode and they are the symbolic forms through which we respond to, understand, apprehend and express our sensuous experience (feeling); they are ways of ordering and developing our sensuous experience. The arts have a biological source in our bodily and cognitive sensations (feeling), thus cohere together as a generic family. Abbs moves from the concepts of aesthetic and the arts to the notions of artist and the artistic, where we can see the crafting of a disciplined elaboration and exploration of the sensuous. For example, dance (the kinaesthetic), fine art (the visual) and drama (the enactive) are arts in which the aesthetic is elaborated and explored through different sensuous priorities. Art uses the aesthetic mode and is an intentional arrangement affording experience in the aesthetic. The basic principles of Abbs' position are:

> First, that the aesthetic represents a particular category of sensuous understanding; second, that the arts cohere intellectually in that they all work through and depend upon the power and logic of aesthetic apprehension; third, that because the arts together form a generic community of understanding they must be conceived ... as an indispensable segment of any balanced curriculum.'
>
> (1989b: xii)

Task 15.3 Considering the generic argument 1

What are your views on Abbs' argument? Write a series of bullets for and against his position.

One of the most fully formed articulations of the generic argument and its implications for classroom practice came through the NCC *Arts in School Project* (NCC 1990), and this has been summarised in Figure 15.1.

The rationale of *'The Arts 5-16, A Curriculum Framework'* NCC Arts in Schools Project

THE ARTS

(the visual, the aural, the kinaesthetic, the verbal, the enactive modes)

engaged in through

MAKING AND APPRAISING

while

EXPLORING – FORMING – PERFORMING – PRESENTING – RESPONDING –

EVALUATING

learning

CONCEPTS (contextual, aesthetic) – SKILLS (perceptual, productive, discursive) –

VALUES AND ATTITUDES (judgements, openness) – INFORMATION (facts)

developing

CREATIVITY AND TECHNIQUE – CRITICISM AND CONTEXT

progressing in

COMPLEXITY – CONTROL – DEPTH – INDEPENDENCE

aiming at the wider educational goals of

INTELLECTUAL DEVELOPMENT

AESTHETIC DEVELOPMENT

EXPLORATION OF VALUES

PHYSICAL AND PERCEPTUAL DEVELOPMENT

PERSONAL AND SOCIAL DEVELOPMENT

ETHOS

Figure 15.1 A rationale for the arts in schools

> **Task 15.4 Considering the generic argument 2**
>
> • What is the connection between the work of Abbs and that of the NCC?
> • What are the practical implications of this rationale for the music classroom?
> • What are the implications for the organisation of the arts in the school curriculum?
>
> Share your thoughts with another beginner teacher.

Other ways in which the notion of 'family' has been assigned to the arts has been through concepts such as creativity (see Ross 1978) and culture. Given the inherent relationship between the arts, the generic family argument has been used to justify a collaborative, integrated or combined approach to the arts in the curriculum. However, there is a fundamental critique targeted at the generic argument, based on the distinctiveness of the arts as opposed to their similarity.

The arts as distinct disciplines

David Best (1992) argues that there is no good philosophical reason why the arts should be grouped together, thus no reason to do so in the school curriculum, and indeed such a grouping could undermine the importance of the arts. Best is particularly concerned with the preoccupation of the generic argument with the aesthetic–feeling relationship, which he argues consigns the arts to the realm of the subjective. For Best, all knowledge has both a felt and cognitive dimension and we can only 'feel' a work of art if we rationally comprehend how it is put together to make its meaning. He suggests that: '. . . the artistic experience is as fully rational, and as fully involves cognition or understanding, as any subject in the curriculum, including the so-called core areas of the sciences and mathematics' (Best 1992: 15).

Furthermore, he maintains that the aesthetic has as much to do with the sciences as it has to do with the arts; scientists are also imaginative and creative. However, while he argues that disciplines have some similar components, he believes that each school subject offers a unique and distinct form of human knowledge and that few of the productive skills and understandings learnt are transferable.

A consequence of the generic position, Best suggests, is that the arts are less likely to be taken seriously in the curriculum unless they can show that they have a rational and cognitive dimension, as with other disciplines.

> **Task 15.5 Music as a distinct discipline**
>
> Taking music as your starting point, make notes on your answers to the following questions:
>
> • What are the distinctive features of music as a discipline?
> • What is the 'rational' dimension to musical knowledge and understanding?
> • Do these distinctive features negate the possibility of any family relationship with other arts or school subjects?
> • Where do you stand on the generic versus distinct debate?

Further support for the arts as distinct argument comes from the work of Howard Gardner (1984), whose theory of multiple intelligences suggest that, for example, we have a separate and discernible musical intelligence.

By and large, most arts educators accept the links between the arts and yet also recognise their distinctive nature. Indeed, Abbs believes in moving from the genus to the species (from the commonalities to the individual differences), and Best is happy for collaborative arts work to take place as long as we do not commit philosophical and epistemological howlers by thinking that they can deliver the same learning. However, in addition to those identified thus far, there is a wider set of reasons why the arts are typically considered together by schools, educators and policy makers alike. These reasons include:

- The political advantage afforded by having a powerful group of subjects when arguing for time, resources and status against other areas of the curriculum such as the sciences and humanities (although some have argued that this actually weakens the case for the individual arts themselves).
- The arts typically work together in the real world and so there are good reasons for curricula and organisational collaboration.
- Some young people may not want or need the specialist teaching associated with a distinct discipline, for example, where a project arises out of the self-directed learning of young people or when a multi-sensory approach is more appropriate for their individual needs.

In the final section of this chapter we argue that there is still an important case to be made for a more connected view of human knowledge that can benefit all students in the day-to-day arts curriculum, and it is to this 'third way' that we now turn.

Twenty-first-century possibilities for music, the arts and education

There is a 'third way' for music, the arts and education which is founded on a more unified conception of *all* knowledge. All symbolic modes, disciplines and subjects enable us to make sense of the world, create the world and re-create the world, and so are at a very deep level related. For example, Robinson maintains that the 'four areas of creative, technical, contextual, and critical development apply equally to all areas of the curriculum' (Robinson and Aronica 2015: 104). On the same theme, Philpott (1996) suggests that imagination, interpretation and values are as much the realm of sciences as the arts. As music (arts) educators, it is possible to accept these relationships and commonalities without negating the distinctiveness of the discipline.

On this account, music will not only have deep connections to knowledge in the arts, but will have relationships to all disciplines as suggested by Best. Having said this, there is a sense in which it is natural for music to look to relationships with the arts, as these relationships are foregrounded within our culture. How do we experience the world through culture where multiple disciplines are always at work? The work of Michael Polanyi provides us with a framework for understanding this.

In any experience, Polanyi suggests that 'we can know more than we can tell' (1967: 25). An example of this is when we know a person or place. We might have a holistic sense of the 'character' of Swindon, say; we have a knowledge 'of' Swindon, and yet might not be fully aware of all that goes into making up this understanding. For Polanyi, much of our knowledge is 'tacit' in this way and in the background when we attend to the 'whole'. We cannot always say or understand what has gone into making the experience 'whole' for us, and yet we foreground what Polanyi calls focal awareness. Our tacit knowledge is subsidiary to our focal awareness of the whole, and yet the human mind integrates our tacit background knowledge into the focal and foregrounded whole.

Such an analysis can easily be translated into our experience of a performance of some type. For example, the symbolism of mathematics in a dance performance is probably part of our subsidiary rather than focal awareness, which is more likely aimed at the kinaesthetic, musical and visual symbolism. In the same way, a scientific theory *might* foreground the logic of maths even though there are kinaesthetic and visual subsidiaries in our understanding of it. In a musical performance, our focal awareness might be on the raw power of a particular passage and how the extravagant lighting and staging provides a frame for this. In the same performance we might subsidiarily be aware of, for example, the gender issues surrounding the imbalance of performers on stage. In our experience of culture (in its widest possible sense), such connections or consiliences are most likely to be a part of our tacit and focal knowledge; this is the way of the world. On this theme, Robinson maintains that:

> In practice, the arts and science overlap in all kinds of ways. Imagination and creativity, properly conceived are as much a part of science as the arts . . . The humanities overlap in many ways with the sciences and the arts, sharing with the arts the primary concern for understanding the human dimension of experience and with the sciences a concern for theoretical analysis, evidence and explanation.
>
> (Robinson and Aronica 2015: 145-146)

Why is this analysis important to music educators and their practice? The reasons include:

1   The way in which a wide range of disciplines are integrated in real life and the wider culture, e.g. film, opera, 'rock' concerts, means that connectedness is always with us. Furthermore, connections between the arts disciplines are also made within particular historical movements, e.g. impressionism and punk, and this is how we experience our world.
2   Making these connections explicit in school is consistent with the encultured, informal learning of our young people, and where formal instruction does not take account of this we risk a disjuncture between their encultured experience of the arts and their experience of the arts (and indeed all subjects) in school, and the possibility of a negative impact on learning, motivation and achievement.
3   The human mind is drawn to making connections when making sense of the world. Making connections can enhance the learning in the 'home' discipline, all disciplines

and also the wider education of the youngster. Wider education here is not just the learning of generic 'soft' skills or the transfer of learning from one subject to another, but relationships between the deep structures of knowledge in the various disciplines through which we make sense of our world, also known as consilience.

4   By being aware of how tacit and focal awareness works in our experience, as teachers we can analyse our knowledge and explicitly plan for exploiting its connectedness.

The implication for you as a music teacher, and indeed all teachers, is that deep connections are always present and we should be open to exploiting them if we aim to enhance the learning within the distinct discipline of music itself. Such a 'third way' suggests that we do not ignore connections (focal or subsidiary), but that we need to be disposed to the potential for learning through both tacit and focal awareness in our music lessons.

Task 15.6 Tacit and focal awareness

Taking a musical performance of your choice, analyse:

*   your focal awareness of musical understanding;
*   your focal and/or tacit awareness of aspects and dimensions of the performance that derive from other artistic disciplines;
*   your focal and/or tacit understanding of aspects and dimensions of the performance that might derive from the sciences and humanities.

Plan an activity for the classroom that, while having a focus on the development of musical understanding, also explicitly draws on a range of other artistic disciplines. What subsidiary understandings from the sciences and humanities are present?

Clearly, the 'third way' has a wide range of imperatives to achieve if it is to be congruent with current educational policy, and this includes: an impact on musical learning, the learning of other disciplines and also the wider learning of youngsters. Music teachers do not need to give up on the distinctness of the discipline, providing they are predisposed to make connections which are an inevitable part of learning in music (and indeed any subject). Few will want to abandon distinct arts teaching, and yet there is much by way of enhanced learning to be gained from the mutual presence of disciplines in any classroom.

There is a sense in which practitioners in all disciplines can become 'precious' about their subject, and this has particularly been the case for music, which is often regarded as 'special' by its advocates. Being 'precious' can be counter-productive and risks the adverse motivation of youngsters. However, by being predisposed to see and accept the power of connections and consilience, we can promote the project that is the distinctiveness of music without losing sight of the bigger picture of human learning and knowledge.

Summary

In this chapter we have:

* identified generic and distinct conceptions of the arts in education and the implications for each;
* suggested a 'third way', implicit in both of these stances, based on the interconnected-ness of the ways in which the human mind makes sense of the world and holds knowledge.

One of the most important implications of the 'third way' is for music teachers not to view themselves in isolation from the wider educational project. This is not just about contributing to a common set of soft skills, such as 'team work', or indeed the transfer of learning into other subjects. But by establishing relationships with, and connections between, the deep structures of knowledge and understanding that underpin the ways in which we make sense of our world, music can both enhance its distinctiveness *and* contribute to the wider development of young people, culture and society.

Further reading

Calouste Gulbenkian Foundation (1982) *The Arts in Schools: Principles, Practice and Provision*, London: Calouste Gulbenkian Foundation.

Plummeridge, C. (2001) Music and combined arts, in C. Philpott and C. Plummeridge (eds) *Issues in Music Teaching*, London: Routledge, pp. 21–31.

Robinson, K. and Aronica, L. (2015) *Creative Schools: Revolutionizing Education from the Ground Up*, London: Allen Lane.

The Warwick Commission (2015) *Enriching Britain: Culture, Creativity and Growth*, The University of Warwick.

Together these texts provide both the background and an up-to-date perspective on music and arts in education.

References

Abbs, P. (ed.) (1987) *The Living Powers: The Arts in Education*, London: Falmer Press.

Abbs, P. (ed.) (1989a) *The Symbolic Order: A Contemporary Reader on the Arts Debate*, London: Falmer Press.

Abbs, P. (1989b) *A is for Aesthetic: Essays on the Creative and Aesthetic*, London: Falmer Press.

Abie, S. (2014) 'Curriculum models: product versus process', *Journal of Education and Practice*, 5, 35: 152-155.

Allsup, R. (2003) 'Transformational education and critical music pedagogy: examining the link between culture and learning', *Music Education Research*, 5, 1: 5-12.

AQA (2015) www.aqa.org.uk/subjects/music/gcse/music-8271 (accessed 27 July 2015).

Arts Council England (2012) *Music Education Hubs: Partnership Working Advice Sheet*. Online, available at: www.artscouncil.org.uk/media/uploads/pdf/partnerships_advice_sheet2.pdf (accessed 31 August 2013).

Auker, P. (1991) 'Pupil talk, musical learning and creativity', *British Journal of Music Education*, 8, 2: 161-166. Online, available at: www.ofsted.gov.uk/resources/music-schools-wider-still-and-wider (accessed 30 December 2015).

Bamford, A. and Glinkowski, P. (2010) *'Wow, it's music next': Impact Evaluation of Wider Opportunities Progamme in Music at Key Stage Two*, Leeds: Federation of Music Services.

Barnes, J. (2011) *Cross-Curricular Learning 3-14*, 2nd edn, London: Sage.

Barrett, M. (1990) 'Music and language in education', *British Journal of Music Education*, 7, 1: 67-73.

Beghetto, R.A. (2012) Expect the unexpected: teaching for creativity in the micromoments, in M.B. Gregerson, H.T. Snyder, and J.C. Kaufman (eds) *Teaching Creatively and Teaching Creativity*, New York: Springer, pp. 133-149.

Berkley, R. (2004) 'Teaching composing as creative problem solving: conceptualising composing pedagogy', *British Journal of Music Education*, 21, 3: 239-263.

Best, D. (1992) *The Rationality of Feeling*, London: Falmer Press.

Black, P., Harrison, C., Lee, C., Marshall, B. and Wiliam, D. (2003) *Assessment for Learning*, Milton Keynes: Open University Press.

Blacking, J. (1987) *A Commonsense View of All Music*, Cambridge: Cambridge University Press.

Board of Education (1927) *Handbook of Suggestions for Teachers*, London: HMSO.

Brewer, J. (1997) *The Pleasures of the Imagination: English Culture in the Eighteenth Century*, London: HarperCollins.

Bruner, J.S. (1986) *Actual Minds: Possible Worlds*, Cambridge, MA: Harvard Educational Press.

Bruner, J.S. (1966) *Towards a Theory of Instruction*, Cambridge, MA: Harvard University Press.

Burnard, P. (2012) *Musical Creativities in Practice*, Oxford: Oxford University Press.

Cain, T. (2013) '"Passing it on": beyond formal or informal pedagogies', *Music Education Research*, 15, 1: 74-91.

Calouste Gulbenkian Foundation (1982) *The Arts in Schools: Principles, Practice and Provision*, London: Calouste Gulbenkian Foundation.

Capel, S., Leask, M. and Turner, T. (2013) *Learning to Teach in the Secondary School: A Companion to School Experience*, 6th edn, London: Routledge.

Carey, J. (2005) *What Good Are The Arts?* London: Faber & Faber.

Claxton, G. (2002) *Building Learning Power: Helping Young People Become Better Learners*, TLO: Bristol. Online, available at: www.buildinglearningpower.co.uk (accessed 30 July 2015).

Cook, N. (1990) *Music, Imagination and Culture*, Oxford: Clarendon Press.

Cornbleth, C. (1990) *Curriculum in Context*, Basingstoke: Falmer Press.

Cringen, A.T. (1889) *The Teacher's Handbook of the Tonic Sol-fa System*, Toronto: Canada Publishing.

Crow, B. (2007) Music-related ICT in education, in P. Philpott, and G. Spruce (eds) *Learning to Teach Music In The Secondary School: A Companion to School Experience*, Abingdon, Oxon: Routledge, pp. 174–192.

Crowe, J. (1996) 'A better class of music', paper presented at Canada: Past Present and Future: A Cross-Disciplinary Conference, University of Calgary, October.

Daubney, A. and Mackrill, D. (2012) 'Mobile technologies in a disconnected educational world? Children's musical experiences using mobile technologies in and out of school', 30th World Conference of the International Society for Music Education (ISME), Thessaloniki, Greece, 15–20 July.

Daubney, A. and Mackrill, D. (2013) *Music Technologies – Playing the Home Advantage*, Music Education UK. Online, available at: http://issuu.com/musiceducationasia/docs/musiceducationuk_issue_04 (accessed 15 August 2015).

D'Amore, A. (ed.) (2009) *Musical Futures: An Approach to Teaching and Learning – Resource Pack*, 2nd edn, London: Paul Hamlyn Foundation.

Davis, B. and Sumara, D. (2006) *Complexity and Education: Inquiries into Learning, Teaching and Research*, Mahwah, NJ: Lawrence Erlbaum Associates.

DeNora, T. (1996) *Beethoven and the Construction of Genius*, Berkeley, CA: University of California Press (French edn, Fayard 1998).

DeNora, T. (2006) *Music in Everyday Life*, Cambridge: Cambridge University Press.

DfE (Department for Education) (2012) *Teachers' Standards*, London: DfE.

DfE (Department for Education) (2013a) *The National Curriculum for England*, London: DfE.

DfE (Department for Education) (2013b) *National Curriculum in England: Music Programmes of Study*, London: Department for Education.

DfE (Department for Education)/DoH (Department of Health) (2015) *Special Educational Needs and Disability Code of Practice: 0–25 Years*, London: DfE/DoH.

DfE (Department for Education)/DCMS (Department for Culture, Media and Sport) (2011) *The Importance of Music: A National Plan for Music Education*, London: DfE/DCMS. Online, available at: www.gov.uk/government/publications/the-importance-of-music-a-national-plan-for-music-education (accessed 31 August 2013).

DfEE (Department for Education and Employment) (1999) *The National Curriculum for England: Music*, London: DfEE.

DfES (Department for Education and Skills) (2001) *Special Education Needs: Code of Practice*, London: DfES.

DfES (Department for Education and Skills) (2004) *National Strategy for Music Programme Foundation Subjects: Key Stage 3 Music*, London: DfES.

DfES (Department for Education and Skills) (2006a) *National Strategy for Music Programme Foundation Subjects: Key Stage 3 Music*, Report No 2, London: DfES.

DfES (Department for Education and Skills) (2006b) *Secondary National Strategy for School Improvement, Foundation Subjects: KS3 Music*, London: DfES.

Dibben, N. (2003) Musical materials, perception and listening, in M. Clayton, T. Herbert and R. Middleton (eds) *The Cultural Study of Music: A Critical Introduction*, London: Routledge, pp. 193–203.

Dickinson, C. and Wright, J. (1993) *Differentiation: A Practical Handbook of Classroom Strategies*, Coventry: NCET.

Didau, D. (2012) *Children Are at School to Learn, not to Behave*, The Guardian, Teacher network. Online, available at: www.theguardian.com/teacher-network/2012/feb/13/learning-behaviour-teaching (accessed 26 August 2013).

Elliott, D.J. (1995) *Music Matters: A New Philosophy of Music Education*, Oxford: Oxford University Press.

Ellis, S. and Tod, J. (2009) *Behaviour for Learning: Proactive Approaches to Behaviour Management*, London: Routledge.

Everitt, A. (1997) *Joining in: An Investigation into Participatory Music*, London: Calouste Gulbenkian Foundation.

Fautley, M. (2010) *Assessment in Music Education*, Oxford: Oxford University Press.

Fautley, M. (2013) *Teaching and Learning Notation*. Online, available at: https://drfautley.wordpress.com/ (*accessed 31 July 2015*).

Fenwick, T., Edwards, R. and Sawchuk, P. (2011) *Emerging Approaches to Educational Research: Tracing the Sociomaterial*, Abingdon, Oxon: Routledge.

Finnegan, R. (2003) Music, experience and the anthropology of emotion, in M. Clayton, T. Herbert and R. Middleton (eds) *The Cultural Study of Music: A Critical Introduction*, London: Routledge, pp. 181–192.

Finney, J. and Philpott, C. (2010) 'Informal learning and meta-pedagogy in initial teacher education in England', *British Journal of Music Education*, 27, 1: 7–19.

Fletcher, P. (1987) *Education and Music*, Oxford: Oxford University Press.

Flynn, G. and Pratt, G. (1995) 'Developing an understanding of appraising music with practising primary teachers', *British Journal of Education*, 12, 2: 127–158.

Folkestad, G. (2005) 'Here, there and everywhere: music education research in a globalised world', *Music Education Research*, 7, 3: 279–287.

Folkestad, G. (2006) 'Formal and informal learning situations or practices vs formal and informal ways of learning', *British Journal of Music Education*, 23, 2: 135–145.

Francis, B. (2000) *Boys, Girls and Achievement: Addressing the Classroom Issues*, London: Routledge Falmer.

Gaines, J. (2004) *Evening in the Palace of Reason*, London: Fourth Estate.

Gardner, H. (1984) *Frames of Mind: The Theory of Multiple intelligences*, London: Heinemann.

Gibson, R. (1986) *Critical Theory and Education*, London: Hodder & Stoughton.

Green, L. (1995) Gender, musical meaning and education, in G. Spruce (ed.) *Teaching Music*, London: Routledge, pp. 123–131.

Green, L. (1996) The emergence of gender as an issue in music education, in C. Plummeridge (ed.) *Music Education: Trends and Issues*, London: Institute of Education, University of London, pp. 41–58.

Green, L. (1997) *Music, Gender, Education*, Cambridge: Cambridge University Press.

Green, L. (2001) *How Pop Musicians Learn: A Way Ahead for Music Education*, Aldershot: Ashgate.

Green, L. (2008) *Music, Informal Learning and the School: A New Classroom Pedagogy*, Aldershot: Ashgate.

Green, L. and O'Neill, S. (2001) Social groups and learning in music education, in British Educational Research Association (BERA) Music Education Review Group, *Mapping Music Education Research in the UK*, Southwell: British Educational Research Association.

Hallam, S. (1998) *Instrumental Teaching: A Practical Guide to better Teaching and Learning*, London: Heinemann.

Hallam, S. (2001) Learning in music: complexity and diversity, in C. Philpott and C. Plummeridge (eds) *Issues in Music Teaching*, London: Routledge, pp. 61–75.

Hallam, S. (2006) Musicality, in G. McPherson (ed.) *The Child as Musician*, New York: Oxford University Press, pp. 93–110.

Hallam, S. (2010) The power of music: its impact on the intellectual, personal and social development of children and young people, in S. Hallam and A. Creech (eds) *Music in the 21st Century in the United Kingdom: Achievements, Analysis and Aspirations*, London: Institute of Education, University of London, pp. 2–17.

Hallam, S. (2015) *The Power of Music*, London: International Music Education Research Centre (iMerc).

Hargreaves, D.J. (1986) *The Developmental Psychology of Music*, Cambridge: Cambridge University Press.

Hargreaves, D.J. and Marshall, N.A. (2003) 'Developing identities in music education', *Music Education Research*, 5, 3: 263–273.

Harland, J., Kinder, K., Lord, P., Stott, A., Schagen, I., Haynes, J., with Cusworth, L., White, R. and Paola, R. (2000) *Arts Education in Secondary Schools: Effects and Effectiveness*, Slough: National Foundation for Educational Research.

Harvey, E. (1988) *Jazz in the Classroom*, London: Boosey & Hawkes.

Higgins, S., Xiao, Z. and Katsipataki, M. (2012) *The Impact of Digital Technology on Learning: A Summary for the Education Endowment Foundation*, Durham: Durham University and Education Endowment Foundation. Online, available at: http://educationendowmentfoundation.org.uk/uploads/pdf/The_Impact_of_Digital_Technologies_on_Learning_FULL_REPORT_(2012).pdf (accessed 30 December 2015).

International Data Corporation (2014) *Worldwide Smartphone Shipments Edge Past 300 Million Units in the Second Quarter; Android and iOS Devices Account for 96% of the Global Market, According to IDC.* Online, available at: www.idc.com/getdoc.jsp?containerId=prUS25037214 (accessed 30 December 2015).

Jaffurs, S. (2004) 'The impact of informal learning practices in the classroom, or how I learned to teach from a garage band', *International Journal of Music Education*, 22, 3: 189–200.

Jorgensen, E. (2003) *Transforming Music Education*, Bloomington, IN: Indiana University Press.

Kendall, I. (1977) The role of literacy in the school music curriculum, in M. Burnett (ed.) *Music Education Review: A Handbook for Music Teachers: Vol. 1*, London: Chappell, pp. 29–44.

Kwami, R. (2000) Non-western Musics: PGCE Knowledge Development Materials, Milton Keynes: Open University (no longer available).

Kwami, R. (2001) Music education in and for a pluralist society, in C. Philpott and C. Plummeridge (eds) *Music Education: Trends and Issues*, London: Institute of Education, pp. 142–155.

Kyriacou, C. (1991) *Essential Teaching Skills*, Cheltenham: Thornes.

Lamont, A., Hargreaves, D.J., Marshall, N.A. and Tarrant, M. (2003) 'Young people's music in and out of school', *British Journal of Music Education*, 20, 3: 229–241.

Laughey, D. (2006) *Music and Youth Culture*, Edinburgh: Edinburgh University Press.

Leppert, R. and McClary, S. (1987) *Music and Society: The Politics of Composition, Performance and Reception*, Cambridge: Cambridge University Press.

McClary, S. (1987) The blasphemy of talking politics in Bach year, in R. Leppert and S. McClary (eds) *Music and Society: The Politics of Composition, Performance and Reception*, Cambridge: Cambridge University Press, pp. 13–62.

Martin, P.J. (1995) *Sounds and Society*, Manchester: Manchester University Press.

Metcalfe, M. (1987) Towards the condition of music, in P. Abbs (ed.) *Living Powers*, London: Falmer, pp. 97–118.

Mills, J. (2005) *Music in the School*, Oxford: Oxford University Press.

Moore, V. (2005) 'One for the rack', *The Guardian Weekend*, 20 August, London: The Guardian.

NAME (National Association of Music Educators) (2000) *Composing in the Classroom: The Creative Dream*, London: NAME.

NACCCE (National Advisory Committee on Creative and Cultural Education) (1999) *All Our Futures: Creativity, Culture and Education*, London: DfEE.

NCC (National Curriculum Council) (1990) *The Arts 5–16: A Curriculum Framework*, Harlow: Oliver & Boyd.

North, A., Hargreaves, D.J. and O'Neill, S. (2000) 'The importance of music to adolescents', *British Journal of Educational Psychology*, 70: 255–272.

O'Brien, T. (1998) *Promoting Positive Behaviour*, London: David Fulton.

Ofsted (2009) *Making More of Music: Improving the Quality of Music Teaching in Secondary Schools*, London: Ofsted.

Ofsted (2012) *Music in Schools: Wider Still and Wider*, London: Ofsted.

Ofsted (2013) *Music Education in Schools: What Hubs Must Do*, London: Ofsted.

Osberg, D. and Biesta, G. (2008) 'The emergent curriculum: navigating a complex course between unguided learning and planned enculturation', *Journal of Curriculum Studies*, 40, 3: 313–328.

Osberg, D., Biesta, G., and Cilliers, P. (2008) From representation to emergence: complexity's challenge to the epistemology of schooling, in M. Mason (ed.) *Complexity Theory and the Philosophy of Education*, Oxford: Wiley-Blackwell, pp. 204–218.

Packer, Y. (1987) *Musical Activities for Children with Behavioural Problems*, London: Disabled Living Foundation.

Packer, Y. (1996) Music with emotionally disturbed children, in G. Spruce (ed.) *Teaching Music*, London: Routledge.

Palmer, P. (1998) *The Courage to Teach*, San Francisco, CA: Jossey-Bass.

Parsons, M., Johnston, M. and Durham, R. (1978) 'Developmental stages in children's aesthetic responses', *Journal of Aesthetic Education*, 12: 83–104.

Pateman, T. (1991) *Key Concepts: A Guide to Aesthetics, Criticism and the Arts in Education*, London: Falmer.

Paynter, J. (1977) The role of creativity in the school music curriculum, in M. Burnett (ed.) *Music Education Review: A Handbook for Music Teachers: Vol. 1*, London: Chappell, pp. 3–28.

Pearson Edexcel (2015) http://qualifications.pearson.com/en/qualifications/edexcel-gcses/music-2016.html (accessed 27 July 2015).

Piaget, J. (1952) *Construction of Reality in the Child*, London: Routledge & Kegan Paul.

Project for Enhancing Effective Learning (PEEL) (2009) www.peelweb.org/index.cfm?resource= good%20behaviours (accessed 26 August 2013).

Philpott, C. (1996) Learning from the arts in the new millennium, in D. Hayes (ed.) *Debating Education: Issues for the New Millennium?* Canterbury: Canterbury Christ Church University College, pp. 118–122.

Philpott, C. (2001) The body and musical literacy, in C. Philpott and C. Plummeridge (eds) *Issues in Music Teaching*, London: RoutledgeFalmer, pp. 79–91.

Philpott, C. (2009) Swanwick, musical development and assessment for learning in the 21st Century, in H. Coll and A. Lamont (eds) *Sound Progress: Exploring Musical Development*, Matlock: NAME, pp. 67–72.

Philpott, C. (2010) The sociological critique of curriculum music in England: is radical change really possible? in R. Wright (ed.) *Sociology and Music Education*, Farnham: Ashgate, pp. 81–92.

Philpott, C. (2012) Assessment for self-directed learning in music education, in C. Philpott and G. Spruce (eds) (2012) *Debates in Music Teaching*, Abingdon, Oxon: Routledge, pp. 153–168.

Philpott, C. and Plummeridge, C. (eds) (2001) *Issues in Music Teaching*, London: Routledge.

Plato (1982) *The Laws*, London: Penguin.

Plummeridge, C. (1991) *Music Education in Theory and Practice*, London: Falmer Press.

Plummeridge, C. (2001) The justification for music education, in C. Philpott and C. Plummeridge (eds) *Issues in Music Teaching*, London: Routledge, pp. 21–31.

Polanyi, M. (1967) *The Tacit Dimension*, London: Routledge.

Pollard, A. (ed.) (2002) *Readings for Reflective Teaching*, London: Continuum.

Pollard, A. and Triggs, P. (1997) *Reflective Teaching in Secondary Education*, London: Continuum.

Powell, S. and Tod, J. (2004) A systematic review of how theories explain learning behaviour in school contexts, in *Research Evidence in Education Library*, London: EPPI-Centre, Social Science Research Unit, Institute of Education.

Pratt, G. and Stephens, J. (eds) (1995) *Teaching Music in the National Curriculum*, London: Heinemann.

QCDA (Qualifications and Curriculum Development Agency) (2007) *The National Curriculum Statutory Requirements for Key Stages 3 and 4*, London: QCDA.

Read, H. (1943) *Education through Art*, London: Faber.

Regelski, T. (2005) Curriculum: implications of aesthetic versus praxial philosophies, in D.J. Elliott (ed.) *Praxial Music Education: Reflections and Dialogues*, Oxford: Oxford University Press, pp. 219–249.

Reid, L.A. (1986) *Ways of Understanding and Education*, London: Heinemann.

Reimer, B. (1989) *A Philosophy of Music Education*, Englewood Cliffs, NJ: Prentice Hall.

Renshaw, P. (2005) *Simply Connect – Next Practice in Group Music Making and Musical Leadership*, London: Paul Hamlyn Foundation.

Robinson, K. and Aronica, L. (2015) *Creative Schools: Revolutionizing Education from the Ground Up*, London: Allen Lane.

Ross, M. (1978) *The Creative Arts*, London: Heinemann.

Ross, M. (1980) *The Arts and Personal Growth*, London: Pergamon.

Ross, M. (ed.) (1982) *The Development of Aesthetic Experience*, Oxford: Pergamon.

Rowntree, D. (1977) *Assessing Students: How Shall We Know Them?* London: Harper.

Rusinek, G. (2008) 'Disaffected learners and school music culture: an opportunity for inclusion', *Research Studies in Music Education*, 30, 9–23.

Russell, D (1987/97) *Popular Music in England 1840–1914*, Manchester: Manchester University Press.

Savage, J. (2013) *The Guided Reader to Teaching and Learning in Music*, Abingdon, Oxon: Routledge.

Sawyer, K. (2007) *Group Genius: The Creative Power of Collaboration*, New York: Basic Books.

Schmidt, P. (2005) 'Music education as transformative practice: creating new frameworks for learning through a Freirean perspective, *Visions of Research in Music Education* (Special Edition), January.

Schools Council (1971) *Music and the Young School Leaver: Problems and Opportunities*, Working Paper 35, London: Methuen Educational.

Schools Council Enquiry 1 (1968) *Music and the Young School Leaver*, London: HMSO.

Scott, D. (2000) *Music, Culture and Society*, Oxford: Oxford University Press.

Scottish Education Department (1955) *Junior Secondary Education*, Edinburgh: HMSO.

Shepherd, J. (1991) *Music as Social Text*, Cambridge: Polity Press.

Shepherd, J., Virden, P., Vulliamy, G. and Wishart, T. (1980) *Whose Music? A Sociology of Musical Languages*, New Brunswick, NJ: Transaction Books.

Sherratt, R.G.A. (1977) Who's for creativity, in C. Cox and R. Boyson (eds) *Black Paper*, London: Temple Smith, pp. 34–37.

Shuter-Dyson, R. and Gabriel, C. (1981) *The Psychology of Musical Ability*, London: Methuen.

Slobada, J. (1985) *The Musical Mind: The Cognitive Psychology of Music*, Oxford: Oxford University Press.

Small, C. (1977) *Music-Society-Education*, London: John Calder.

Small, C. (1998) *Musicking: The Meanings of Performing and Listening*, Middletown, CT: Wesleyan University Press.

Small, C. (1999) 'Musicking - the meanings of performance and listening: a lecture', *Music Education Research*, 1, 1: 9–22.

Small, C. (2011) Prologue: misunderstanding and reunderstanding, in F. Laurence and O. Urbain (eds) *Music and Solidarity*, London: Transaction.

Smith, A. (1973) 'Feasibility of tracking musical form as cognitive listening objective', *Journal of Research in Music Education*, 4: 373–391.

Smith, C., Dakers, J., Dow, W., Head, G., Sutherland, M. and Irwin, R. (2005) A systematic review of what pupils, aged 11–16, believe impacts on their motivation to learn in the classroom, in *Research Evidence in Education Library*, London: EPPI-Centre, Social Science Research Unit, Institute of Education, University of London.

Smith, M.K. (2000) Curriculum theory and practice, in *The Encyclopedia of Informal Education*. Online, available at: www.infed.org/biblio/b-curric.htm (accessed 2 July 2015).

Spruce, G. (2009) Teaching and learning for critical thinking and understanding, in J. Evans and C. Philpott (eds) *A Practical Guide to Teaching Music in the Secondary School*, Abingdon, Oxon: Routledge.

Spruce, G. (2015) Music education, social justice, and the 'student voice': addressing student alienation through a dialogical conception of music education, in C. Benedict, P. Schmidt, G. Spruce and P. Woodford (eds) *The Oxford Companion to Social Justice in Music Education*, New York: Routledge, pp. 287–301.

Street, J. (2012) *Music and Politics*, Cambridge: Polity Press.

Swanwick, K. (1979) *A Basis for Music Education*, Windsor: NFER Nelson.

Swanwick, K. (1988) *Music, Mind and Education*, London: Routledge.

Swanwick, K. (1991) 'Musical criticism and musical development', *British Journal of Music Education*, 8, 2: 139–148.

Swanwick, K. (1994) *Musical Knowledge: Intuition, Analysis and Music Education*, Abingdon, Oxon: Routledge.

Swanwick, K. (1997) Editorial, *British Journal of Music Education*, 14, 1: 3–4.

Swanwick, K. (1999) *Teaching Music Musically*, London: Routledge.

TEEP (Teacher Effectiveness Enhancement Model) (2009) www.teep.org.uk/teep_model.asp (accessed 26 August 2013).

UNESCO (2003) *Overcoming Exclusion through Inclusive Approaches in Education: A Challenge and a Vision*, Concept Paper, Paris: UNESCO.

Vulliamy, G. (1978) What counts as school music? in G. Whitty and M.F.D. Young (eds) *Explorations in the Politics of School Knowledge*, Driffield: Nafferton, pp. 19–34.

Vulliamy, G. and Shepherd, J. (1984) 'The application of critical sociology to music education', *British Journal of Music Education*, 1, 3: 247–266.

Vygotsky, L.S. (1986) *Thought and Language*, rev. edn, trans. A. Kozulin, Cambridge, MA: MIT Press.

Walker, R. (1996) 'Music education freed from colonialism: a new praxis', *International Journal of Music Education*, 27: 2–15.

Walker, R. (2005) 'A worthy function for music in education', *International Journal of Music Education*, 23, 2: 135–137.

Wallas, G. (1926) *The Art of Thought*, London: Watts.

Warnock, M. (1978) *The Warnock Report: Special Educational Needs*, London: HMSO. Online, available at: www.educationengland.org.uk/documents/warnock (accessed 17 August 2015).

The Warwick Commission (2015) *Enriching Britain: Culture, Creativity and Growth*, Warwick: The University of Warwick.

Welsh, G., Purves, R., Hargreaves, D. and Marshall, N. (2011) 'Early career challenges in secondary school music teaching', *British Educational Research Journal*, 37, 2: 285–315.

Whittaker, W.G. (1925) *Class-Singing*, Oxford: Oxford University Press.

Woodford, P. (2005) *Democracy and Music Education*, Bloomington, IN: Indiana University Press.

Wright, R. (2001) 'Gender and achievement: the view from the classroom', *British Journal of Music Education*, 18, 3: 275–291.

Younger, M. and Warrington, M. (1996) 'Differential achievement of girls and boys at GCSE', *British Journal of Sociology of Education*, 17, 3: 299–313.

Index

Page numbers in *italics* refer to figures

Printed in Great Britain
by Amazon

64054881R10151